MATTERS
OF FACT AND
OF FICTION

GORE VIDAL

MATTERS OF FACT AND OF FICTION

Essays
1973–1976

Random House   New York

Library of Congress Cataloging in Publication Data
Vidal, Gore, 1925–
Matters of fact and of fiction.
I. Title.
AC8.V43   814'.5'4
ISBN 0-394-41128-5   76-53459

"The Top Ten Best Sellers" ("The Ashes of Hollywood, I & II"), "The Great World
and Louis Auchincloss" ("Real Class"), "Clavino's Novels" ("Fabulous Clavino"),
"American Plastic: The Matter of Fiction," "Some Memories of the Glorious Bird
and An Earlier Self" ("Selected Memories of the Glorious Bird and the Golden Age"),
"The Four Generations of the Adams Family" ("The Adams' Fall"), "President and
Mrs. U.S. Grant" ("The Grants"), "West Point," "The Art and Arts of E. Howard
Hunt," and "What Robert Moses did to New York City" ("Emperor of Concrete")
were originally published in *The New York Review of Books*. "The State of the Union"
was first published in *Esquire Magazine*. "Professor V. Nabokov" first appeared in *The
Observer*. "French Letters: Theories of the New Novel" was originally published in
Encounter. "The Hacks of Academe" was first published in *The Times Literary
Supplement*. "Contagious Self-Love" and "Conglomerates" first appeared in the *New
Statesman*.

Manufactured in the United States of America
2 4 6 8 9 7 5 3
First Edition

For Diana Phipps

Note

I have divided this collection of pieces into two parts. The first deals with fiction. The second with the world in general and politics in particular. Fiction and fact, then, are the matters at hand. I have included one already reprinted essay, "French Letters" (what Mr. R.Z. Shepherd would call one of my "golden oldies"), because it is relevant to the argument that I make about the nature of fiction. The other pieces have not, until now, been published in book form.

I realize that commentaries on politics and the affairs of the day tend to date, but what does not? One writer of book-chat complained that my collected essays *(Homage to Daniel Shays)* were not very interesting because the subjects were often old and so lacked urgency. But that of course is the very nature of both criticism and journalism.

"Criticism," wrote Sainte-Beuve, "by itself, does nothing and can do nothing. The best of it can act only in concert, and almost in collaboration, with public feeling. I shall venture to say that the critic is only the *secretary* of the public—though a secretary who does not wait to be dictated to, but each morning divines and redacts the general opinion. Even when he has actually expressed the thought which everybody has (or would like to have), a great and living part of his allusions, of his conclusions, and of their consequences, remains in the wits of his readers. I maintain that in reading over old papers and their most successful critiques we never find more than half the article in print—the other was written only in the reader's mind. You are to suppose a sheet printed of which we only read one side—the other has disappeared, is blank."

Since there is no specific memory of much of anything in the United States (or in any television culture), why revive the forgotten? Because it is the nature of secretaries to report, as this one does in the following half-pages.

G.V.

Contents

One

The Matter of Fiction

The Top Ten Best Sellers
According to the Sunday New York Times
as of January 7, 1973

"Shit has its own integrity." The Wise Hack at the Writers' Table in the MGM commissary used regularly to affirm this axiom for the benefit of us alien integers from the world of Quality Lit. It was plain to him (if not to the front office) that since we had come to Hollywood only to make money, our pictures would entirely lack the one basic homely ingredient that spells boffo world-wide grosses. The Wise Hack was not far wrong. He knew that the sort of exuberant badness which so often achieves perfect popularity cannot be faked even though, as he was quick to admit, no one ever lost a penny underestimating the intelligence of the American public. He was cynical (so were we); yet he also truly believed that children in jeopardy *always* hooked an audience, that Lana Turner was convincing when she rejected the advances of Edmund Purdom in *The Prodigal* "because I'm a priestess of Baal," and he thought that Irving Thalberg was a genius of Leonardo proportion because he had made such tasteful "products" as *The Barretts of Wimpole Street* and *Marie Antoinette.*

In my day at the Writers' Table (mid-fifties) television had shaken the industry and the shit-dispensers could now . . . well, flush their products into every home without having to worry about booking a theater. In desperation, the front office started hiring alien integers whose lack of reverence for the industry distressed the Wise Hack who daily lectured us as we sat at our long table eating the specialty of the studio, top-billed as the *Louis B. Mayer Chicken Soup with Matzoh Balls* (yes, invariably, the dumb starlet would ask, What do they do with the rest of the matzoh?). Christopher Isherwood and I sat on one side of the table; John O'Hara on the other. Aldous Huxley worked at home. Dorothy Parker drank at home.

The last time I saw Dorothy Parker, Los Angeles had been on fire for three days. As I took a taxi from the studio I asked the driver, "How's the fire doing?" "You mean," said the Hollywoodian, "the holocaust." The style, you see, must come as easily and naturally as that. I found Dorothy standing in front of her house, gazing at the smoky sky; in one hand she held a drink, in the other a comb which absently she was passing through her short straight hair. As I came toward her, she gave me a secret smile. "I am combing," she whispered, "Los Angeles out of my hair." But of course that was not possible. The ashes of Hollywood are still very much in our hair, as the ten best sellers I have just read demonstrate.

The bad movies we made twenty years ago are now regarded in altogether too many circles as important aspects of what the new illiterates want to believe is the only significant art form of the twentieth century. An entire generation has been brought up to admire the product of that era. Like so many dinosaur droppings, the old Hollywood films have petrified into something rich, strange, numinous—golden. For any survivor of the Writers' Table (alien or indigenous integer), it is astonishing to find young directors like Bertolucci, Bogdanovich, Truffaut reverently repeating or echoing or paying homage to the sort of kitsch we created first time around with a good deal of "help" from our producers and practically none at all from the directors—if one may quickly set aside the myth of the director as *auteur*. Golden-age movies were the work of producer(s) and writer(s). The director was given a finished shooting script with each shot clearly marked, and woe to him if he changed MED CLOSE SHOT to MED SHOT without permission from the front office, which each evening, in serried ranks, watched the day's rushes with script in hand ("We've got some good pages today," they would say; never good film). The director, as the Wise Hack liked to observe, is the brother-in-law.

I think it is necessary to make these remarks about the movies of the thirties, forties, and fifties as a preface to the ten best-selling novels under review since most of these books reflect to some degree the films each author saw in his formative years, while at least seven of the novels appear to me to be deliberate attempts not so much to re-create new film product as to suggest old movies that will make the reader (and publisher and reprinter and, to come full circle, film-maker) recall past success and respond accordingly. Certainly none of the ten writers (save the noble engineer Solzhenitsyn and the classicist Mary Renault) is in any way rooted in literature. For the eight, storytelling began with *The Birth of a Nation.* Came to high noon with, well, *High Noon* and *Mrs. Miniver* and *Rebecca* and *A Farewell to Arms.* Except for the influence of the dead Ian Fleming (whose own work was a curious amalgam of old movies in the Eric Ambler–Hitchcock style with some sado-masochist games added), these books connect not at all with other books. But with the movies . . . ah, the movies!

Let us begin with number ten on your Hit Parade of Fiction, *Two from Galilee,* by Marjorie Holmes. Marjorie is also the author of *I've Got to Talk to Somebody, God* and *Who Am I, God? Two from Galilee* is subtitled significantly, "A Love Story of Mary and Joseph." Since the film *Love Story* really took off: what about a love story starring the Mother and the Stepfather of Our Lord? A super idea. And Marjorie has written it. We open with the thirteen-year-old Mary menstruating ("a bloody hand had smitten her in the night"). " 'I am almost fourteen, Father,' she said, 'and I have become nubile this day.' " She is "mad for" Joseph, a carpenter's son; he is mad for her.

Shrewdly Marjorie has taken two young Americans of the lower middle class and placed them in old Galilee. I recognize some of the descriptions as being from the last version of *Ben Hur* to which I made a considerable contribution. "The couches covered with a silken stuff threaded with gold. The glow from a hanging alabaster lamp. . . ." Luckily, I was on the set at the beginning of the shooting and so was able to persuade the art director to remove tomatoes from Mrs. Ben Hur Senior's kitchen.

Otherwise, Marjorie might have had Hannah prepare a tomato and bacon sandwich for her daughter Mary.

Since Miss Holmes is not an experienced writer, it is difficult to know what, if anything, she had in mind when she decided to tell the Age-Old Story with nothing new to add. True, there are some domestic crises and folksy wrinkles like Joseph's father being a drunk. Incidentally, Joseph and Mary are known by their English names while the other characters keep their Hebrew names. Mary's mother Hannah is fun: a Jewish mother as observed by a gentile housewife in McLean, Virginia, who has seen some recent movies on the subject and heard all the jokes on television.

Hannah worries for her daughter. Will Joseph get into Mary *before* the wedding? "Hannah had no idea what it was like to be a man—this waiting. No woman could comprehend physical passion." Helen Gurley Brown and Germaine Greer will no doubt set Miss Holmes straight on that sexist point. But perhaps the author is reflecting her audience (Who are they, by the way? *Where* are they? Baptists in Oklahoma City? Catholics in Duluth suburbs?) when she writes that Hannah "did not have the faintest concept of the demon-god that entered a youth's loins at puberty and gave him no peace thereafter." Yes, I checked the last noun for spelling. Joseph, incidentally, is such a stud that when Mary is with him "the thing that was between them chimed and quivered and lent discomfort to all."

Suddenly between that chiming, quivering thing and Mary falls the shadow of the Holy Ghost. "Mary's flesh sang," as she experienced "the singing silence of God." Miss Holmes rises to lyricism. "The Holy Spirit came upon her, invaded her body, and her bowels stirred and her loins melted." Obviously entry was not made through the ear as those Renaissance painters who lacked Miss Holmes's powerful realism believed. Mary soon starts wondering why "the blood pumps so painfully in my breast and my bowels run so thin?" She finds out in due course. Joseph has a hard time believing her story until the Holy Spirit tells him to get it together and accept his peculiar role as the antlered saint of a new cult.

At census time the young marrieds set out for Bethlehem, where the local Holiday Inn is full up or, as a passer-by says, " 'The Inn? You'll be lucky to find a corner for the ass at the inn.' " As these quotations demonstrate, Miss Holmes's style is beyond cliché. But when it comes to scene-making, she is sometimes betrayed by the familiarity of her subject matter. If the Story is to be told truly there must be a birth scene, and so she is obliged to write, " 'Some hot water if you can get it,' " adding, " 'Go no further even to fetch a midwife.' " To which a helpful stranger replies, " 'I'll send one of them for one.' " Reminding us of the Joan Crawford interview some decades ago when the living legend asked with quiet majesty, "Whom is fooling whom?" Finally, "Each night the great star stood over the stable's entrance. Joseph had never seen such a star, flaming now purple, now white. . . ."

I am told that religioso fiction has a wide audience around the country, and though these books rarely appear on best-seller lists in sinks of corruption like New York City, their overall sales in the country remind us that the enormous audience which flocked to see *Ben Hur, The Robe, The Ten Commandments* is still waiting to have its simple faith renewed and stimulated with, as the sage at the Writers' Table would say, teats and sand.

Number nine, *The Eiger Sanction,* by Trevanian (just one name) is light years distant from *Two from Galilee.* For one thing, it is sometimes well-written, though hardly, as the blurb tells us, "vintage Huxley." Actually *The Eiger Sanction* is an Ian Fleming by-blow and of its too numerous kind pretty good. Fleming once remarked that he wrote his books for warm-blooded heterosexuals. I suspect that Mr. Trevanian (Ms. Trevanian?) is writing for tepid-blooded bisexuals—that is to say, a majority of those who prefer reading kinky thrillers to watching that television set before whose busy screen 90 percent of all Americans spend a third of their waking hours.

Mr. Trevanian's James Bond is called Dr. Jonathan Hemlock. A professor of art, he "moonlights" as a paid assassin for the Search and Sanction Division of CII, an aspect (presumably invented) of the CIA. Dr. Hemlock is engaged to kill those who kill CII agents. With the proceeds from these murders, he buys paintings to hang in the renovated church where he lives on Long Island. He drinks Pichon-Longueville-Baron, worships his "beloved Impressionists" (his taste in pictures is duller than the author suspects), and as for sex, well, he's a tough cookie and finds it temporarily satisfying, "like urination" or "a termination of discomfort, not an achievement of pleasure." This drives women mad.

Mr. Trevanian has a nice gift for bizarre characters. The chief of Search and Sanction is an albino who lives in darkness; he must also undergo periodic changes of blood because he is "one of nature's rarest genealogical phenomena," presumably related to a cadet branch of the Plantagenet family. It seems only yesterday that Sidney Greenstreet was growing orchids in a most sinister greenhouse and chuckling mirthlessly. Actually, that was thirty years ago and writers are now having a difficult time thinking up unlikely traits . . . not to mention names. Unhappily the mind that created Pussy Galore cloned before it went to ashes, and Mr. Trevanian brightly offers us Felicity Arce, Jean-Paul Bidet, Randie Nickers, and a host of other cute names.

But he is also capable of writing most engagingly. "His line of thought was severed by the paternal and the plebeian voice of the pilot assuring him that he knew where they were going." Or, "He intended to give [the book] a handsome review in obedience to his theory that the surest way to maintain position at the top of the field was to advance and support men of clearly inferior capacities." More of this and Mr. Trevanian will write himself out of the genre and into Quality Lit, Satire Division. But he must refrain from writing beautifully: "mountain stars still crisp and cold despite the threat of dawn to mute their brilliance," not to mention "organic viscosity of the dark around him"—an inapplicable description of a night in the high Alps worthy of Nathalie Sarraute, as is "Time had been viscous for Ben, too."

It is sad to report that Mr. Trevanian cannot resist presenting in thin disguise Mr. and Mrs. Burton and Mr. and Mrs. Onassis. There is nothing wrong with this if you have a point to make about them. But he has nothing to say; he simply mentions them in order to express disdain. No doubt they deserve his Olympian disgust, but he should leave to Suzy the record of their doings and to the really bad writers the exploitation of their famous legends. It is interesting, incidentally, to observe the curiously incestuous feedback of the so-called media. About a dozen people are known to nearly everyone capable of reading a simply written book. Therefore the golden dozen keep cropping up in popular books with the same insistence that their doings dominate the press, and the most successful exploiters of these legends are the very primitive writers like Harold Robbins who not only do not know the golden dozen at first or even second hand but, inexcusably, lack the imagination to think up anything exciting to add to what the reader has already learned from gossip columns and magazine interviews. At times while reading these best sellers I had the odd sensation that I was actually reading a batch of old Leonard Lyons gossip columns or a copy of *Photoplay* or anything except a book. But then it is a characteristic of today's writers (serious as well as commercial) to want their books to resemble "facts" rather than fiction. *The Odessa File, August 1914, The Eiger Sanction* are nonfiction titles.

Mr. Trevanian has recourse to that staple of recent fiction the Fag Villain. Since kikes and niggers can no longer be shown as bad people, only commies (pre-Nixon) and fags are certain to arouse the loathing of all decent fiction addicts. I will say for Mr. Trevanian that his Fag Villain is pretty funny—an exquisite killer named Miles Mellough with a poodle named Faggot. In fact, Mr. Trevanian in his comic mood is almost always beguiling, and this bright scenario ought to put new life into the Bond product. I think even the Wise Hack would have applauded the screenplay I automatically started preparing in my head. LONG SHOT the Eiger mountain. DAY. As titles begin, CUT TO . . .

On the Night of the Seventh Moon belongs to a genre I know very little about: the Gothic novel for ladies. But I do recall the films made from the novels of Daphne du Maurier, the queen of this sort of writing. In fact, I once wrote the screenplay for one of her most powerful works, *The Scapegoat*, in which the dogged (and in this case hounded) Alec Guinness played two people. Although Miss du Maurier had written an up-to-date variation on *The Prisoner of Zenda*, she had somehow got the notion that she had written the passion of St. Theresa. She used to send me helpful memos; and though she could not spell the simplest words or adhere to any agreed-upon grammar, her prose surged with vulgar invention and powerful feeling of the sort that cannot be faked.

I suspect Victoria Holt is also serious about her work. The publishers tell us that she is very popular; certainly she has written many books with magical titles. This one starts rather like *Rebecca:* "Now that I have reached the mature age of twenty-seven I look back on the fantastic adventure of my youth and can almost convince myself that it did not happen. . . ." A sense of warm security begins to engulf the reader at this point. Even the heroine's name inspires confidence: Helena Trant . . . so reminiscent of Helen Trent, whose vicissitudes on radio kept my generation enthralled, not to mention the ever so slight similarity to the name Trapp and all that that truly box-office name suggests; we are almost in the same neck of the woods, too, the Black Forest, 1860. And here is Helen, I mean Helena, asking herself a series of fascinating questions. "Did I suffer some mental aberration? Was it really true—as they tried to convince me—that I, a romantic and rather feckless girl, had been betrayed as so many had before? . . ."

Helena's mother was German (noble); her father English (donnish). Mother dies; girl goes to school in Germany. On a misty day she gets lost in the Black Forest. She is nubile, as Marjorie Holmes would say. Suddenly, riding toward her, "like a hero of the forest on his big white horse," was a godlike young man. He was "tall, broad, and immediately I was aware of what I could only describe then as authority." (How right she was! Though Maximilian is incognito he is really the heir to the local Grand Duchy and—but we are ahead of our story.)

He offers to take her to his hunting lodge. She sits in front of him on his horse ("He held me tightly against him which aroused in me a strange emotion which I had never felt before and which should, of course, have been a warning"). A nice old woman retainer gets her into dry things ("my hair fell about my shoulders; it was thick, dark and straight"). She wants to go back to school but "the mist is too thick." Supper. " 'Allow me to serve you some of this meat,' " says the randy prince. "He did so and I took a piece of rye bread which was hot and crusty and delicious. There was a mixture of spicy pickle and a kind of sauerkraut such as I had never tasted before." Miss Holt knows her readers like a good din from time to time along with romance, and terror. As it turns out, Max doesn't lay Helena despite the demongod in his loins. A virgin, Helena departs not knowing whom it was she met.

Back to England. Father dead, Helena lives with two aunts. A couple arrive from Germany; they say that they are cousins of her late mother. She goes back to Germany with them. Festival in a small town known as The Night of the Seventh Moon. *He* appears; takes her away with him into the forest. He sends for the couple. They witness his marriage to Helena. She is in a state of ecstasy. For one thing, she is well-groomed. "My best dress; it was of a green silky material with a monk's collar of velvet of a slightly darker shade of green." Remember Joan Fontaine at

Manderley? The new clothes? And, ah, the mystery? But Helena has done better than Joan's Max de Winter. She is now Countess Lokenburg. She gloats: "I wondered what the aunts would say when they heard that I had become the wife of a count."

But almost as good as social climbing, there is lust. Max's kiss "made me feel exalted and expectant all at once. It was cruel and yet tender; it was passionate and caressing." Can such happiness last? Certainly not. A mysterious illness; she is out of her head. When she recovers, she is told that on the night of the seventh moon she was taken into the forest and . . . "there criminally assaulted." Those blissful days with Max were all a dream, brought on by a doctor's drug. Meanwhile, she is knocked up. She has the baby; goes back to England. A clergyman falls in love with her and wants to marry her but Helena feels that her past will ruin his career. He is noble: " 'I'd rather have a wife than a bishopric.' "

The plot becomes very complex. Hired to be governess to children of what turns out to be a princely cousin of Max who is married to Wilhelmina because he thinks Helena dead because Wilhelmina's colleagues the supposed cousins of Helena were in a plot to . . . Enough! All turns out well, though it is touch-and-go for a while when her child, the heir to the principality, is kidnapped by the wicked cousin (Raymond Massey in *The Prisoner of Zenda*) who then attacks her. " 'You *are* mad,' I said." He cackles: " 'You will not live to see me rule Rochenstein, but before you die I am going to show you what kind of lover you turned your back on.' " (Mailer's *American Dream?*)

Finally, Helena takes her place at Maximilian's side as consort. Each year they celebrate the night of the seventh moon, and in the year Cousin Victoria Regina dies, "What a beautiful night! With the full moon high in the sky paling the stars to insignificance . . ." Those stars keep cropping up in these books, but then as Bette Davis said to Paul Henreid in the last but one frame of *Now Voyager*, "Don't ask for the moon when we have" (a beat) "the stars!" FADE OUT on night sky filled with stars.

I have never before read a book by Herman Wouk on the sensible ground that I could imagine what it must be like: solid, uninspired, and filled with rabbinical lore. After all, one knows of his deep and abiding religious sense, his hatred of sex outside marriage, his love for the American ruling class. I did see the film of *The Caine Mutiny* (from Queequeg to Queeg, or the decline of

American narrative); and I found the morality disturbing. Mr. Wouk has an embarrassing passion for the American goyim, particularly the West Point–Annapolis crowd who stand, he would seem to believe, between him and the Cossacks. In his lowbrow way he reflects what one has come to think of as the *Commentary* syndrome or: all's right with America if you're not in a gas chamber, and making money.

I did see the film *Youngblood Hawke* four times, finding something new to delight in at each visit. When James Franciscus, playing a raw provincial genius like Thomas Wolfe, meets Suzanne Pleshette in a publisher's office, he is told, "She will be your editor and stylist." Well, she pushes these heavy glasses up on her forehead and, my God, she's pretty as well as brilliant and witty, which she proves by saying, "Shall I call you Youngy or Bloody?" The Wise Hack at the Writers' Table always maintained that when boy meets girl they've *got* to meet cute.

The Winds of War: 885 pages of small type in which Herman Wouk describes the family of a naval captain just before America enters the Second World War (there is to be a sequel). As I picked up the heavy book, I knew terror, for I am that rarest of reviewers who actually reads every word, and rather slowly. What I saw on the first page was disquieting. The protagonist's name Victor Henry put me off. It sounded as if he had changed it from something longer, more exotic, more, shall we say, *Eastern*. But then Henry was the family name of the hero of *A Farewell to Arms* so perhaps Mr. Wouk is just having a little fun with us. Mrs. Henry is called Rhoda; the sort of name someone in New York would think one of *them* would be called out there west of the Hudson. "At forty-five, Rhoda Henry remained a singularly attractive woman, but she was rather a crab." This means that she is destined for extramarital high jinks. "In casual talk [Rhoda] used the swooping high notes of smart Washington women." I grew up in Washington at exactly the same period Mr. Wouk is writing about and I must demur: smart Washington ladies sounded no different from smart New York ladies (no swooping in either city).

Captain Henry is stationed at the War Department. He is "a squat Navy fullback from California, of no means or family." Mr. Wouk quotes from the letter he wrote his congressman asking for an appointment to the Naval Academy. "My life aim is to serve as an officer in the US Navy." We are told he speaks Russian learned from "Czarist settlers in Fort Ross, California." Anyway he got appointed; has risen; is gung ho and wants to command a battleship. The marriage? "Rhode returned an arch glance redolent of married sex." Elsewhere—the Nazis are on the march.

There are three children. Son Warren was involved in "an escapade involving an older woman and a midnight car crash. The parents had never raised the topic of women, partly from bashfulness—they were both prudish churchgoers, ill at ease with such a topic. . . ." Son Byron is in Siena carrying on with one Nathalie, niece of a famed American Jewish writer, author of *A Jew's Jesus.* Byron has recently turned against his Renaissance studies because " 'I don't believe David looked like Apollo, or Moses like Jupiter.' " Further, " 'The poor idealistic Jewish preacher from the back hills. That's the Lord I grew up with. My father's a religious man; we had to read a chapter of the Bible every morning at home.' "

At this point my worst fears about Mr. Wouk seemed justified. The Russian-speaking Victor Henry who reads a chapter of the Bible every morning to his family and is prudish about sexual matters is, Mr. Wouk wants us to believe, a typical gallant prewar goyisher American naval officer. If I may speak from a certain small knowledge (I was born at West Point, son of an instructor and graduate), I find Mr. Wouk's naval officer incredible—or "incredulous," as they say in best-seller land. There may have been a few religious nuts here and there in the fleet but certainly a naval officer who is about to be posted as an attaché to the American embassy in Berlin would not be one of them. In those days Annapolis was notoriously snobbish and no matter how simple and fundamentalist the background of its graduates, they tended toward worldliness; in fact, a surprising number married rich women. West Pointers were more square but also rowdier. Mr. Wouk's failure to come to terms with the American gentile is not unusual. Few American Jewish writers have been able to put themselves into gentile skins—much less foreskins. With ecumenical relish, Mr. Wouk tells us that son Byron (who marries a Jewish girl) is circumcised.

With an obviously bogus protagonist, Mr. Wouk must now depend upon the cunning of his narrative gift to propel these characters through great events: Berlin under Hitler, Poland during the Nazi invasion, London in the Blitz, Pearl Harbor on December 7, 1941; and not only must he describe the sweep of military and political action but also give us close-ups of Roosevelt, Churchill, Stalin, Hitler, Mussolini. It is Upton Sinclair all over again and, to my astonishment, it is splendid stuff. The detail is painstaking and generally authentic. The naïve portraits of the great men convince rather more than subtler work might have done.

Henry's reports from Berlin attract Roosevelt's attention. Mr. Wouk's portrait of FDR is by no means as sycophantish as one might expect. No doubt the recent revelations of the late President's sexual irregularities have forced the puritan Mr. Wouk to revise his estimate of a man I am sure he regarded at the time as a god, not to mention shield against the Cossacks. With hindsight he now writes, "Behind the jolly aristocratic surface, there loomed a grim ill-defined personality of distant visions and hard purpose, a tough son of a bitch to whom nobody meant very much, except perhaps his family; and maybe not they either." This is not at all bad, except as prose. Unfortunately, Mr. Wouk has no ear for "jolly aristocratic" speech patterns. I doubt if FDR would have called Pug "old top" (though when my father was in the administration the President used to address him, for some obscure reason, as "brother Vidal").

Also, Mr. Wouk makes strange assumptions. For instance, FDR "wore pince-nez glasses in imitation of his great relative, President Teddy Roosevelt, and he also imitated his booming manly manner; but a prissy Harvard accent made this heartiness somewhat ridiculous." The pince-nez was worn by a good many people in those days, but if FDR was consciously imitating anyone it would have been his mentor the pince-nezed Woodrow Wilson. T. Roosevelt's voice was not booming but thin and shrill. FDR's accent was neither prissy nor Harvard but Dutchess County and can still be heard among the American nobles now, thank God, out of higher politics.

With extraordinary ease, Mr. Wouk moves from husband to wife to sons to daughter, and the narrative never falters. His reconstruction of history is painless and, I should think, most useful to simple readers curious about the Second War. Yet there is a good deal of pop-writing silliness. We get the Mirror Scene (used by all pop-writers to tell us what the characters look like): "the mirror told her a different story, but even it seemed friendly to her that night: it showed . . ." We get the Fag Villain. In this case an American consul at Florence who will not give the good

Jew Jastrow a passport because "people don't see departmental circulars about consuls who've been recalled and whose careers have gone *poof!*" Sumner Welles is briefly glimpsed as a villain (and those who recall the gossip of the period will know why).

Then, of course, there is the problem of Mr. Wouk and sex. Daughter Madeline rooms with two girls and "both were having affairs—one with a joke writer, the other with an actor working as a bellhop. Madeline had found herself being asked to skulk around, stay out late, or remain in her room while one or another pair copulated. . . . She was disgusted. Both girls had good jobs, both dressed with taste, both were college graduates. Yet they behaved like sluts. . . ." But then to Madeline, "sex was a delightful matter of playing with fire, but enjoying the blaze from a safe distance, until she could leap into the hallowed white conflagration of a bridal night. She was a middle class good girl, and not in the least ashamed of it."

Incidentally, Mr. Wouk perpetuates the myth that the SS were all fags. This is now an article of faith with many uneducated Americans on the ground that to be a fag is the worst thing that could befall anyone next to falling into the hands of a fag sadist, particularly the SS guards who were as "alike as chorus boys . . . with blond waved hair, white teeth, bronzed skin, and blue eyes." Actually the SS guards in 1939 were not particularly pretty; they were also not fags. Hitler had eliminated that element.

Mr. Wouk's prose is generally correct if uninspired. The use of the ugly verb "shrill" crops up in at least half the best sellers under review and is plainly here to stay. Also, I suppose we must stop making any distinction between "nauseous" and "nauseated." The book ends with Pearl Harbor in flames and . . . yes, you've guessed it. The stars! "Overhead a clear starry black sky arched" (at least the sky was overhead and not underfoot), "with Orion setting in the west, and Venus sparkling in the east. . . . The familiar religious awe came over him, the sense of a Presence above this pitiful little earth. He could almost picture God the Father looking down with sad wonder at this mischief."

The films *Since You Went Away* and *The Best Years of Our Life* come to mind; not to mention all those *March of Times* in the Trans-Lux theaters of the old republic as it girded itself for war. But for all Mr. Wouk's idiocies and idiosyncrasies, his competence is most impressive and his professionalism awe-inspiring in a world of lazy writers and TV-stunned readers. I did not in the least regret reading every word of his book, though I suspect he is a writer best read swiftly by the page in order to get the sweep of his narrative while overlooking the infelicities of style and the shallowness of mind. I realize my sort of slow reading does a disservice to this kind of a book. But then I hope the author will be pleased to know that at least one person has actually read his very long best seller. Few people will. There is evidence that a recent best seller by a well-known writer was never read by its publisher or by the book club that took it or by the film company that optioned it. Certainly writers of book-chat for newspapers *never* read long books and seldom do more than glance at short ones.

Number six on the best-seller list, *The Camerons,* by Robert Crichton, is a mystifying work. One understands the sincerity of Herman Wouk, number seven, as he tries to impose his stern morality on an alien culture, or even that of the dread Marjorie Holmes, number ten, exploiting Bible Belt religiosity with what I trust is some degree of seriousness (all those chats with God must have made her a fan). But Mr. Crichton has elected to address himself to characters that seem to be infinitely remote from him, not to mention his readers. A UK mining town in what I take to be the 1870s (there is a reference to Keir Hardie, the trade unionist). With considerable fluency Mr. Crichton tells the story of a miner's sixteen-year-old daughter who goes to the Highlands to find herself a golden youth to give her children. She captures a Highland fisherman, locks him up in the mines for twenty years, and has a number of children by him who more or less fulfill her "genealogical" (as Trevanian would say) dream.

Of all these books this one is closest to the movies. The characters all speak with the singing cadences of Culver City's *How Green Was My Valley.* Another inspiration is *None But the Lonely Heart,* in which Ethel Barrymore said to Cary Grant, "Love's not for the poor, son." Mr. Cameron plays a number of variations on that theme, among them "Love, in everyday life, is a luxury."

One reads page after page, recalling movies. As always the Mirror Scene. The Food Scene (a good recipe for finnan haddie). There is the Fever Breaks Scene (during this episode I *knew* that there would have to be a tracheotomy and sure enough the doctor said that it was sometimes necessary but that in this case . . .). The Confrontation between Mr. Big and the Hero. Cameron has been injured while at work; the mine owner will give him no compensation. Cameron sues; the miners strike. He wins but not before the Confrontation with the Mob Scene when the miners turn on him for being the cause of their hunger. There is even the Illiterate Learning about Literature Scene, inspired by *The Corn Is Green,* in which Bette Davis taught the young Welsh miner John Dall to read Quality Lit so that he could grow up to be Emlyn Williams. Well, Cameron goes to the library and asks for *Macbeth* and reads it to the amazement of the bitter drunken librarian (Thomas Mitchell).

There is the Nubile Scene ("For a small girl she had large breasts and the shirt was tight and made her breasts stand out, and she kept the jacket near at hand because she didn't want to embarrass her father if he came into the room. She had only recently become that way and both she and her father weren't quite sure how to act about it"). Young Love Scene (the son's girl friend is named Allison—from *Peyton Place*). At the end, the Camerons sail for the New World. The first night out Cameron "wouldn't go down to her then and so he stayed at the rail and watched the phosphorescent waves wash up against the sides of the ship and explode in stars."

There is something drastically wrong with this smoothly executed novel and I cannot figure out what it is other than to suspect that the author lacks the integrity the Wise Hack insists upon. Mr. Crichton has decided to tell a story that does not seem to interest him very much. At those moments when the book almost comes alive (the conflict between labor and management), the author backs away from his true subject because socialism cannot be mentioned in best-seller land except as something innately wicked. Yet technically Mr. Crichton is a good writer and he ought to do a lot better than this since plainly he lacks the "integrity" to do worse.

Can your average beautiful teen-age Persian eunuch find happiness with your average Greek world conqueror who is also a dish and aged only twenty-six? The answer Mary Renault triumphantly gives us in *The Persian Boy* is *ne!* Twenty-five years ago *The City and the Pillar* was considered shocking because it showed what two nubile boys did together on a hot summer afternoon in McLean, Virginia. Worse, one of them went right on doing that sort of thing for the rest of his life. The scandal! The shame! In 1973 the only true love story on the best-seller list is about two homosexuals, and their monstrous aberration (so upsetting to

moralists like Mr. Wouk) is apparently taken for granted by those
ladies who buy hardcover novels.

At this point I find myself wishing that one had some way of
knowing just who buys and who reads what sort of books. I am
particularly puzzled (and pleased) by the success of Mary Renault. Americans have always disliked history (of some fifty subjects offered in high school the students recently listed history
fiftieth and least popular) and know nothing at all of the classical
world. Yet in a dozen popular books Mary Renault has made the
classical era alive, forcing even the dullest of book-chat writers to
recognize that bisexuality was once our culture's norm and that
Christianity's perversion of this human fact is the aberration and
not the other way around. I cannot think how Miss Renault has
managed to do what she has done, but the culture is the better for
her work.

I am predisposed to like the novel dealing with history and find
it hard to understand why this valuable genre should be so much
disdained. After all, every realistic novel is historical. But somehow, describing what happened last summer at Rutgers is for our
solemn writers a serious subject, while to re-create Alexander the
Great is simply frivolous. Incidentally, I am here concerned only
with the traditional novel as practiced by Updike, Tolstoy,
George Eliot, Nabokov, the Caldwells (Taylor and Erskine) as
well as by the ten writers under review. I leave for another and
graver occasion the matter of experimental high literature and its
signs.

In *The Persian Boy* Miss Renault presents us with Alexander at
the height of his glory as seen through the eyes of the boy eunuch
Bagoas. Miss Renault is good at projecting herself and us into
strange cultures. With ease she becomes her narrator Bagoas; the
book is told in the first person (a device *not* invented by Robert
Graves as innocent commentators like to tell us but a classroom
exercise going back more than two millennia: write as if you were
Alexander the Great addressing your troops before Tyre). Bagoas's father is murdered by political enemies; the boy is en-
slaved; castrated; rented out as a whore by his first master. Because of his beauty he ends up in the bed of the Great King of
Persia Darius. Alexander conquers Persia; sets fire to Persepolis.
The Great King is killed by his own people and Bagoas is presented by one of the murderers to Alexander, who, according to
historical account, never took advantage sexually of those he cap-

tured. Bagoas falls in love with the conqueror and, finally, seduces him. The love affair continues happily to the end, although there is constant jealousy on Bagoas's side because of Alexander's permanent attachment to his boyhood friend Hephaestion, not to mention the wives he picks up en route.

The effect of the book is phantasmagoric. Marvelous cities, strange landscapes, colliding cultures, and at the center the golden conqueror of the earth as he drives on and on past the endurance of his men, past his own strength. Today when a revulsion against war is normal, the usual commercialite would be inclined to depict Alexander as a Fag Villain-Killer, but in a note Miss Renault makes the point: "It needs to be borne in mind today that not till more than a century later did a handful of philosophers even start to question the morality of war." Alexander was doing what he thought a man in his place ought to do. The world was there to be conquered.

The device of observing the conqueror entirely through the eyes of an Oriental is excellent and rather novel. We are able to see the Macedonian troops as they appeared to the Persians: crude gangsters smashing to bits an old and subtle culture they cannot understand, like today's Americans in Asia. But, finally, *hubris* is the theme; and the fire returns to heaven. I am not at all certain that what we have here is the "right" Alexander, but right or not, Miss Renault has drawn the portrait of someone who *seems* real yet unlike anyone else, and that divinity the commercialites are forever trying for in their leaden works really does gleam from time to time in the pages of this nice invention.

August 1914 has already been dealt with at sympathetic but cautious length in these pages and I shall touch on it only as it relates to other best sellers. As a fiction the novel is not as well managed as Mr. Wouk's *Winds of War*. I daresay as an expression of one man's indomitable spirit in a tyrannous society we must honor if not the art the author. Fortunately the Nobel Prize is designed for just such a purpose. Certainly it is seldom bestowed for literary merit; if it were, Nabokov and not the noble engineer Solzhenitsyn would have received it when the Swedes decided it was Holy Russia's turn to be honored.

Solzhenitsyn is rooted most ambitiously in literature as well as in films. Tolstoy appears on page 3 and Tolstoy hangs over the work like a mushroom cloud. In a sense the novel is to be taken as a dialogue between the creator of *War and Peace* and Solzhenit-

syn; with the engineer opposing Tolstoy's view of history as a
series of great tides in which the actions of individuals matter not
at all. I'm on Solzhenitsyn's side in this debate but cannot get
much worked up over his long and wearisome account of Russian
military bungling at the beginning of the First World War. The
characters are impossible to keep straight, though perhaps future
volumes will clarify things. Like *Winds of War*, this is the first of
a series.

The book begins with dawn on the Caucasus, towering "so vast
above petty human creation, so elemental . . ." The word "vast"
is repeated in the next paragraph to get us in the mood for a
superspectacle. Then we learn that one of the characters has
actually met Tolstoy, and their meeting is recalled on page 17.
" 'What is the aim of man's life on earth?' " asks the young man.
Tolstoy's reply is prompt: " 'To serve good and thereby to build
the Kingdom of Heaven on earth.' " How? " 'Only through love!
Nothing else. No one will discover anything better.' " This is
best-seller writing with a vengeance.

In due course we arrive at the Mirror Scene: "She was not even
comforted by the sight of her naturally rosy skin, her round
shoulders, the hair which fell down to her hips and took four
buckets of rain water to wash." The Nubile Scene: "She had
always avoided undressing even in front of other women, because
she was ashamed of her breasts, which were large, big and generous even for a woman of her build." Wisdom Phrases: "The
dangers of beauty are well known: narcissism, irresponsibility,
selfishness." Or "Evil people always support each other; that is
their chief strength." Like Hitler and Stalin? Also, *Christian* Wisdom Phrases: "There is a justice which existed before us, without
us and for its own sake. And our task is to *divine* what it is." Not
since Charles Morgan's last novel has there been so much profun-
dity in a best seller.

As for the movies, the best Russian product is recalled, particularly *Battleship Potemkin*. Also, boldly acknowledging the cinema's
primacy, Solzhenitsyn has rendered his battle scenes in screenplay form with "=" meaning CUT TO. These passages are particularly inept. *"Mad tearing sound of rifle fire, machine-gun fire, artillery
fire!/ Reddened by fire, THE WHEEL still rolls./ = The firelight glitters
with savage joy/"* and so on. The Wise Hack would have been
deeply disturbed by the presumption of this member of the audience who ought to be eating popcorn in the second balcony and

not parodying the century's one true art form that also makes money. From time to time Solzhenitsyn employs the Dos Passos device of random newspaper cuttings to give us a sense of what is going on in August 1914. This works a bit better than the mock screenplay.

At the book's core there is nothing beyond the author's crypto-Christianity, which is obviously not going to please his masters; they will also dislike his astonishing discovery that "the best social order is not susceptible to being arbitrarily constructed, or even to being scientifically constructed." To give the noble engineer his due he is good at describing how things work, and it is plain that nature destined him to write manuals of artillery or instructions on how to take apart a threshing machine. Many people who do not ordinarily read books have bought this book and mention rather proudly that they are reading it, but so far I have yet to meet anyone who has finished it. I fear that the best one can say of Solzhenitsyn is *goré vidal* (a Russian phrase meaning "he has seen grief").

A peculiarity of American sexual mores is that those men who like to think of themselves as exclusively and triumphantly heterosexual are convinced that the most masculine of all activities is not tending to the sexual needs of women but watching other men play games. I have never understood this aspect of my countrymen but I suppose there is a need for it (bonding?), just as the Romans had a need to see people being murdered. Perhaps there is a connection between the American male's need to watch athletes and his fatness: according to a W.H.O. report the American male is the world's fattest and softest; this might explain why he also loves guns—you can always get your revolver up.

I fear that I am not the audience Mr. Dan Jenkins had in mind when he wrote his amiable book *Semi-Tough,* but I found it pleasant enough, and particularly interesting for what it does *not* go into. The narrator is a pro football player who has been persuaded "that it might be good for a pro football stud to have a book which might have a healthy influence on kids." Question: Do young people watch football games nowadays? It seems to me that "jock-sniffers" (as Mr. Jenkins calls them) are of Nixonian age and type—though few have the thirty-seventh president's nose for such pleasures. The unfat and the unsoft young must have other diversions. One wonders, too, if they believe that "a man makes himself a man by whatever he does with himself, and in pro football that means busting his ass for his team."

Semi-Tough tells of the preparation for the big game. Apparently, training involves an astonishing amount of drink, pot, and what the narrator refers to as "wool," meaning cunt. There is one black player who may or may not like boys and the narrator clams up on what is a very delicate subject in jock circles. I am not sure Mr. Jenkins is aware of all the reverberations set off by the jokes of one of his white players. Asked why he is an athlete, the stud says, " 'Mainly, we just like to take showers with niggers.' " It is a pity Mary Renault did not write this book. And a pity, come to think of it, that Mr. Jenkins did not write *August 1914*, a subject suitable for his kind of farce. No movie in *Semi-Tough*. As the Wise Hack knows all too well, sports movies bomb at the box office. Perhaps the Warhol factory will succeed where the majors have failed. SHOWER ROOM—LONG SHOT. CUT TO: CLOSE SHOT—SOAP.

At first glance *The Odessa File*, by Frederick Forsyth, looks to be just another bold hard-hitting attack on the Nazis in the form of a thriller masked as a pseudo-documentary. But the proportions of this particular bit of nonsense are very peculiarly balanced. First, the book is dedicated "to all press reporters." The dust jacket tells us that the author worked for Reuters in the early 1960s; it does not give us his nationality but from the odd prose that he writes I suspect his first language is not English. Also the book's copyright is in the name of a company: a tax dodge not possible for American citizens. Next there is an Author's Note. Mr. Forsyth tells us that although he gives "heartfelt thanks" to all those who helped him in his task he cannot name any of them for three reasons. Apparently some were former members of the SS and "were not aware at the time either whom they were talking to, or that what they said would end up in a book." Others asked not to be mentioned; still others are omitted "for their sakes rather than for mine." This takes care of the sources for what he would like us to believe is a true account of the way Odessa (an organization of former SS officers) continues to help its members in South America and the Federal Republic.

After the Author's Note there is a Foreword (by the author). We are told who Adolf Hitler was and how he and the Nazis ruled Germany from 1933 to 1945 and how they organized the SS in order to kill fourteen million "so-called enemies of the Reich," of which six million were Jews. When Germany began to lose the war, "vast sums of gold were smuggled out and deposited in numbered bank accounts, false identity papers were prepared, escape channels opened up. When the Allies finally conquered Germany, the bulk of the mass-murderers had gone."

Well, one knows about Eichmann, and of course Martin Bormann is a minor industry among bad journalists; so presumably there are other "important" SS officers growing old in Paraguay. But do they, as Mr. Forsyth assures us, have an organization called Odessa whose aim is "fivefold"? Firstfold is "to rehabilitate former SS men *into the professions* of the Federal Republic"; second, "to infiltrate at least the lower echelons of political party activity"; third, to provide "legal defense" for any SS killer hauled before a court and in every way possible to stultify the course of justice in West Germany; fourth, to promote the fortunes of former SS members (this seems to be a repeat of the first of the fivefolds); and, five, "to propagandize the German people to the viewpoint that the SS killers were in fact none other than ordinary patriotic soldiers."

This is food for thought. Yet why has one never heard of Odessa? Mr. Forsyth anticipates that question: "changing its name several times" (highly important for a completely secret society), "the Odessa has sought to deny its own existence as an organization, with the result that many Germans are inclined to say that Odessa does not exist. The short answer is: it exists. . . ." We are then assured that the tale he is about to tell represents one of their failures. Obviously fun and games; presumably, there is no such thing as the Odessa but in the interest of making a thriller look like a document (today's fashion in novels) the author is mingling true with "false facts," as Thomas Jefferson would say.

Now for the story. But, no, after the Dedication and the Author's Note and the Foreword there comes a Publisher's Note. Apparently many of the characters in the book are "real people" but "the publishers do not wish to elucidate further because it is in this ability to perplex the reader as to how much is true and how much false that much of the grip of the story lies." The publishers, Viking, write suspiciously like Mr. Forsyth. "Nevertheless, the publishers feel the reader may be interested or assisted to know that the story of former SS Captain Eduard Roschmann, the commandant of the concentration camp at Riga from 1941 to 1944, from his birth in Graz, Austria, in 1908, to his present exile in South America, is completely factual and drawn from SS and West German records." So let us bear this Publisher's Note in mind as we contemplate the story Mr. Forsyth tells.

After the fall of Hitler, Roschmann was harbored at "the enormous Franciscan Monastery in Rome in Via Sicilia." There is no such establishment according to my spies in the order. "Bishop Alois Hudal, the German Bishop in Rome" (Mr. Forsyth seems to think that this is some sort of post) "spirited thousands [of SS] to safety." "The SS men traveled on Red Cross travel documents, issued through the intervention of the Vatican." After a period in Egypt, Roschmann returns to Germany in 1955 under a pseudonym. Thanks to Odessa, he becomes the head of an important firm. He conducts secret research "aimed at devising a teleguidance system for those rockets [he] is now working on in West Germany. His code name is Vulkan."

Why is Roschmann at work on the rockets? Because Odessa and its evil scientists "have proposed to President Nasser" (whose predecessor Mr. Forsyth thinks was named Naguil), and he "accepted with alacrity, that these warheads on the Kahiras and Zafiras be of a different type. Some will contain concentrated cultures of bubonic plague, and the others will explode high above the ground, showering the entire territory of Israel with irradiated cobalt-sixty. Within hours they will all be dying of the pest or of gamma-ray sickness."

This is splendid Fu Manchu nonsense (infecting the Israelis with bubonic plague would of course start a world epidemic killing the Egyptians, too, while spreading radioactive cobalt in the air would probably kill off a large percentage of the world's population, as any story conference at Universal would quickly conclude). Next Mr. Forsyth presents us with the classic thriller cliché: only one man holds this operation together. Roschmann. Destroy him and Israel is saved.

The plot of course is foiled by a West German newspaperman and its details need not concern us: it is the sort of storytelling that propels the hero from one person to the next person, asking questions. As a stylist, Mr. Forsyth is addicted to the freight-car sentence: "This time his destination was Bonn, the small and boring town on the river's edge that Konrad Adenauer had chosen as the capital of the Federal Republic, because he came from it." (Adenauer came from Cologne but Mr. Forsyth is not one to be deterred by small details: after all, he is under the impression that it was Martin Bormann "on whom the mantle of the Führer had fallen after 1945.") What is important is that Mr. Forsyth and Viking Press want us to believe that the Vatican knowingly saved thousands of SS men after 1945, that six of the ten high-ranking Hamburg police officers in 1964 were former SS men, that President Nasser authorized a clandestine SS organization to provide him with the means to attack Israel with bubonic plague, and that when this plot failed, the Argentine government presumably offered asylum to Captain Roschmann. *Caveat emptor.*

The boldness of author and publisher commands . . . well, awe and alarm. Is it possible now to write a novel in which Franklin Roosevelt secretly finances the German American Bund because he had been made mad by infantile paralysis? Can one write a novel in which Brezhnev is arranging with the American army defectors in Canada to poison Lake Michigan (assuming this is not a redundancy)? Viking would probably say, yes, why not? And for good measure, to ensure success, exploit the prejudices, if possible, of American Jewish readers, never letting them forget that the guilt of the Germans ("dreaming only in the dark hours of the ancient gods of strength and lust and power") for having produced Hitler is now as eternal in the works of bad writers and greedy publishers as is the guilt of the Jews for the death of Jesus in the minds of altogether too many simple Christians. Exploitation of either of these myths strikes me as an absolute evil and not permissible even in the cheapest of fiction brought out by the most opportunist of publishers.

The number one best seller is called *Jonathan Livingston Seagull.* It is a greeting card bound like a book with a number of photographs of seagulls in flight. The brief text celebrates the desire for excellence of a seagull who does not want simply to fly in order to eat but to fly beautifully for its own sake. He is much disliked for this by his peers; in fact, he is ostracized. Later he is translated to higher and higher spheres where he can spend eternity practicing new flight techniques. It is touching that this little story should be so very popular because it is actually celebrating art for art's sake as well as the virtues of nonconformity; and so, paradoxically, it gives pleasure to the artless and to the conforming, to the drones who dream of honey-making in their unchanging hive.

Unlike the other best sellers this work is not so much a reflection of the age of movies as it is a tribute to Charles Darwin and his high priestess, the incomparable creatrix of *The Fountainhead* (starring Gary Cooper and Patricia Neal), Ayn Rand.

There is not much point in generalizing further about these best sellers. The authors prefer fact or its appearance to actual invention. This suggests that contemporary historians are not doing their job if to Wouk and Solzhenitsyn falls the task of telling today's reader about two world wars and to Forsyth and Trevanian current tales of the cold war. As Christianity and Judaism sink into decadence, religioso fictions still exert a certain appeal. It will surprise certain politicians to learn that sex is of no great interest to best-selling authors. Only *Semi-Tough* tries to be sexy, and fails. Too much deodorant.

Reading these ten books one after the other was like being trapped in the "Late Late Show," staggering from one half-remembered movie scene to another, all the while beginning to suspect with a certain horror that the Wise Hack at the Writers' Table will be honored and remembered for his many credits on numerous profitable pix long after Isherwood (adapted "The Gambler," with Gregory Peck), Faulkner (adapted *The Big Sleep*, with Humphrey Bogart), Huxley (adapted *Pride and Prejudice*, with Greer Garson), Vidal (adapted *Suddenly Last Summer*, with Elizabeth Taylor) take their humble places below the salt, as it were, for none of us regarded with sufficient seriousness the greatest art form of all time. By preferring perversely to write books that reflected not the movies we had seen but life itself, not as observed by that sterile machine the camera but as it is netted by the protean fact of a beautiful if diminishing and polluted language, we were, all in all, kind of dumb. Like Sam, one should've played it again.

The New York Review of Books,
May 17 and May 31, 1973

The Great World
and Louis Auchincloss

"What a dull and dreary trade is that of critic," wrote Diderot. "It is so difficult to create a thing, even a mediocre thing; it is so easy to detect mediocrity." Either the great philosophe was deliberately exaggerating or Americans have always lived in an entirely different continuum from Europe. For us the making of mediocre things is the rule while the ability to detect mediocrity or anything else is rare. A century ago, E. L. Godkin wrote in *The Nation:* "The great mischief has always been that whenever our reviewers deviate from the usual and popular course of panegyric, they start from and end in personality, so that the public mind is almost sure to connect unfavorable criticism with personal animosity."

Don't knock, boost! was the cry of Warren Harding. To which the corollary was plain: anyone who knocks is a bad person with a grudge. As a result, the American has always reacted to the setting of standards rather the way Count Dracula responds to a clove of garlic or a crucifix. Since we are essentially a nation of hustlers rather than makers, any attempt to set limits or goals,

rules or standards, is to attack a system of free enterprise where
not only does the sucker not deserve that even break but the
honest man is simply the one whose cheating goes undetected.
Worse, to say that one English sentence might be better made
than another is to be a snob, a subverter of the democracy, a
Know Nothing enemy of the late arrivals to our shores and its
difficult language.

I doubt if E. L. Godkin would find our American book-chat
scene any better today than it was when he and his literary editor
Wendell Phillips Garrison did their best to create if not common
readers uncommon reviewers. Panegyric is rarer today than it
was in the last century but personality is still everything, as the
Sunday *New York Times Book Review* demonstrates each week: who
can ever forget the *Times*'s gorgeous tribute not so much to the
book by Mr. Saul Bellow under review but to its author's admittedly unusual physical beauty? What matters is not if a book is
good or bad (who, after all, would know the difference?) but
whether or not the author is a good person or a bad person. It is
an article of faith among us that only a good person can write a
good book; certainly, a bad person will only write bad books (the
continuing Ezra Pound debate is full of fine examples of this
popular wisdom).

But then, moralizing is as natural to the American book-chat
writer as it is to the rest of our countrymen—a sort of national
tic. Naturally, there are fashions in goodness owing to changes
in the Climate of Opinion (current forecast: Chomsky occluded,
low pressure over the black experience, small Stravinsky-Craft
warnings). Also, since Godkin's time, the American university
has come into its terrible own. Departments of English now
produce by what appears to be parthenogenesis novels intended
only for the classroom; my favorite demonstrated that the universe is—what else?—the university. Occasionally, a university
novel (or U-novel) will be read by the general (and dwindling)
public for the novel; and sometimes a novel written for that same
public (P-novel) will be absorbed into Academe, but more and
more the division between the two realms grows and soon what
is written to be taught in class will stay there and what is written
to be read outside will stay there, too. On that day the kingdom
of prose will end, with an exegesis.

Meanwhile, book-chat, both P and U, buzzes on like some
deranged bumblebee with a taste for ragweed; its store of bitter

honey periodically collected and offered the public (?) in books with titles like *Literary Horizons: A Quarter Century of American Fiction*, by Granville Hicks, one of the most venerable bees in the business, a nice old thing who likes just about everything that's "serious" but tends to worry more about the authors than their books. Will X develop? Get past the hurdle of The Second Novel (everyone has One Novel in him, the First) or will fashion destroy him? Drink? Finally, does he deserve to be memorialized in *Literary Horizons?* Mr. Hicks's list of approved novelists contains one black, one Catholic, one Southern Wasp and six Jews. That is the standard mix for the seventies. The fifties mix would have been six Southern Wasps, one Jew, no black, etc.

For those who find puzzling the high favor enjoyed by the Jewish novelist in today's book-chat land, I recommend Mr. Alfred Kazin's powerful introduction to *The Commentary Reader*, "The Jew as Modern American Writer." Mr. Kazin tells us, with pardonable pride, that not only are Jews "the mental elite of the power age" but "definitely it was now [1966] the thing to be Jewish." As a result, to be a Jew in America is the serious subject for a P- or even U-novel, while to be a Wasp is to be away from the creative center; the born Catholic (as opposed to a convert) is thought at best cute (if Irish), at worst silly (if drunken Irish). In the permissive sixties, Negroes were allowed to pass themselves off as blacks and their books were highly praised for a time, but then there was all that trouble in the schools and what with one thing or another the black writers faded away except for James Baldwin, Mr. Hicks's token nigger. Yet even Mr. Hicks is worried about Mr. Baldwin. Does he *really* belong on the List? Is it perhaps time for his "funeral service" as a writer? Or will he make one final titanic effort and get it all together and write The Novel?

Like Bouvard, like Pécuchet, like every current book-chatterer, Hicks thinks that there really is something somewhere called The Novel which undergoes periodic and progressive change (for the better—this is America!) through Experiments by Great Masters. Consequently the Task of the Critic is to make up Lists of Contenders and place his bets accordingly. Not for Mr. Hicks Brigid Brophy's truism: there is no such thing as The Novel, only novels.

At any given moment the subject or the matter of American fiction is limited by the prevailing moral prejudices and assumptions of the residents in book-chat land. U-novels must always be predictably experimental (I reserve for another occasion a scrutiny of those interesting cacti) while the respectable P-novel is always naturalistic, usually urban, often Jewish, always middle-class, and, of course, deeply, sincerely heterosexual.

Conscious of what the matter of fiction *ought* to be, Mr. Hicks somewhat nervously puts Louis Auchincloss on his list. On the one hand, Auchincloss deals entirely with the American scene, writes in a comfortably conventional manner, and is one of the few intellectuals who write popular novels. On the other hand, despite these virtues, Auchincloss is not much thought of in either the P or the U world and Mr. Hicks is forced to buzz uneasily: "Although I have read and reviewed most of Louis Auchincloss's work in the past twelve years, I hesitated about including him in this volume." So the original Debrett must have felt when first called upon to include the Irish peerage. "Certainly he has not been one of the movers and shakers of the postwar period." As opposed, presumably, to Reynolds Price, Wright Morris, Herbert Gold, Bernard Malamud, and the other powerhouses on Mr. Hicks's list. Actually, only two or three of Mr. Hicks's writers could be said to have made any contribution at all to world literature. But that is a matter of taste. After all, what, Pontius, *is* literature?

Mr. Hicks returns worriedly to the *matter* of fiction. Apparently Auchincloss "has written for the most part about 'good' society, the well-to-do and the well-bred. And he has written about them with authority. What bothers me is not that he writes about this little world but that he seems to be aware of no other. Although he is conscious of its faults, he never questions its values in any serious way." This is fascinating. I have read all of Auchincloss's novels and I cannot recall one that did not in a most serious way question the values of his "little world." Little world!

It is a tribute to the cunning of our rulers and to the stupidity of our intellectuals (book-chat division, anyway) that the world Auchincloss writes about, the domain of Wall Street bankers and lawyers and stockbrokers, is thought to be irrelevant, a faded and fading genteel-gentile enclave when, in actual fact, this little world comprises the altogether too vigorous and self-renewing ruling class of the United States—an oligarchy that is in firm control of the Chase Manhattan Bank, American foreign policy, and the decision-making processes of both the Republican and

Democratic parties; also, most "relevantly," Auchincloss's characters set up and administer the various foundations that subsidize those universities where academics may serenely and dully dwell like so many frogs who think their pond the ocean—or the universe the university.

Of all our novelists, Auchincloss is the only one who tells us how our rulers behave in their banks and their boardrooms, their law offices and their clubs. Yet such is the vastness of our society and the remoteness of academics and book-chatterers from actual power that those who should be most in this writer's debt have no idea what a useful service he renders us by revealing and, in some ways, by betraying his class. But then how can the doings of a banker who is white and gentile and rich be *relevant* when everyone knows that the only meaningful American experience is to be Jewish, lower-middle-class, and academic? Or (in Mr. Hicks's words), "As I said a while ago and was scolded for saying, the characteristic hero of our time is a misfit." Call me Granville.

Ignorance of the real world is not a new thing in our literary life. After the Second World War, a young critic made a splash with a book that attributed the poverty of American fiction to the lack of a class system—a vulgar variation on Henry James's somewhat similar but usually misunderstood observations about American life. This particular writer came from a small town in the Midwest; from school, he had gone into the service and from there into a university. Since he himself had never seen any sign of a class system, he decided that the United States was a truly egalitarian society. It should be noted that one of the charms of the American arrangement is that a citizen can go through a lifetime and never know his true station in life or who his rulers are.

Of course our writers know that there are rich people hidden away somewhere (in the gossip columns of Suzy, in the novels of Louis Auchincloss), but since the Depression the owners of the country have played it cool, kept out of sight, consumed inconspicuously. Finally, no less a P (now P-U)-writer than that lifelong little friend of the rich Ernest Hemingway felt obliged to reassure us that the rich are really just folks. For the P-writer the ruling class does not exist as a subject for fiction if only because the rulers are not to be found in his real world of desperate suburbs. The U-writer knows about the Harkness plan—but then what is a harkness? Something to do with horse racing?

While the names that the foundations bear do not suggest to him our actual rulers—only their stewards in the bureaucracy of philanthropy, the last stronghold of the great immutable fortunes.

The serious P-writer knows that he must reflect the world he lives in: the quotidian of the average man. To look outside that world is to be untrue and, very possibly, undemocratic. To write about the actual rulers of the world we live in (assuming that they exist, of course) is to travel in fantasy land. As a result, novels to do with politics, the past, money, manners, power are as irrelevant to the serious P-writer as are the breathy commercial fictions of all the Irvingses—so unlike the higher relevancies of all the Normans.

In a society where matters of importance are invariably euphemized (how can an antipersonnel weapon actually kill?) a writer like Louis Auchincloss who writes about the way money is made and spent is going to have a very hard time being taken seriously. For one thing, it is now generally believed in book-chat land that the old rich families haven't existed since the time of Edith Wharton while the new-rich are better suited for journalistic exposés than for a treatment in the serious P- or U-novel. It is true that an indiscriminate reading public enjoys reading Auchincloss because, unlike the well-educated, they suspect that the rich are always with us and probably up to no good. But since the much-heralded death of the Wasp establishment, the matter of Auchincloss's fiction simply cannot be considered important.

This is too bad. After all, he is a good novelist, and a superb short-story writer. More important, he has made a brave effort to create his own literary tradition—a private oasis in the cactus land of American letters. He has written about Shakespeare's penchant for motiveless malignity (a peculiarly American theme), about Henry James, about our women writers as the custodians and caretakers of the values of that dour European tribe which originally killed the Indians and settled the continent.

Mr. Hicks, with his eerie gift for misunderstanding what a writer is writing about, thinks that Auchincloss is proudly showing off his class while bemoaning its eclipse by later arrivals. Actually, the eye that Auchincloss casts on his own class is a cold one and he is more tortured than complacent when he records in book after book the collapse of the Puritan ethical system and its replacement by—as far as those of us now living can tell—nothing. As for the ruling class being replaced by later arrivals, he knows (though they, apparently, do not) that regardless of the considerable stir the newcomers have made in the peripheral worlds of the universities, showbiz, and book-chat, they have made almost no impact at all on the actual power structure of the country.

Auchincloss deals with the masters of the American empire partly because they are the people he knows best and partly, I suspect, because he cannot figure them out to his own satisfaction. Were they better or worse in the last century? What is good, what is bad in business? And business (money) is what our ruling class has always been about; this is particularly obvious now that the evangelical Christian style of the last century has been abandoned by all but the most dull of our rulers' employees (read any speech by any recent president to savor what was once the very sound of Carnegie, of Gould, and of Rockefeller).

Finally, most unfashionably, Auchincloss writes best in the third person; his kind of revelation demands a certain obliqueness, a moral complexity which cannot be rendered in the confessional tone that marks so much of current American fiction, good and bad. He plays God with his characters, and despite the old-fashionedness of his literary method he is an unusually compelling narrator, telling us things that we don't know about people we don't often meet in novels—what other novelist went to school with Bill and McGenghis Bundy? Now, abruptly, he ceases to play God. The third person becomes first person as he describes in *A Writer's Capital* the world and the family that produced him, a world and family not supposed either by their own standards or by those of book-chat land to produce an artist of any kind.

I must here confess to an interest. From the time I was ten until I was sixteen years old my stepfather was Hugh D. Auchincloss, recently saluted by a society chronicler as "the first gentleman of the United States"—to the enormous pleasure and true amazement of the family. The Auchinclosses resemble the fictional Primes in *The Embezzler*, a family that over the years has become extraordinarily distinguished for no discernible reason or, as Louis puts it, "There was never an Auchincloss fortune . . . each generation of Auchincloss men either made or married its own money."

Plainly, even sharply, Louis chronicles the family's history from their arrival in America (1803) to the present day. He is realistic about the family's pretensions though he does not seem to be aware of the constant chorus of criticism their innumerable in-laws used to (still do?) indulge in. I can recall various quasi-humorous rebellions on the part of the in-laws (once led by Wilmarth Lewis) at the annual clan gathering in New York. What the in-laws could never understand was the source of the family's self-esteem. After all, what had they ever *done?* And didn't they come to America a bit late by true "aristocratic" standards? And hadn't they been peddlers back in Scotland who had then gone into *dry goods* in New York? And what was so great about making blue jeans? Besides, weren't they all a bit too dark? What about "those grave, watery eyes over huge aquiline noses"? And wasn't there a rumor that they had Italian blood? And when you come right down to it didn't they look (this was only whispered at Bailey's Beach, muttered in the men's room of the Knickerbocker) *Jewish?*

In the various peregrinations of the branch of the family that I was attached to (I almost wrote "assigned to": sooner or later the Auchinclosses pick up one of everything, including the chicest of the presidents), I never came across Louis, who was, in any case, eight years older than I. Right after the war when I was told that a Louis Auchincloss had written a novel, I said: Not possible. No Auchincloss could write a book. Banking and law, power and money—that is their category.

From reading Louis's memoir I gather that that was rather his own view of the matter. He had a good deal to overcome and this is reflected in the curiously tense tone of his narrative. He had the bad luck, for a writer, to come from a happy family, and there is no leveler as great as a family's love. Hatred of one parent or the other can make an Ivan the Terrible or a Hemingway; the protective love, however, of two devoted parents can absolutely destroy an artist. This seems to have been particularly true in the case of Louis's mother. For one thing she knew a good deal about literature (unlike every other American writer's mother) and so hoped that he would not turn out to be second-rate, and wretched.

From the beginning, Louis was a writer: word-minded, gossip-prone, book-devouring. In other words, a sissy by the standards of the continuing heterosexual dictatorship that has so perfectly perverted in one way or another just about every male in the country. The sensitive, plump, small boy like Louis has a particularly grim time of it but, happily, as the memoir shows, he was able eventually to come to grips with himself and society in a way that many of the other sensitive, plump boys never could. A somber constant of just about every American literary gathering is the drunk, soft, aging writer who bobs and weaves and jabs pathetically at real and imagined enemies, happy in his ginny madness that he is demonstrating for all the world to see his so potent manliness.

By loving both parents more or less equally, Auchincloss saw through the manly world of law and finance; saw what it did to his father, who suffered, at one point, a nervous breakdown. Not illogically, "I came to think of women as a privileged happy lot. With the right to sit home all day on sofas and telephone, and of men as poor slaves doomed to go downtown and do dull, soul-breaking things to support their families." As for Wall Street, "never shall I forget the horror inspired in me by those narrow dark streets and those tall sooty towers. . . ." The story of Auchincloss's life is how he reconciled the world of father with that of mother; how he became a lawyer and a novelist; how the practice of law nourished his art and, presumably, the other way around, though I'm not so sure that I would want such a good novelist creating a trust for me.

Groton, Yale, Virginia Law School, the Navy during the Second World War, then a Manhattan law firm, psychoanalysis, marriage, children, two dozen books. Now from the author's middle age, he looks back at himself and our time, holding the mirror this way and that, wondering why, all in all, he lacked the talent early on for being happy, for being himself. With characteristic modesty, he underplays his own struggle to reconcile two worlds, not to mention the duality of his own nature. Yet I suspect that having made himself a writer, he must have found demoralizing the fact that the sort of writing he was interested in doing was, simply, not acceptable to the serious U- or even the serious P-book-chatterers.

The literary line to which Auchincloss belongs was never vigorous in the United States—as demonstrated by its master Henry James's wise removal to England. Edith Wharton moved to France, but remained an American; even so, to this day, she is regarded as no more than pale James. Since Mrs. Wharton, the novel of manners has been pretty much in the hands of commercialites. Neither the insider Marquand nor the outsider O'Hara is taken seriously in U-land while in P-land they were particularly denigrated after the war when book-chat was no longer written by newspapermen who were given books to review because they were not good enough to write about games but by young men and women who had gone to universities where the modern tradition *(sic)* was entirely exotic: Joyce and Lawrence, Proust and Kafka were solemnly presented to them as the models worth honoring or emulating. It is true that right after the war James made a comeback, but only as an elaborate maker of patterns: *what* Maisie knew was not so important as her way of telling what she knew.

The early fifties was not a good time for a writer like Louis Auchincloss. But it could have been worse: at least he did not have to apologize for his class because, pre-Camelot, no American writer had a clue who or what an Auchincloss was. Yet even then his novels never much interested his fellow writers or those who chatted them up because he did not appear to deal with anything that really mattered, like the recent war, or being Jewish-/academic/middle-class/heterosexual in a world of ball-cutters. No one was prepared for dry ironic novels about our rulers—not even those social scientists who are forever on the lookout for the actual bill of sale for the United States.

Auchincloss himself was no help. He refused to advertise himself. If the book-chatterers had no idea what Sullivan and Cromwell was he wasn't going to tell them. He just showed the firm in action. He also knew, from the beginning, what he was doing: "I can truly say that I was never 'disillusioned' by society. I was perfectly clear from the beginning that I was interested in the story of money: how it was made, inherited, lost, spent." Not since Dreiser has an American writer had so much to tell us about the role of money in our lives. In fascinating detail, he shows how generations of lawyers have kept intact the great fortunes of the last century. With Pharaonic single-mindedness they have filled the American social landscape with pyramids of tax-exempt money, to the eternal glory of Rockefeller, Ford, et al. As a result, every American's life has been affected by the people Auchincloss writes so well about.

I cannot recall where or when I first met Louis. He lists me among a dozen writers he met twenty years ago at the Greenwich Village flat of the amiable novelist Vance Bourjaily and his wife. I do recall the curiosity I had about him: how on earth was he going to be both a lawyer and a writer (a question entirely subjective: how could I write what I did and be an effective politician? Answer: forget it). I can't remember how he answered the question or if he did. I was amused by the reaction of other writers to him. They knew—particularly the wives or girl friends—that there was something "social" about him but that was neither a plus nor a minus in the Eisenhower era. Earlier it would have been a considerable handicap. In my first years as a writer, I was often pleased to be identified with the protagonist of *The City and the Pillar*—a male prostitute. After all, that was a *real* identity, I thought, sharing the collective innocence.

Louis moved through these affairs with considerable charm and he exaggerates when he writes: "The fact that I was a Wall Street lawyer, a registered Republican, and a social registrite was quite enough for half the people at any one party to cross me off as a kind of duckbill platypus not to be taken seriously." Rather wistfully, he observes: "I am sure I had read more books by more of the guests at any one party than anyone else." I am sure that he had. But then it has always been true that in the United States the people who ought to read books write them. Poor Louis who *knew* French and American literature, who "kept up" with what was going on, now found himself in a literary society of illiterate young play-actors. Overexcited by the publicity surrounding Hemingway and Fitzgerald, they had decided to imitate these "old masters." At least a dozen were playing Hemingway—and several grizzled survivors still are. Certainly no one was himself —but then selves are hard to come by in America. So, in a way, Louis was indeed like a platypus in that farmyard of imitation roosters. After all, he didn't resemble any famous writer we had ever heard of. He was simply himself, and so odd man out to the young counterfeiters.

Since then, Auchincloss has learned (through psychoanalysis, he tells us) that "a man's background is largely of his own creating." Yet pondering the response to this discovery as expressed in his work, he writes,

> American critics still place a great emphasis on the fact of background on character, and by background they mean something absolute which is the same for all those in the foreground. Furthermore, they tend to assume that the effect of any class privilege in a background must be deleterious to a character and that the author has introduced such a background only to explain the harm done. Now the truth is that the background to most of my characters has

been selected simply because it is a familiar one to me and is hence
more available as a model. . . . I cannot but surmise that the stubborn
refusal on the part of many critics to see this is evidence of a resentment on their part against the rich, a resentment sometimes carried
to the point of denying that a rich man can be a valid subject for
fiction. . . . Such a point of view would have been, of course, ridiculous in the eighteenth or nineteenth centuries when the great bulk
of the characters of fiction came from the upper or upper middle
class. Critics did not resent Anna Karenina or Colonel Newcome.

Louis Auchincloss's latest book, *The Partners,* is a collection of
related short stories set in a New York law firm. A merger has
been proposed between the demure firm of the partners and a
larger, flashier firm. Old values (but are they really values?) combat new forces. Invariably those who do the right self-sacrificing
thing end up echoing Mrs. Lee in Henry Adams's *Democracy:*
"The bitterest part of all this horrid story is that nine out of ten
of your countrymen would say I have made a mistake." By not
marrying a blackguard senator.

The author's virtues are well displayed: almost alone among
our writers he is able to show in a convincing way men at work
—men at work discreetly managing the nation's money, selecting
its governors, creating the American empire. Present, too, are his
vices. Narrative is sometimes forced too rapidly, causing characters to be etiolated while the profound literariness of the author
keeps leaking into the oddest characters. I am sure that not even
the most civilized of these Wall Street types is given to quoting
King Lear and Saint-Simon quite as often as his author has him
do. Also, there are the stagy bits of writing that recur from book
to book—hands are always "flung up" by Auchincloss characters;
something I have never seen done in real life west of Naples.

One small advance: in each of Auchincloss's previous books
sooner or later the author's Jacobite fascination with the theater
intrudes and, when it does, I know with terrible foreboding that
I shall presently see upon the page that somber ugly word
"scrim." I am happy to report that in *The Partners* there is no
scrim; only the author's elegant proscenium arch framing our
proud, savage rulers as they go single-mindedly about their principal task: the preserving of fortunes that ought to be broken up.

The New York Review of Books,
July 18, 1974

Calvino's Novels

Between the end of the Second World War in 1945 and the beginning of the Korean War in 1950, there was a burst of creative activity throughout the American empire as well as in our client states of Western Europe. From Auden's *Age of Anxiety* to Carson McCullers' *Reflections in a Golden Eye* to Paul Bowles's *The Sheltering Sky* to Tennessee Williams's *A Streetcar Named Desire* to Tudor's ballets and to Bernstein's enthusiasms, it was an exciting time. The cold war was no more than a nip in the air while the junior senator from Wisconsin was just another genial pol with a drinking problem and an eye for the boys. In that happy time the young American writer was able to reel in triumph through the old cities of Europe—the exchange rate entirely in his favor.

Twenty-six years ago this spring I arrived in Rome. First impressions: Acid-yellow forsythia on the Janiculum. Purple wisteria in the Forum. Chunks of goat on a plate in a trattoria. Samuel Barber at the American Academy, talking Italian accurately. Harold Acton politely deploring our barbarous presence in *his* Europe. Frederick Prokosch at Doney's, eating cakes. Streets empty of cars. Had there been traffic of any kind, Tennessee Williams would have been planted long since in the Protestant cemetery, for he drove a jeep although "I am practically *blind* in one eye," he would say proudly, going through the occasional red light, treating sidewalk and street as one.

I visited George Santayana in his hospital cell at the Convent of the Blue Nuns. He wore a dressing gown; Lord Byron collar open at the withered neck; faded mauve waistcoat. He was genial; made a virtue of his deafness. "*I* will talk. You will listen." A sly smile; black glittering eyes—he looked exactly like my grandmother gone dramatically bald.

"Have you met my young *new* friend Robert Lowell?" I said no. "He will have a difficult life. To be a Lowell. From Boston. A Catholic *convert.*" The black eyes shone with a lovely malice. "And a poet, too! Oh, dear. Now tell me who is a Mr. Edmund Wilson? He came to see me. I think that he must be very important. In fact, I believe he *said* that he was very important. You sent me a book, he said. I said that I had not. He said but you did, and got very angry. I tried to tell him that I do not *send* books. But later I recalled that when we were rescued by the American army—and how *glad* we were to see you!" A fond glance at me (one still wore khakis, frayed army belt). "A major, a very forceful man, came to see me, with a number of my books. He stood over me and *made* me sign them . . . for this one, for that one. I was terrified and did as he requested. Perhaps one of those books was for Mr. Wilson."

The only books in Santayana's cell were his own—and a set of Toynbee's recently published history, which he was reading characteristically; that is, he first broke (or foxed) the spine of the book and undid the sections; then, as he finished reading each section, he would throw it in the wastebasket. "Some sort of preacher, I should think," he said of Toynbee. "But the footnotes are not entirely worthless."

Santayana signed a copy of *The Middle Span* for me; he wrote "from" before his name. "I almost never do that," he said. An appraising look. "You look younger than you are because your head is somewhat small in proportion to your body." That was in 1948, when the conquering Americans lived in Rome and Paris and strolled streets as yet uncrowded with automobiles or with the billion or so human beings who have since joined us.

In that far-off time, the people one met talked about novels and

novelists the way they now talk of movies and directors. Young
people today think that I am exaggerating. But novelists mattered
then and the Italian novel, in particular, was having a fine flower-
ing. Yet the American writers in Rome and Paris saw little of
their counterparts. For one thing, the Italians were just getting
around to reading Dos Passos and Steinbeck—the generation that
had gone untranslated during the Fascist era. Also, few Italian
writers then (or now) spoke or read English with any ease while
the American writers then (though not so much now) proudly
spoke no language but English.

I do remember in 1948 coming across a book by Italo Calvino.
An Italian Calvin, I said to myself, fixing permanently his name
in my memory. Idly, I wondered what a man called Italo Calvino
would write about. I glanced at his first novel, *Il sentiero dei nidi
di ragno* (1947). Something about partisans in Liguria. A fellow
war novelist. No, I thought; and put it down. I did note that he
was two years older than I, worked for the publisher Einaudi,
lived in Turin.

During the last year, I have read Calvino straight through,
starting with the book I only glanced at in 1948, now translated
as *The Path to the Nest of Spiders*.

Calvino's first novel is a plainly told, exuberant sort of book.
Although the writing is conventional, there is an odd intensity
in the way Calvino sees things, a closeness of scrutiny much like
that of William Golding. Like Golding he knows how and when
to occupy entirely, with all senses functioning, landscape, state
of mind, act. In *The Spire* Golding makes the flawed church so real
that one smells the mortar, sees the motes of dust, fears for the
ill-placed stones. Calvino does the same in the story of Pin, a boy
living on the Ligurian coast of Italy, near San Remo (although
Calvino was brought up in San Remo, he was actually born in
Cuba, a detail given by none of his American publishers; no
doubt in deference to our recent attempted conquest of that unfortunate island).

Pin lives with his sister, a prostitute. He spends his days at a
low-life bar where he amuses with songs and taunts the grownups, a race of monsters as far as he is concerned, but he has no
other companions, for "Pin is a boy who does not know how to
play games, and cannot take part in the games either of children
or grownups." Pin dreams, however, of "a friend, a real friend
who understands him and whom he can understand, and then to

him, and only to him, will he show the place where the spiders have their lairs."

> It's on a stony little path which winds down to the torrent between earthy grassy slopes. There, in the grass, the spiders make their nests, in tunnels lined with dry grass. But the wonderful thing is that the nests have tiny doors, also made of dried grass, tiny round doors which can open and shut.

This sort of precise, quasi-scientific observation keeps Calvino from the sort of sentimentality that was prevalent in the forties, when wise children learned compassion from a black mammy as she deep-fried chitlins and Jesus in equal parts south of the Mason-Dixon line.

Pin joins the partisans in the hills above the Ligurian coast. I have a suspicion that Calvino is dreaming all this, for he writes like a bookish, near-sighted man who has mislaid his glasses: objects held close-to are vividly described but the middle and far distances of landscape and war tend to blur. It makes no difference, however, for the dreams of a near-sighted young man at the beginning of a literary career can be more real to the reader than the busy reportage of those journalist-novelists who were so entirely there and, seeing it all, saw nothing.

Although Calvino manages to inhabit the skin of the outraged and outrageous child, his men and women are almost always shadowy. Later in his career, Calvino will eliminate men and women altogether as he re-creates the cosmos. Meanwhile, as a beginning, he is a vivid, if occasionally clumsy, writer. Two thirds of the way through the narrative he shifts the point of view from Pin to a pair of commissars who would have been more effective had he observed them from outside. Then, confusingly, he shifts again, briefly, into the mind of a traitor who is about to be shot. Finally, he returns to Pin just as the boy finds the longed-for friend, a young partisan called Cousin who takes him in hand not only literally but, presumably, for the rest of the time Pin will need to grow up. Calvino's last paragraphs are almost always jubilant—the sort of cheerful codas that only a deep pessimist about human matters could write. But then Calvino, like one of Pin's friends, Red Wolf, "belongs to the generation brought up on strip cartoons; he has taken them all seriously and life has not disproved them so far."

In 1952 Calvino published *The Cloven Viscount,* one of the three
short novels he has since collected under the title *Our Ancestors.*
They are engaging works, written in a style somewhat like that
of T. H. White's Arthurian novels. The narrator of *The Cloven
Viscount* is, again, an orphan boy. During a war between Austria
and Turkey (1716) the boy's uncle Viscount Medardo was cloven
from pate to crotch by a cannonball. Saved by doctors on the
battlefield, the half Viscount was sent home with one leg, one
arm, one eye, half a nose, mouth, etc. En route, Calvino pays
homage (ironic?) to Malaparte ("The patch of plain they were
crossing was covered with horses' carcasses, some supine with
hooves to the sky, others prone with muzzles dug into the earth"
—a nice reprise of those dead horses in *The Skin*).

The story is cheerfully, briskly told. The half Viscount is a
perfect bastard and takes pleasure in murder, fire, torture. He
burns down part of his own castle, hoping to incinerate his old
nurse Sebastiana; finally, he packs her off to a leper colony. He
tries to poison his nephew. He never stops slashing living creatures in half. He has a thing about halfness.

> "If only I could halve every thing like this," said my uncle, lying
> face down on the rocks, stroking the convulsive half of an octopus,
> "so that everyone could escape from his obtuse and ignorant whole-
> ness. I was whole and all things were natural and confused to me,
> stupid as the air; I thought I was seeing all and it was only the
> outside rind. If you ever become a half of yourself, and I hope you
> do for your own sake, my boy, you'll understand things beyond the
> common intelligence of brains that are whole. You'll have lost half
> of yourself and of the world, but the remaining half will be a
> thousand times deeper and more precious."

I note that the publisher's blurb would have us believe that this
is "an allegory of modern man—alienated and mutilated—this
novel has profound overtones. As a parody of the Christian para-
bles of good and evil, it is both witty and refreshing." Well, at
least the book is witty and refreshing. Actually the story is less
Christian than a send-up of Plato and his ideas of the whole.

In due course the other half of the Viscount hits town; this half
is unbearably good and deeply boring. He, too, is given to celebrating halfness because "One understands the sorrow of every
person and thing in the world at its own incompleteness. I was

whole and did not understand. . . ." A charming young girl named Pamela (homage to Richardson) is beloved by both halves of the Viscount; but she has serious reservations about each. "Doing good together is the only way to love," intones the good half. To which the irritable girl responds, "A pity. I thought there were other ways." When the two halves are finally united, the resulting whole Viscount is the usual not very interesting human mixture. In a happy ending, he marries Pamela. But the boy-narrator is not content. "Amid all this fervor of wholeness, [I] felt myself growing sadder and more lacking. Sometimes one who thinks himself incomplete is merely young."

The Cloven Viscount is filled with many closely observed natural images like "The subsoil was so full of ants that a hand put down anywhere came up all black and swarming with them." I don't know which was written first, *The Cloven Viscount* (1952) or "The Argentine Ant," published in *Botteghe Oscure* (1952), but Calvino's nightmare of an ant-infested world touched on in the novel becomes the subject of "The Argentine Ant" and I fear that I must now trot out that so often misused word "masterpiece." Or, put another way, if "The Argentine Ant" is not a masterpiece of twentieth-century prose writing, I cannot think of anything better. Certainly it is as minatory and strange as anything by Kafka. It is also hideously funny. In some forty pages Calvino gives us "the human condition," as the blurb writers would say, in spades. That is, the human condition *today*. Or the dilemma of modern man. Or the disrupted environment. Or nature's revenge. Or an allegory of grace. Whatever . . . But a story is, finally, what it tells and no more.

Calvino's first sentence is rather better than God's "in the beginning was the word." God (as told to Saint John) has always had a penchant for cloudy abstractions of the sort favored by American novelists, heavyweight division—unlike Calvino, who simply tells us what's what: "When we came to settle here we did not know about the ants." No nonsense about "here" or "we." *Here* is a place infested with ants and *we* are the nuclear family: father, mother, child. No names.

"We" have rented a house in a town "where our Uncle Augusto used to hang out. Uncle Augusto rather liked the place, though he did say, 'You should see the ants over there . . . they're not like the ones here, those ants. . . .' But we paid no attention at the time." As the local landlady Signora Mauro shows the young couple about the house they have just rented from her, she distracts their attention from the walls with a long dissertation on the gas meter. When she has gone, the baby is put to bed and the young couple take a stroll outside. Their next-door neighbor is spraying the plants in his garden with a bellows. The ants, he explains, "as if not wanting to make it sound important."

The young couple return to their house and find it infested with ants. The Argentine ants. The husband-narrator suddenly recalls that this country is known for them. "It comes from South America," he adds, helpfully, to his distraught wife. Finally, they go to bed without "the feeling we were starting a new life, only a sense of dragging on into a future full of new troubles."

The rest of the story deals with the way that the others in the valley cope with the ants. Some go in for poisons; others make fantastic contraptions to confuse or kill the insects while for twenty years the Argentine Ant Control Corporation's representative has been putting out molasses ostensibly to control (kill) the ants but many believe that this is done to *feed* the ants. The frantic young couple pay a call on Signora Mauro in her dim palatial drawing room. She is firm; ants do not exist in well-tended houses, but from the way she squirms in her chair it is plain that the ants are crawling about under her clothes.

Methodically, Calvino describes the various human responses to The Condition. There is the Christian Scientist ignoring of all evidence; the Manichaean acceptance of evil; the relentless Darwinian faith that genetic superiority will prevail. But the ants prove indestructible and the story ends with the family going down to the seaside where there are no ants; where

> The water was calm, with just a slight continual change of color, blue and black, darker farthest away. I thought of the expanses of water like this, of the infinite grains of soft sand down there at the bottom of the sea where the currents leave white shells washed clean by the waves.

I don't know what this coda means. I also see no reason for it to mean. A contrast has been made between the ant-infested valley and the cool serenity of mineral and of shell beneath the sea, that other air we can no longer breathe since our ancestors chose to live upon the land.

In 1956 Calvino edited a volume of Italian fables, and the local critics decided that he was true heir to Grimm. Certainly the bright, deadly fairy tale attracts him and he returned to it with *The Baron in the Trees* (1957). Like the other two tales in the trilogy, the story is related in the first person; this time by the eponymous baron's brother. The year is 1767. The place Liguria. The Baron is Cosimo Piovasco di Rondò, who after an argument at dinner on June 15 decides to live in the trees. The response of family and friends to this decision is varied. But Cosimo is content. Later he goes in for politics; deals with Napoleon himself; becomes legend.

Calvino has now developed two ways of writing. One is literally fabulous. The other makes use of a dry, rather didactic style in which the detail is as precisely observed as if the author were writing a manual for the construction of a solar heating unit. Yet the premises of the "dry" stories are often quite as fantastic as those of the fairy tales.*

"Smog" was published in 1958, a long time before the current preoccupation with man's systematic destruction of the environment. The narrator comes to a large city to take over a small magazine called *Purification*. The owner of the magazine, Commendatore Cordà, is an important manufacturer who produces the sort of air pollution that his magazine would like to eliminate. Cordà has it both ways and his new editor settles in nicely. The prevailing image of the story is smog: gray dust covers everything; nothing is ever clean. The city is very like the valley of the Argentine ants but on a larger scale, for now a vast population is slowly strangling in the fumes of its industry, of the combustion engine.

Calvino is finely comic as he shows us the publisher instructing his editor in how to strike the right tone. "We are not utopians, mind you, we are practical men." Or, "It's a battle for an ideal." Or, "There will not be (nor has there ever been) any contradiction between an economy in free, natural expansion and the hygiene necessary to the human organism . . . between the smoke of our productive factories and the green of our incomparable natural beauty. . . ." Finally, the editorial policy is set. "We are one of the cities where the problem of air pollution is most seri-

---

*I have not read *La speculazione edilizia* (1957). From the description of it in *Dizionario della letteratura italiana contemporanea*, it is a general indictment of Italy's postwar building boom and of the helplessness of the intellectual Quinto Anfossi to come to terms with "cement fever."

ous, but at the same time we are the city where most is being done
to counteract the situation. At the same time, you understand!"
By some fifteen years, Calvino anticipated Exxon's double-talk
ads on American television.

This is the first of Calvino's stories where a realistic affair takes
place between a man and a woman—well, fairly realistic. We
never know how the elegant and wealthy Claudia came to meet
the narrator or what she sees in him; yet, periodically, she de-
scends upon him, confuses him ("to embrace her, I had removed
my glasses"). One day they drive out of the city. The narrator
comments on the ugliness of the city and the ubiquitous smog.
Claudia says that "people have lost the sense of beauty." He
answers, "Beauty has to be constantly invented." They argue; he
finds everything cruel. Later, he meets a proletarian who is in
arms against Cordà. The narrator admires the worker Omar,
admires "the stubborn ones, the tough ones." But Calvino does
not really *engage*, in Sartre's sense. He suspects that the trap we
are in is too great for mere politics to spring.

The narrator begins to write about atomic radiation in the
atmosphere; about the way the weather is changing in the world.
Is there a connection? Even Cordà is momentarily alarmed. But
then life goes on, for is not Cordà himself "the smog's master? It
was he who blew it out constantly over the city," and his magazine was "born of the need to give those working to produce the
smog some hope of a life that was not all smog, and yet, at the
same time, to celebrate its power."

The story's coda resembles that of "The Argentine Ant." The
narrator goes to the outskirts of the city where the women are
doing laundry. The sight is cheering. "It wasn't much, but for
me, seeking only images to retain in my eyes, perhaps it was
enough."

The next year Calvino switched to his other manner. *The
Nonexistent Knight* is the last of the Our Ancestors trilogy though
it comes first chronologically, in the age of Charlemagne. Again
a war is going on. We are not introduced to the narrator until
page 34—Sister Theodora is a nun in a convent who has been
assigned to tell this story "for the health of the soul." Unfortunately, the plot is giving her a good deal of trouble because "we
nuns have few occasions to speak with soldiers. . . . Apart from
religious ceremonies, triduums, novenas, gardening, harvesting,
vintaging, whippings, slavery, incest, fires, hangings, invasions,

sacking, rape and pestilence, we have had no experience."

Sister Theodora does her best with the tale of Agiluf, a knight who does not exist. What does exist is a suit of white armor from which comes the voice of Agiluf. He is a devoted knight in the service of Charlemagne who thinks him a bit much but graciously concedes, "for someone who doesn't exist, you seem in fine form." Since Agiluf has no appetites or weaknesses, he is the perfect soldier and so disliked by all. As for Agiluf, "people's bodies gave him a disagreeable feeling resembling envy, but also a stab of pride of contemptuous superiority." A young man (an older version of Pin, of the cloven Viscount's nephew) named Raimbaut joins the army to avenge his father's death. Agiluf gives him dull advice. There are battles. General observations. "What is war, after all, but this passing of more and more dented objects from hand to hand?" Then a meeting with a man who confuses himself with things outside himself. When he drinks soup, he becomes soup; thinks he is soup to be drunk in turn: "the world being nothing but a vast shapeless mass of soup in which all things dissolved."

Calvino now strikes a theme which will be developed in later works. The confusion between "I"/"it"; "I"/"you"; the arbitrariness of naming things, of categorizing, and of setting apart, particularly when "World conditions were still confused in the era when this book took place. It was not rare then to find names and thoughts and forms and institutions that corresponded to nothing in existence. But at the same time the world was polluted with objects and capacities and persons who lacked any name or distinguishing mark."

A triangle occurs. Raimbaut falls in love with a knight who proves to be a young woman, Bradamante. Unfortunately, *she* falls in love with Agiluf, the nonexistent knight. At this point there is rather too much plot for Sister Theodora, who strikes the professional writer's saddest note. "One starts off writing with a certain zest, but a time comes when the pen merely grates in dusty ink, and not a drop of life flows, and life is all outside, outside the window, outside oneself, and it seems that never more can one escape into a page one is writing, open out another world, leap the gap."

But the teller finally gets a grip on the tale; closes the gap. Knightly quests are conducted, concluded. Agiluf surrenders his armor and ceases to be; Raimbaut is allowed to inhabit the armor.

Bradamante has vanished, but with a fine *coup de théâtre* Sister
Theodora reveals to us that *she* is Bradamante, who is now rush-
ing the narrative to its end so that she can take the beloved white
armor in her arms: aware that it now contains the young and
passionate Raimbaut, her true love. "That is why my pen at a
certain point began running on so. I rush to meet him. . . . A page
is good only when we turn it and find life urging along. . . ."

With the completion of the trilogy, Calvino took to his other
manner and wrote "The Watcher," the most realistic of his stories and the most overtly political. The narrator has a name,
Amerigo Ormea. He is a poll watcher in Turin for the Communist party during the national election of 1953. Amerigo's poll is
inside the vast "Cottolengo Hospital for Incurables." Apparently
the mad and the senile and even the comatose are allowed to vote
("hospitals, asylums and convents had served as great reservoirs
of votes for the Christian Democrat party"). Amerigo is a serene
observer of democracy's confusions, having "learned that change,
in politics, comes through long and complex processes"; he also
confesses that "acquiring experience had meant becoming
slightly pessimistic."

In the course of the day, Amerigo observes with fine dispassion
the priests and nuns as they herd their charges into the polling
booths that have been set up inside the hospital. Despite the
grotesqueries of the situation, Amerigo takes some pleasure in the
matter-of-factness of the voting, for "in Italy, which had always
bowed and scraped before every form of pomp, display, sumptu-
ousness, ornament, this seemed to him finally the lesson of an
honest, austere morality, and a perpetual, silent revenge on the
Fascists . . .; now they had fallen into dust with all their gold
fringe and their ribbons, while democracy, with its stark ceremony of pieces of paper folded over like telegrams, of pencils
given to callused or shaky hands, went ahead."

But for the watcher boredom eventually sets in; it is a long day.
"Amerigo felt a yearning need for beauty, which became focused
in the thought of his mistress Lia." He contemplates Lia in reverie. "What is this need of ours for beauty? Amerigo asks himself." Apparently Calvino has not advanced much beyond the last
dialogue in "Smog." He contemplates the perfection of classical
Greece but recalls that the Greeks destroyed deformed children,
redundant girls. Obviously placing beauty too high in the scale
of values is "a step toward an inhuman civilization, which will

then sentence the deformed to be thrown off a cliff."

When another poll watcher remarks to Amerigo that the mad all must recognize one another in Cottolengo, he slips into reverie: "They would remember that humanity could be a different thing, as in fables, a world of giants, an Olympus. . . . As we do: and perhaps, without realizing it, we are deformed, backward, compared to a different, forgotten form of existence. . . ." What is human, what is real?

Calvino's vision is usually presented in fantastic terms but now he becomes unusually concrete. Since he has elected to illuminate an actual time and place (Italy between 1945 and the election of 1953), he is able to spell it out. "In those years the Italian Communist party, among its many other tasks, had also assumed the position of an ideal liberal party, which had never really existed. And so the bosom of each individual communist could house two personalities at once: an intransigent revolutionary and an Olympian liberal." Amerigo's pessimism derives from the obvious fact that the two do not go together. I am reminded of Alexander Herzen's comment about the Latins: they do not want liberty, they want to sue for liberty.

Amerigo goes home to lunch (he has a maid who cooks and serves! Written in 1963 about the events of 1953, this is plainly a historical novel). He looks for a book to read. "Pure literature" is out. "Personal literature now seemed to him a row of tombstones in a cemetery; the literature of the living as well as of the dead. Now he sought something else from books: the wisdom of the ages or simply something that helped to understand something." He takes a stab at Marx's *Youthful Writings.* "Man's universality appears, practically speaking, in that same universe that makes all nature man's *inorganic body.* . . . Nature is man's *inorganic body* precisely because it is not his human body." Thus genius turns everything into itself. As Marx invented *Kapital* from capitalism, so Calvino turns a passage of Marx into Calvino himself: the man who drinks soup is the soup that drinks him. Wholeness is all.

Fortified with this reassuring text, Amerigo endures a telephone conversation with Lia. It is the usual quibbling conversation between Calvino protagonist and Calvino mistress. She tells him that she is pregnant. "Amerigo was an ardent supporter of birth control, even though his party's attitude on the subject was either agnostic or hostile. Nothing shocked him so much as the

ease with which people multiply, and the more hungry and backward, the more they keep having children. . . ." In the land of
Margaret Sanger this point of view is not exactly startling, but
for an Italian communist a dozen years ago, the sense of a world
dying of too many children, of too much "smog" was a monstrous
revelation. At this point, Amerigo rounds on both the Bible and
Marx as demented celebrators of human fecundity.

Amerigo returns to the hospital; observes children shaped like
fish and again wonders at what point is a human being human.
Finally the day ends; the voting is done. Amerigo looks out over
the complex of hospital buildings and notes that the reddish sun
appeared to open "perspectives of a city that had never been
seen." Thus the Calvino coda strikes its first familiar chord.
Laughing women cross the courtyard with a cauldron, "perhaps
the evening soup. Even the ultimate city of imperfection has its
perfect hour, the watcher thought, the hour, the moment, when
every city is the City."

Most realistic and specific of Calvino's works, "The Watcher"
has proved (to date) to be the last of the "dry" narratives. In 1965
Calvino published *Cosmicomics:* twelve brief stories dealing in a
fantastic way with the creation of the universe, man, society. Like
Pin's young friend who decided that life indeed resembles the
strip cartoon, Calvino has deployed his complex prose in order
to compose in words a super strip cartoon narrated by Qfwfq
whose progress from life inside the first atom to mollusk on the
earth's sea floor to social-climbing amphibian to dinosaur to
moon-farmer is told in a dozen episodes that are entirely unlike
anything that anyone else has written since, well, let us say Lu-
cian.

"At Daybreak" is the story of the creation of the universe as
viewed by Qfwfq and his mysterious tribe consisting of a father,
mother, sister, brother, Granny, as well as acquaintances—form-
less sentiencies who inhabit the universal dust that is in the verge
of becoming the nebula which will contain our solar system.
Where and who *they* are is, literally, obscure, since light has not
yet been invented. So "there was nothing to do but wait, keep
covered as best we could, doze, speak out now and then to make
sure we were all still there; and, naturally, scratch ourselves;
because—they can say what they like—all those particles spinning around had only one effect, a troublesome itching." That
itch starts to change things. Condensation begins. Also, confu-

sion: Granny loses her cushion, "a little ellipsoid of galactic matter." Things clot; nickel is formed; members of the tribe start flying off in all directions. Suddenly the condensation is complete and light breaks. The sun is now in its place and the planets begin their orbits "and, above all, it was deathly hot."

As the earth starts to jell, Qfwfq's sister takes fright and vanishes inside the planet and is not heard from again "until I met her, much later, at Canberra in 1912, married to a certain Sullivan, a retired railroad man, so changed I hardly recognized her."

The early Calvino was much like his peers Pavese and Vittorini —writers who tended to reflect the realistic storytelling of Hemingway and Dos Passos. Then Calvino moved to Paris, where he found his own voice or voices and became, to a degree, infected by the French. Since the writing of *Our Ancestors* and the three stories that make up *The Watcher*, Calvino has been influenced, variously, by Barthes and the semiologists, by Borges and by the now old New Novel. In *Cosmicomics* these influences are generally benign, since Calvino is too formidable and original an artist to be derailed by theoreticians or undone by the example of another creator. Nevertheless the story "A Sign in Space" comes perilously close to being altogether too reverent an obeisance to semiology.

As the sun takes two hundred million years to revolve around the galaxy, Qfwfq becomes obsessed with making a sign in space, something peculiarly his own to mark his passage as well as something that would impress anyone who might be watching. His ambition is the result of a desire to think because "to think something had never been possible, first because there were no things to think about, and second because signs to think of them by were lacking, but from the moment there was that sign, it was possible for someone thinking to think of a sign, and therefore that one, in the sense that the sign was the thing you could think about and also the sign of the thing thought, namely, itself." So he makes his sign ("I felt I was going forth to conquer the only thing that mattered to me, sign and dominion and name . . .").

Unfortunately, a spiteful contemporary named Kgwgk erases Qfwfq's sign and replaces it with his own. In a rage, Qfwfq wants "to make a new sign in space, a real sign that would make Kgwgk die of envy." So, out of competitiveness, art is born. But the task of sign-making is becoming more difficult because the world "was beginning to produce an image of itself, and in everything a form was beginning to correspond to a function" (a theme from *The Nonexistent Knight*) and "in this new sign of mine you could perceive the influence of our new way of looking at things, call it style if you like. . . ."

Qfwfq is delighted with his new sign but as time passes he likes it less and less, thinks it is a bit pretentious, old-fashioned; decides he must erase it before his rival sees it (so writers revise old books or make new ones that obliterate earlier works—yes, call it style if you like). Finally, Qfwfq erases the inadequate sign. For a time he is pleased that there is nothing in space which might make him look idiotic to a rival—in this, he resembles so many would-be writers who contrive to vanish into universities and, each year, by not publishing that novel or poem, increase their reputations.

But doing nothing is, finally, abhorrent to the real artist: Qfwfq starts to amuse himself by making *false* signs, "to annoy Kgwgk . . . notches in space, holes, stains, little tricks that only an incompetent creature like Kgwgk could mistake for signs." So the artist masochistically mocks his own art, shatters form (the sign) itself, makes jokes to confuse and exploit 57th Street. But then things get out of hand. To Qfwfq's horror, every time he passes what he thinks was one of his false signs, there are a dozen other signs, all scribbled over his.

Finally, everything was now so obscured by a crisscross of meaningless signs that "world and space seemed the mirror of each other, both minutely adorned with hieroglyphics and ideograms" including the badly inked tail of the letter *R* in an evening newspaper joined to a thready imperfection in the paper, one among the eight hundred thousand flakings of a tarred wall in the Melbourne docks. . . . In the universe now there was no longer a container and a thing contained, but only a general thickness of signs superimposed and coagulated."

Qfwfq gives up. There is no longer a point of reference "because it was clear that, independent of signs, space didn't exist and perhaps had never existed." So the story concludes; and the rest is the solipsism of art. To the old debate about being and non-being, Calvino adds his own vision of the multiplicity of signs which obliterates *all* meaning. Too many names for a thing is like no name for a thing; therefore, no thing, nothing.

"How Much Shall We Bet?" continues the theme. At the beginning Qfwfq "bet that there was going to be a universe, and I hit the nail on the head." This was the first bet he won with Dean (k)yK. Through the ages the two continue to make bets and Qfwfq usually wins because "I bet on the possibility of a certain event's taking place, whereas the Dean almost always bet against it."

Qfwfq kept on winning until he began to take wild leaps into the future. "On February 28, 1926, at Santhia, in the Province of Vercelli—got that? At number 18 in Via Garibaldi—you follow me? Signorina Giuseppina Pensotti, aged twenty-two, leaves her home at quarter to six in the afternoon; does she turn right or left?" Qfwfq starts losing. Then they begin to bet about characters in unwritten novels . . . will Balzac make Lucien de Rubempré kill himself at the end of *Les illusions perdues?* The Dean wins that one.

The two bettors end up in charge of vast research foundations which contain innumerable reference libraries. Finally, like man's universe itself, they begin to drown in signs and Qfwfq looks back nostalgically to the beginning, "How beautiful it was then, through that void, to draw lines and parabolas, pick out the precise point, the intersection between space and time when the event would spring forth, undeniable in the prominence of its glow; whereas now events come flowing down without interruption, like cement being poured, one column next to the other . . . a doughy mass of events without form or direction, which surrounds, submerges, crushes all reasoning."

In another story the last of the dinosaurs turns out to be Qfwfq, who meets and moves in with the next race. The New Ones don't realize that he is one of their dread enemies from the past. They think him remarkably ugly but not unduly alien. Qfwfq's attitude is like that of the protagonist in William Golding's *The Inheritors* except that in Calvino's version the last of the Old Ones merges with the inheritors. Amused, Qfwfq listens to the monstrous, conflicting legends about his race, tribute to the power of man's imagination, to the words he uses, to the signs he recognizes.

Finally, "I knew that the more the Dinosaurs disappear, the more they extend their dominion, and over forests far more vast than those that cover the continents: in the labyrinth of the survivors' thoughts." But Qfwfq was not at all sentimental about being the last dinosaur and at the story's end he left the New Ones and "travelled through valleys and plains. I came to a station, caught the first train, and was lost in the crowd."

In "The Spiral," the last of the *Cosmicomics*, Qfwfq is a mollusk on a rock in the primeval sea. The theme is again *in ovo omnes*. Calvino describes with minuteness the sensations of the mollusk on the rock, "damp and happy. . . . I was what they call a narcissist to a slight extent; I mean I stayed there observing myself all the time, I saw all my good points and all my defects, and I liked myself for the former and for the latter; I had no terms of comparison, you must remember that, too." Such was Eden. But then the heat of the sun started altering things; there were vibrations from another sex; there were eggs to be fertilized: love.

In response to the new things, Qfwfq expresses himself by making a shell which turns out to be a spiral that is not only very good for defense but unusually beautiful. Yet Qfwfq takes no credit for the beauty: "My shell made itself, without my taking any special pains to have it come out one way rather than another." But then the instinctive artist in the mollusk asserts itself: "This doesn't mean that I was absent-minded during that time; I applied myself instead, to the act of secreting. . . ." Meanwhile, *she*, the beloved, is making *her* shell, identical with his.

Ages pass. The shell-Qfwfq is on a railroad embankment as a train passes by. A party of Dutch girls looks out the window. Qfwfq is not startled by anything, for "I feel as if, in making the shell, I had also made the rest." But one new element has entered the equation. "I had failed to foresee one thing: the eyes that finally opened to see us didn't belong to us but to others." So dies Narcissus. "They developed eyes at our expense. So sight, *our* sight, which we were obscurely waiting for, was the sight that the others had of us."

But the artist who made the spiral-shaped shell is not to be outdone by miscalculation or by fate. Proudly he concludes: "All these eyes were mine. I had made them possible; I had had the active part; I furnished them the raw material, the image." Again the gallant coda, for fixed in the watcher's eye is not only the fact of the beautiful shell that *he* made but also "the most faithful image of her" who had inspired the shell and was the shell: thus male and female are at last united in the retina of a stranger's eye.

In 1967, Calvino published more of Qfwfq's adventures in *Time and the Hunter*. For the most part they are engaging cartoons, but one is disconcerted to encounter altogether too many bits of Sarraute, of Robbe-Grillet, of Borges (far too much of Borges) incorporated in the prose of what I have come to regard as a true modern master. On page 6 occurs "viscous"; on page 11 "acid mucus." I started to feel queasy: these are Sarraute words. I decided that their use was simply a matter of coincidence. But when, on page 29, I saw the dread word "magma" I knew that Calvino has been too long in Paris, for only Sarrautistes use "magma," a word the great theoretician of the old New Novel so arbitrarily and uniquely appropriated from the discipline of science. Elsewhere in the stories, Robbe-Grillet's technique of recording the minutiae of a banal situation stops cold some of Calvino's best effects.

"The Chase," in fact, could have been written by Robbe-Grillet. This is not a compliment. Take the beginning:

> That car chasing me is faster than mine; inside there is one man, alone, armed with a pistol, a good shot. . . . We have stopped at a traffic signal, in a long column. The signal is regulated in such a way that on our side the red light lasts a hundred and eighty seconds and the green light a hundred and twenty, no doubt based on the premise that the perpendicular traffic is heavier and slower.

And so on for sixteen pages, like a movie in slow motion.

The theory behind this sort of enervating prose is as follows, since to write is to describe, with words, why not then describe words themselves (with other words)? Or, glory be! words describing words describing an action of no importance (the corner of that room in Robbe-Grillet's *Jalousie*). This sort of "experiment" has always seemed to me to be of more use to students of language than to readers of writing. On his own and at his best, Calvino does what very few writers can do: he describes imaginary worlds with the most extraordinary precision and beauty (a word he has single-handedly removed from that sphere of suspicion which the old New Novelists maintain surrounds all words and any narrative).

In *Cosmicomics* Calvino makes it possible for the reader to inhabit a meson, a mollusk, a dinosaur; makes him for the first time see light ending a dark universe. Since this is a unique gift, I find all the more alarming the "literariness" of *Time and the Hunter*. I was particularly put off by the central story "t zero," which could have been written (and rather better) by Borges.

With a bow and arrow, Qfwfq confronts a charging lion. In his head he makes an equation: Time zero is where he Qfwfq is;

where the Lion-o is. All combinations of a series which may be finite or infinite pass through Qo's head, exactly like the man before the firing squad in Borges's celebrated story. Now it is possible that these stories will appeal to minds more convergent than mine (students of mathematics, engineers, Young Republicans are supposed to think convergently while novelists, gourmets, and non-Christian humanists think divergently) but to me this pseudo-scientific rendering of a series of possibilities is deeply boring.

But there are also pleasures in this collection. Particularly "The Origin of the Birds." "Now these stories can be told better with strip drawings than with a story composed of sentences one after the other." So the crafty Calvino by placing one sentence after another *describes* a strip cartoon and the effect is charming even though Qfwfq's adventure among the birds is not really a strip cartoon but the description of a cartoon *in words.*

The narrator's technique is like that of *The Nonexistent Knight.* He starts to draw a scene; then erases it the way Sister Theodora used to eliminate oceans and forests as she hurried her lovers to their inevitable rendezvous. Calvino also comes as close as any writer can to saying that which is sensed about creation but may not be put into words or drawn in pictures.

"I managed to embrace in a single thought the world of things as they were and of things as they could have been, and I realized that a single system included all." In the arms of Or, the queen of the birds, Qfwfq begins to *see* that "the world is single and what exists can't be explained without . . ." But he has gone too far. As he is about to say the unsayable, Or tries to smother him. But he is still able to blurt out, "There's no difference. Monsters and non-monsters have always been close to one another! What hasn't been continues to be. . . ." At that point, the birds expel him from their paradise; and like a dreamer rudely awakened, he forgets his vision of unity. "(The last strip is all photographs: a bird, the same bird in close-up, the head of the bird enlarged, a detail of the head, the eye. . . .)" It is the same eye that occurs at the end of *Cosmicomics,* the eye of—cosmic consciousness for those who recall that guru of a past generation, Dr. Richard M. Bucke.

Calvino ends these tales with his own *The Count of Monte Cristo.* The problem he sets himself is how to get out of Château d'If. Faria keeps making plans and tunneling his way through an endless, exitless fortress. Dantès, on the other hand, broods on the nature of the fortress as well as on the various drafts of the novel that Dumas is writing. In some drafts, Dantès will escape and find a treasure and get revenge on his enemies. In other drafts, he suffers a different fate. The narrator contemplates the possibilities of escape by considering the way a fortress (or a work of art) is made. "To plan a book—or an escape—the first thing to know is what to exclude." This particular story is Borges at his very best and, taking into account the essential unity of the multiplicity of all things, one cannot rule out that Calvino's version of *The Count of Monte Cristo* by Alexandre Dumas is indeed the finest achievement of Jorge Luis Borges as imagined by Italo Calvino.

Calvino's seventh and latest novel (or work or meditation or poem), *Invisible Cities,* is perhaps his most beautiful work. In a garden sit the aged Kublai Khan and the young Marco Polo— Tartar emperor and Venetian traveler. The mood is sunset. Prospero is holding up for the last time his magic wand: Kublai Khan has sensed the end of his empire, of his cities, of himself.

Marco Polo, however, diverts the emperor with tales of cities that he has seen within the empire and Kublai Khan listens, searches for a pattern in Marco Polo's Cities and memory, Cities and desire, Cities and signs, Thin Cities, Trading Cities, Cities and eyes, Cities and names, Cities and the dead, Cities and the sky, Continuous Cities, Hidden Cities. The emperor soon determines that each of these fantastic places is really the same place.

Marco Polo agrees: " 'Memory's images, once they are fixed in words, are erased,' Polo said." (So does Borges, repeatedly!) " 'Perhaps I am afraid of losing Venice all at once, if I speak of it, or perhaps, speaking of other cities, I have already lost it, little by little.' " Again the theme of multiplicity and wholeness, "when every city," as Calvino wrote at the end of "The Watcher," "is the City."

Of all tasks, describing the contents of a book is the most difficult and in the case of a marvelous creation like *Invisible Cities,* perfectly irrelevant. I shall spare myself the labor; noting, however, that something new and wise has begun to enter the Calvino canon. The artist seems to have made a peace with the tension between man's idea of the many and of the one. He could now, if he wanted, stop.

Yet Calvino is obliged to go on writing just as his Marco Polo goes on traveling because

> he cannot stop; he must go on to another city, where another of his pasts awaits him, or something perhaps that had been a possible future of his and is now someone else's present. Futures not achieved are only branches of the past: dead branches.
>
> "Journeys to relive your past?" was the Khan's question at this point, a question which could also have been formulated: "Journeys to recover your future?"
>
> And Marco's answer was: "Elsewhere is a negative mirror. The traveler recognizes the little that is his, discovering the much he has not had and will never have."

Later, after more descriptions of his cities, Kublai Khan decides that "the empire is nothing but a zodiac of the mind's phantasms."

> "On the day when I know all the emblems," he asked Marco, "shall I be able to possess my empire, at last?"
>
> And the Venetian answered, "Sire, do not believe it. On that day you will be an emblem among emblems."

Finally, Kublai Khan recognizes that all cities are tending toward the concentric circles of Dante's hell.

> He said: "It is all useless, if the last landing place can only be the infernal city, and it is there that, in ever-narrowing circles, the current is drawing us."
>
> And Polo said: "The inferno of the living is not something that will be; if there is one, it is what is already here, the inferno where we live every day, that we form by being together. There are two ways to escape suffering it. The first is easy for many: accept the inferno and become such a part of it that you can no longer see it. The second is risky and demands constant vigilance and apprehension; seek and learn to recognize who and what, in the midst of the inferno, are not inferno, then make them endure, give them space."

During the last quarter century Italo Calvino has advanced far beyond his American and English contemporaries. As they continue to look for the place where the spiders make their nests, Calvino has not only found that special place but learned how

himself to make fantastic webs of prose to which all things adhere. In fact, reading Calvino, I had the unnerving sense that I
was also writing what he had written; thus does his art prove his
case as writer and reader become one, or One.

The New York Review of Books,
May 30, 1974

Professor V. Nabokov

Professor Vladimir Nabokov's beautiful memoir *Speak Memory* has now been succeeded by *Strong Opinions*—a collection of press clippings in which he has preserved for future classes what looks to be every interview granted during the last decade. Plainly he has not taken to heart Turgenev's "Never try to justify yourselves (whatever libelous stories they may tell about you). Don't try to explain a misunderstanding, don't be anxious, yourselves, either to say or hear 'the last word.' "

Alas, the Black Swan of Swiss-American letters has a lot of explaining to do (no singing, however: we need the swan for many a future summer). In addition to the bubbling interviews, Professor Nabokov recounts the many misunderstandings between him and the French publisher of *Lolita*, between him and the critics of his translation of Pushkin's *Eugene Onegin*, between him and various adversaries in the form of Letters to the Editor (by slyly omitting the pretext for each letter, he creates a loony Kafka-like mood). Included, too, are examples of his own book-chat: Sartre's *La Nausée* "belongs to that tense-looking but really very loose type of writing, which has been popularized by many second-raters—Barbusse, Céline, and so forth." Finally, he gives us several meticulous portraits of those butterflies he murdered ("with an expert nip of its thorax") during his celebrated tours of America's motels.

Professor Nabokov's answers to the questions posed him by a dozen or so interviewers are often amusing, sometimes illuminating, and always—after the third or fourth performance—unbearable in their repetitiveness. Never again do I want to read that he writes in longhand with a hard pencil while standing at a lectern until he tires and sits or lies down, that he writes on Bristol cards which are lined on only one side so that he will not mistake a used card for a fresh card. Reading and rereading these descriptions, one understands why he thinks Robbe-Grillet a great writer.

Admittedly, interviewers are always eager to know how a writer writes (*what* he writes holds less magic for them). But the Swan of Lac Léman in the course of what he admits has been a good deal of editing might have spared us so many repetitions. "I demanded of my students the passion of science and the patience of poetry." Superb—but only the first time. ("Aphoristicism is a symptom of arteriosclerosis.") And of course the synoptic interviews tell and retell the sacred story of all that was lost by the noble family of "squires and soldiers" (perhaps descended from Genghis Khan) in the Russian revolution, and of their heir's hegira (Germany, England, America) and metamorphosis at Cornell from "lean lecturer into full professor," from obscure Russian emigré novelist into the creator of *Lolita*, considered by Isherwood to be the best travel book ever written about America.

Professor Nabokov's public appearances and occasional commentaries are always looked forward to because he likes to attack celebrated writers. Hemingway and Conrad are, essentially, "writers of books for boys." "I cannot abide Conrad's souvenir-shop style, bottled ships and shell necklaces of romanticist clichés." Nor can he abide Mann's "asinine *Death in Venice* or Pasternak's melodramatic and vilely written *Zhivago* or Faulkner's corn-cobby chronicles" . . . while at Cornell, "I remember the delight of tearing apart *Don Quixote*, a cruel and crude old book . . ." or "that awful Monsieur Camus," or "the not quite first-rate Eliot . . . and definitely second-rate Pound." Or "the so-called 'realism' of old novels, the easy platitudes of Balzac or Somerset Maugham, or D. H. Lawrence . . ." The Professor does admit to admiring Borges, Salinger (J.D., not Pierre), Updike, and at one point he pays a nice tribute to several other *New Yorker* writers while *"My* greatest masterpieces of twentieth-century prose are, in this order, Joyce's *Ulysses,* Kafka's *Transformations,* Biely's *Petersburg* and the first half of Proust's fairy tale in search of lost time." Class dismissed.

Strong Opinions reminds one to what extent the author is still very much a part of the American academic machine. Certainly the best bit of material in this ragbag of a book is a description of giving an examination to a large class at Cornell on a winter's day. Although sensibly stern about "the symbolism racket in schools [which] attracts computerised minds but destroys plain intelligence as well as poetical sense," Nabokov himself has become just the sort of writer the racketeers most like to teach. Not only is his prose full of trilingual puns and word-play but "as I just like composing riddles with elegant solutions," there are bound to be symbols galore and much, much more beneath those Tartar arbors, amongst those Scythian mists.

The best of the interviews are the ones with Alfred Appel, Jr. —plainly a Nabokovian invention—the "Jr" is one giveaway. Another is that Mr. Appel's questions are often longer and wittier than the Professor's answers. Can this mean that an intellectual comedy team is being discreetly tried out in these pages? A brand-new Stravinsky and Craft? Certainly, teacher provides pupil with the most elegant *cache-cache* as well as *cache-sexe.* Periodically, the Professor is obliged to note that he himself is not *repeat* not attracted to those very young girls who keep cropping up in his work. ("Lewis Carroll liked little girls. I don't.") At these moments, our proud Black Swan becomes an uneasy goose, fearful of being cooked by Cornell's board of regents.

Despite occasional pleasures, this is not a book for those who admire Nabokov's novels. But for students who will write about him in American universities, it is probably useful to have all this twaddle in one volume. For myself, I am rereading *Transparent Things,* that perfect radiogram of found objects, precisely set in the artist's own Time. If only for this lovely work, Nabokov will never be forced to echo an earlier American culture hero who wrote, sadly:

Yet do I find it perceptible—here to riot in understatement—that I, who was once a leading personage in and about those scanty playgrounds of human interest which we nickname literature seem now to have become, for all practical results, unheard-of thereabouts.

Readers who can correctly identify the author of the above passage will be given a letter of introduction to Professor V. Nabokov, Palace Hotel, Montreux, Vaud, Switzerland.

The Observer
May 12, 1974

French Letters:
Theories of the New Novel

To say that no one now much likes novels is to exaggerate very little. The large public which used to find pleasure in prose fictions prefers movies, television, journalism, and books of "fact." But then, Americans have never been enthusiastic readers. According to Dr. Gallup, only 5 percent of our population can be regarded as habitual readers. This 5 percent is probably a constant minority from generation to generation, despite the fact that at the end of the nineteenth century there were as many bookstores in the United States as there are today. It is true that novels in paperback often reach a very large audience. But that public is hardly serious, if one is to believe a recent *New York Times* symposium on paperback publishing. Apparently novels sell not according to who wrote them but according to how they are presented, which means that *Boys and Girls Together* will out-sell *Pale Fire*, something it did not do in hard cover. Except for a handful of entertainers like the late Ian Fleming, the mass audience knows nothing of authors. They buy titles, and most of those titles are not of novels but of nonfiction: books about the

Kennedys, doctors, and vivid murders are preferred to the work of anyone's imagination no matter how agreeably debased.

In this, if nothing else, the large public resembles the clerks, one of whom, Norman Podhoretz, observed nine years ago that "A feeling of dissatisfaction and impatience, irritation and boredom with contemporary serious fiction is very widespread," and he made the point that the magazine article is preferred to the novel because the article is useful, specific, relevant—something that most novels are not. This liking for fact may explain why some of our best-known novelists are read with attention only when they comment on literary or social matters. In the highest intellectual circles, a new novel by James Baldwin or William Gass or Norman Mailer—to name at random three celebrated novelists—is apt to be regarded with a certain embarrassment, hostage to a fortune often too crudely gained, and bearing little relation to its author's distinguished commentaries.

An even odder situation exists in the academy. At a time when the works of living writers are used promiscuously as classroom texts, the students themselves do little voluntary reading. "I hate to read," said a Harvard senior to a *New York Times* reporter, "and I never buy any paperbacks." The undergraduates' dislike of reading novels is partly due to the laborious way in which novels are taught: the slow killing of the work through a close textual analysis. Between the work and the reader comes the explication, and the explicator is prone to regard the object of analysis as being, somehow, inferior to the analysis itself.

In fact, according to Saul Bellow, "Critics and professors have declared themselves the true heirs and successors of the modern classic authors." And so, in order to maintain their usurped dignity, they are given "to redescribing everything downward, blackening the present age and denying creative scope to their contemporaries." Although Mr. Bellow overstates the case, the fact remains that the novel as currently practiced does not appeal to the intellectuals any more than it does to the large public, and it may well be that the form will become extinct now that we have entered the age which Professor Marshall McLuhan has termed post-Gutenberg. Whether or not the Professor's engaging generalities are true (that linear type, for centuries a shaper of our thought, has been superseded by electronic devices), it is a fact that the generation now in college is the first to be brought up entirely within the tradition of television and differs significantly from its predecessors. Quick to learn through sight and sound, today's student often experiences difficulty in reading and writing. Linear type's warm glow, so comforting to Gutenberg man, makes his successors uncomfortably hot. Needless to say, that bright minority which continues the literary culture exists as always, but it is no secret that even they prefer watching movies to reading novels. John Barth ought to interest them more than Antonioni, but he doesn't.

For the serious novelist, however, the loss of the audience should not be disturbing. "I write," declared one of them serenely. "Let the reader learn to read." And contrary to Whitman, great audiences are not necessary for the creation of a high literature. The last fifty years have been a particularly good time for poetry in English, yet even that public which can read intelligently knows very little of what has been done. Ideally, the writer needs no audience other than the few who understand. It is immodest and greedy to want more. Unhappily, the novelist, by the very nature of his coarse art, is greedy and immodest; unless he is read by everyone, he cannot delight, instruct, reform, destroy a world he wants, at the least, to be different for his having lived in it. Writers as various as Dickens and Joyce, as George Eliot and Proust, have suffered from this madness. It is the nature of the beast. But now the beast is caged, confined by old forms that have ceased to attract. And so the question is: Can those forms be changed, and the beast set free?

Since the Second World War, Alain Robbe-Grillet, Nathalie Sarraute, Michel Butor, Claude Simon, and Robert Pinget, among others, have attempted to change not only the form of the novel but the relationship between book and reader, and though their experiments are taken most seriously on the Continent, they are still too little known and thought about in those countries the late General de Gaulle believed to be largely populated by Anglo-Saxons. Among American commentators, only Susan Sontag in *Against Interpretation, and Other Essays,* published in 1966, has made a sustained effort to understand what the French are doing, and her occasional essays on their work are well worth reading, not only as reflections of an interesting and interested mind but also because she shares with the New Novelists (as they loosely describe themselves) a desire for the novel to become "what it is not in England and America, with rare and unrelated exceptions: a form of art which people with serious and sophisticated [*sic*] taste in the other arts can take seriously." Certainly Miss Sontag finds nothing adventurous or serious in "the work of the American writers most admired today: for example, Saul Bellow, Norman Mailer, James Baldwin, William Styron, Philip Roth, Bernard Malamud." They are "essentially unconcerned with the problems of the novel as an art form. Their main concern is with their 'subjects.' " And because of this, she finds them "essentially unserious and unambitious." By this criterion, to be serious and ambitious in the novel the writer must create works of prose comparable to those experiments in painting which have brought us to Pop and Op art and in music to the strategic silences of John Cage. Whether or not these experiments succeed or fail is irrelevant. It is enough, if the artist is serious, to attempt new forms; certainly he must not repeat old ones.

The two chief theorists of the New Novel are Alain Robbe-Grillet and Nathalie Sarraute. As novelists, their works do not much resemble one another or, for that matter, conform to each other's strictures. But it is as theorists not as novelists that they shall concern us here. Of the two, Alain Robbe-Grillet has done the most to explain what he thinks the New Novel is and is not, in *Snapshots* and *For a New Novel*, translated by Richard Howard (1965). To begin with, he believes that any attempt at controlling the world by assigning it a meaning (the accepted task of the traditional novelist) is no longer possible. At best, meaning was

> an illusory simplification; and far from becoming clearer and clearer because of it, the world has only, little by little, lost all its life. Since it is chiefly in its presence that the world's reality resides, our task is now to create a literature which takes that presence into account.

He then attacks the idea of psychological "depth" as a myth. From the Comtesse de La Fayette to Gide, the novelist's role was to burrow "deeper and deeper, to reach some ever more intimate strata." Since then, however, "something" has been "changing totally, definitively in our relations with the universe." Though he does not define that ominous "something," its principal effect is that "we no longer consider the world as our own, our private property, designed according to our needs and readily domesticated." Consequently:

> the novel of characters belongs entirely to the past; it describes a period: and that which marked the apogee of the individual. Perhaps

this is not an advance, but it is evident that the present period is rather one of administrative numbers. The world's destiny has ceased, for us, to be identified with the rise or fall of certain men, of certain families.

Nathalie Sarraute is also concerned with the idea of man the administrative number in *Tropisms* and in *The Age of Suspicion*, translated by Maria Jolas (1964). She quotes Claude-Edmonde Magny: "Modern man, overwhelmed by mechanical civilization, is reduced to the triple determinism of hunger, sexuality and social status: Freud, Marx and Pavlov." (Surely in the wrong order.) She, too, rejects the idea of human depth: "The deep uncovered by Proust's analyses had already proved to be nothing but a surface."

Like Robbe-Grillet, she sees the modern novel as an evolution from Dostoevsky-Flaubert to Proust-Kafka; and each agrees (in essays written by her in 1947 and by him in 1958) that one of its principal touchstones is Camus's *The Stranger*, a work which she feels "came at the appointed time," when the old psychological novel was bankrupt because, paradoxically, psychology itself, having gone deeper than ever before, "inspired doubts as to the ultimate value of all methods of research." *Homo absurdus*, therefore, was Noah's dove, the messenger of deliverance. Camus's stranger is shown entirely from the inside, "all sentiment or thought whatsoever appears to have been completely abolished." He has been created without psychology or memory; he exists in a perpetual present. Robbe-Grillet goes even further in his analysis:

> It is no exaggeration to claim that it is things quite specifically which ultimately lead this man to crime: the sun, the sea, the brilliant sand, the gleaming knife, the spring among the rocks, the revolver . . . as, of course, among these things, the leading role is taken by Nature.

Only the absolute presence of things can be recorded; certainly the depiction of human character is no longer possible. In fact, Miss Sarraute believes that for both author and reader, character is "the converging point of their mutual distrust," and she makes of Stendhal's "The genius of suspicion has appeared on the scene" a leitmotiv for an age in which "the reader has grown wary of practically everything. The reason being that for some time now he has been learning too many things and he is unable to forget entirely all he had learned." Perhaps the most vivid thing he has learned (or at least it was vivid when she was writing in 1947) is the fact of genocide in the concentration camps:

> Beyond these furthermost limits to which Kafka did not follow them but to where he had the superhuman courage to precede them, all feeling disappears, even contempt and hatred; there remains only vast, empty stupefaction, definitive total, don't understand.
>   To remain at the point where he left off or to attempt to go on from there are equally impossible. Those who live in a world of human beings can only retrace their steps.

The proof that human life can be as perfectly meaningless in the scale of a human society as it is in eternity stunned a generation, and the shock of this knowledge, more than anything else (certainly more than the discoveries of the mental therapists or the new techniques of industrial automation), caused a dislocation of human values which in turn made something like the New Novel inevitable.

Although Nathalie Sarraute and Alain Robbe-Grillet are formidable theorists, neither is entirely free of those rhetorical plangencies the French so often revert to when their best *aperçus* are about to slip the net of logic. Each is very much a part of that French intellectual tradition so wickedly described in *Tristes Tropiques* by Lévi-Strauss (1964, translated by John Russell):

> First you establish the traditional "two views" of the question. You then put forward a common-sensical justification of the one, only to refute it by the other. Finally, you send them both packing by the use of a third interpretation, in which both the others are shown to be equally unsatisfactory. Certain verbal maneuvers enable you, that is, to line up the traditional "antitheses" as complementary aspects of a single reality: form and substance, content and container, appearance and reality, essence and existence, continuity and discontinuity, and so on. Before long the exercise becomes the merest verbalizing, reflection gives place to a kind of superior punning, and the "accomplished philosopher" may be recognized by the ingenuity with which he makes ever-bolder play with assonance, ambiguity, and the use of those words which sound alike and yet bear quite different meanings.

Miss Sarraute is not above this sort of juggling, particularly when she redefines literary categories, maintaining that the traditional novelists are formalists, while the New Novelists, by eschewing old forms, are the true realists because

> their works, which seek to break away from all that is prescribed, conventional and dead, to turn towards what is free, sincere and alive, will necessarily, sooner or later, become ferments of emancipation and progress.

This demagoguery does not obscure the fact that she is obsessed with form in a way that the traditional writer seldom is. It is she, not he, who dreams

> of a technique that might succeed in plunging the reader into the stream of those subterranean dreams of which Proust only had time to obtain a rapid aerial view, and concerning which he observed and reproduced nothing but the broad motionless lines. This technique would give the reader the illusion of repeating these actions himself, in a more clearly aware, more orderly, distinct and forceful manner than he can do in life, without their losing that element of indetermination, of opacity and mystery, that one's own actions always have for the one who lives them.

This is perilously close to fine lady-writing (Miss Sarraute is addicted to the triad, particularly of adjectives), but despite all protestations, she is totally absorbed with form; and though she dislikes being called a formalist, she can hardly hope to avoid the label, since she has set herself the superb task of continuing consciously those prose experiments that made the early part of the twentieth century one of the great ages of the novel.

In regard to the modern masters, both Robbe-Grillet and Miss Sarraute remark with a certain wonder that there have been no true heirs to Proust, Joyce, and Kafka; the main line of the realistic novel simply resumed as though they had never existed. Yet, as Robbe-Grillet remarks:

> Flaubert wrote the new novel of 1860, Proust the new novel of 1910. The writer must proudly consent to bear his own date, knowing that there are no masterpieces in eternity, but only works in history, and that they have survived only to the degree that they have left the past behind them and heralded the future.

Here, as so often in Robbe-Grillet's theorizing, one is offered a
sensible statement, followed by a dubious observation about survival (many conventional, even reactionary works have survived
nicely), ending with a look-to-the-dawn-of-a-new-age chord,
played fortissimo. Yet the desire to continue the modern tradition is perfectly valid. And even if the New Novelists do not
succeed (in science most experiments fail), they are at least "really
serious," as Miss Sontag would say.

There is, however, something very odd about a literary movement so radical in its pronouncements yet so traditional in its
references. Both Miss Sarraute and Robbe-Grillet continually
relate themselves to great predecessors, giving rise to the suspicion that, like Saul Bellow's literary usurpers, they are assuming
for themselves the accomplishments of Dostoevsky, Flaubert,
Proust, Joyce, and Beckett. In this, at least, they are significantly
more modest than their heroes. One cannot imagine the Joyce of
Finnegans Wake acknowledging a literary debt to anyone or Flaubert admitting—as Robbe-Grillet does—that his work is "merely
pursuing a constant evolution of a genre." Curiously enough, the
writers whom Robbe-Grillet and Miss Sarraute most resemble
wrote books which were described by Arthur Symons for the
Encyclopaedia Britannica as being

> made up of an infinite number of details, set side by side, every
> detail equally prominent. . . . [the authors] do not search further
> than "the physical basis of life," and they find everything that can
> be known of that unknown force written visibly upon the sudden
> faces of little incidents, little expressive movements. . . . It is their
> distinction—the finest of their inventions—that, in order to render
> new sensations, a new vision of things, they invented a new lan-
> guage.

They, of course, are the presently unfashionable brothers Ed-
mond and Jules de Goncourt, whose collaboration ended in 1870.

In attacking the traditional novel, both Robbe-Grillet and Miss
Sarraute are on safe ground. Miss Sarraute is particularly effective when she observes that even the least aware of the tradition-
alists seems "unable to escape a certain feeling of uneasiness as
regards dialogue." She remarks upon the self-conscious way in
which contemporary writers sprinkle their pages with "he saids"
and "she replieds," and she makes gentle fun of Henry Green's

hopeful comment that perhaps the novel of the future will be largely composed in dialogue since, as she quotes him, people don't write letters any more: they use the telephone.

But the dialogue novel does not appeal to her, for it brings "the novel dangerously near the domain of the theater, where it is bound to be in a position of inferiority"—on the ground that the nuances of dialogue in the theater are supplied by actors while in the novel the writer himself must provide, somehow, the sub-conversation which is the true meaning. Opposed to the dialogue novel is the one of Proustian analysis. Miss Sarraute finds much fault with this method (no meaningful depths left to plumb in the wake of Freud), but concedes that "In spite of the rather serious charges that may be brought against analysis, it is difficult to turn from it today without turning one's back on progress."

"Progress," "*New* Novel," "permanent creation of tomorrow's world," "the discovery of reality will continue only if we abandon outward forms," "general evolution of the genre" . . . again and again one is reminded in reading the manifestos of these two explorers that we are living (one might even say that we are trapped) in the age of science. Miss Sarraute particularly delights in using quasi-scientific references. She refers to her first collection of pieces as "Tropisms." (According to authority, a tropism is "the turning of an organism, or part of one, in a particular direction in response to some special external stimulus.") She is also addicted to words like "larval" and "magma," and her analogies are often clinical: "Suspicion, which is by way of destroying the character and the entire outmoded mechanism that guaranteed its force, is one of the morbid reactions by which an organism defends itself and seeks another equilibrium. . . ."

Yet she does not like to be called a "laboratory novelist" any more than she likes to be called a formalist. One wonders why. For it is obvious that both she and Robbe-Grillet see themselves in white smocks working out new formulas for a new fiction. Underlying all their theories is the assumption that if scientists can break the atom with an equation, a dedicated writer ought to be able to find a new form in which to redefine the "unchanging human heart," as Bouvard might have said to Pécuchet. Since the old formulas have lost their efficacy, the novel, if it is to survive, must become something new; and so, to create that something new, they believe that writers must resort to calculated invention and bold experiment.

It is an interesting comment on the age that both Miss Sarraute and Robbe-Grillet take for granted that the highest literature has always been made by self-conscious avant-gardists. Although this was certainly true of Flaubert, whose letters show him in the laboratory, agonizing over that double genitive which nearly soured the recipe for *Madame Bovary*, and of Joyce, who spent a third of his life making a language for the night, Dostoevsky, Conrad, and Tolstoy—to name three novelists quite as great— were not much concerned with laboratory experiments. Their interest was in what Miss Sontag calls "the subject"; and though it is true they did not leave the form of the novel as they found it, their art was not the product of calculated experiments with form so much as it was the result of their ability, by virtue of what they were, to transmute the familiar and make it rare. They were men of genius unobsessed by what Goethe once referred to as "an eccentric desire for originality." Or as Saul Bellow puts it: "Genius is always, without strain, avant-garde. Its departure from tradition is not the result of caprice or of policy but of an inner necessity."

Absorbed by his subject, the genius is a natural innovator—a fact which must be maddening to the ordinary writer, who, because he is merely ambitious, is forced to approach literature from the outside, hoping by the study of a masterpiece's form and by an analysis of its content to reconstruct the principle of its composition in order that he may create either simulacra or, if he is furiously ambitious, by rearranging the component parts, something "new." This approach from the outside is of course the natural way of the critic, and it is significant that the New Novelists tend to blur the boundary between critic and novelist. "Critical preoccupation," writes Robbe-Grillet, "far from sterilizing creation, can on the contrary serve it as a driving force."

In the present age the methods of the scientist, who deals only in what can be measured, demonstrated and proved, are central. Consequently, anything as unverifiable as a novel is suspect. Or, as Miss Sarraute quotes Paul Tournier:

> There is nobody left who is willing to admit that he invents. The only thing that matters is the document, which must be precise, dated, proven, authentic. Works of the imagination are banned, because they are invented. . . . The public, in order to believe what it is told, must be convinced that it is not being "taken in." All that counts now is the "true fact."

This may explain why so many contemporary novelists feel they must apologize for effects which seem unduly extravagant or made up ("but that's the way it really happened!"). Nor is it to make a scandal to observe that most "serious" American novels are autobiographies, usually composed to pay off grudges. But then the novelist can hardly be held responsible for the society he reflects. After all, much of the world's reading consists of those weekly news magazines in which actual people are dealt with in fictional terms. It is the spirit of the age to believe that any fact, no matter how suspect, is superior to any imaginative exercise, no matter how true. The result of this attitude has been particularly harrowing in the universities, where English departments now do their best to pretend that they are every bit as fact-minded as the physical scientists (to whom the largest appropriations go). Doggedly, English teachers do research, publish learned findings, make breakthroughs in F. Scott Fitzgerald and, in their search for facts, behave as if no work of literature can be called complete until each character has been satisfactorily identified as someone who actually lived and had a history known to the author. It is no wonder that the ambitious writer is tempted to re-create the novel along what he believes to be scientific lines. With admiration, Miss Sontag quotes William Burroughs:

> I think there's going to be more and more merging of art and science. Scientists are already studying the creative process, and I think that the whole line between art and science will break down and that scientists, I hope, will become more creative and writers more scientific.

Recently in France the matter of science and the novel was much debated. In an essay called *Nouvelle Critique ou Nouvelle Imposture*, Raymond Picard attacked the new critic Roland Barthes, who promptly defended himself on the ground that a concern with form is only natural since structure precedes creation (an insight appropriated from anthropology, a discipline recently become fashionable). Picard then returned to the attack, mocking those writers who pretend to be scientists, pointing out that they

> improperly apply to the literary domain methods which have proved fruitful elsewhere but which here lose their efficiency and rigor. . . . These critical approaches have a scientific air to them, but the resemblance is pure caricature. The new critics use science

roughly as someone ignorant of electricity might use electronics.
What they're after is its prestige: in other respects they are at opposite poles to the scientific spirit. Their statements generally sound
more like oracles than useful hypotheses: categorical, unverifiable,
unilluminating.

Picard is perhaps too harsh, but no one can deny that Robbe-
Grillet and Nathalie Sarraute often appropriate the language of
science without understanding its spirit—for instance, one can
verify the law of physics which states that there is no action
without reaction, but how to prove the critical assertion that
things in themselves are what caused Camus's creature to kill? Yet
if to revive a moribund art form writers find it helpful to pretend
to be physicists, then one ought not to tease them unduly for
donning so solemnly mask and rubber gloves. After all, Count
Tolstoy thought he was a philosopher. But whether pseudo-scien-
tists or original thinkers, neither Robbe-Grillet nor Miss Sarraute
finds it easy to put theory into practice. As Robbe-Grillet says
disarmingly: "It is easier to indicate a new form than to follow it
without failure." And he must be said to fail a good deal of the
time: is there anything more incantatory than the repetition of the
word *"lugubre"* in *Last Year at Marienbad?* Or more visceral than
the repetition of the killing of the centipede in *Jealousy?* While
Miss Sarraute finds that her later essays are "far removed from the
conception and composition of my first book"—which, nevertheless, she includes in the same volume as the essays, with the
somewhat puzzling comment that "this first book contains *in nuce*
all the raw material that I have continued to develop in my later
works."

For Robbe-Grillet, the problem of the novel is—obviously—
the problem of man in relation to his environment, a relationship
which he believes has changed radically in the last fifty years. In
the past, man attempted to personalize the universe. In prose, this
is revealed by metaphor: "majestic peaks," "huddled villages,"
"pitiless sun." "These anthropomorphic analogies are repeated
too insistently, too coherently, not to reveal an entire metaphysical system." And he attacks what he holds to be the humanistic
view: "On the pretext that man can achieve only a subjective
knowledge of the world, humanism decides to elect man the
justification of everything." In fact, he believes that humanists
will go so far as to maintain that "it is not enough to show man
where he is: it must further be proclaimed that man is every-

where." Quite shrewdly he observes: "If I say 'the world is man,' I shall always gain absolution; while if I say things are things, and man is only man, I am immediately charged with a crime against humanity."

It is this desire to remove the falsely human from the nature of things that is at the basis of Robbe-Grillet's theory. He is arguing not so much against what Ruskin called "the pathetic fallacy," as against our race's tendency to console itself by making human what is plainly nonhuman. To those who accuse him of trying to dehumanize the novel, he replies that since any book is written by a man "animated by torments and passion," it cannot help but be human. Nevertheless, "suppose the eyes of this man rest on things without indulgence, insistently: he sees them but he refuses to appropriate them." Finally, "man looks at the world but the world does not look back at him, and so, if he rejects communion, he also rejects tragedy." Inconsistently, he later quotes with admiration Bousquet's "We watch things pass by in order to forget that they are watching us die."

Do those things watch or not? At times Miss Sarraute writes as if she thought they did. Her *Tropisms* are full of things invested with human response ("The crouched houses standing watch all along the gray streets"), but then she is not so strict as Robbe-Grillet in her apprehension of reality. She will accept "those analogies which are limited to the instinctive irresistible nature of the movements . . . produced in us by the presence of others, or by objects from the outside world." For Robbe-Grillet, however, "All analogies are dangerous."

Man's consciousness has now been separated from his environment. He lives in a perpetual present. He possesses memory but it is not chronological. Therefore the best that the writer can hope to do is to impart a precise sense of man's being in the present. To achieve this immediacy, Miss Sarraute favors "some precise dramatic action shown in slow motion"; a world in which "time was no longer the time of real life but of a hugely amplified present." While Robbe-Grillet, in commenting upon his film *Last Year at Marienbad*, declares:

> The Universe in which the entire film occurs is, characteristically, in a perpetual present which makes all recourse to memory impossible. This is a world without a past, a world which is self-sufficient at every moment and which obliterates itself as it proceeds.

To him, the film is a ninety-minute fact without antecedents. "The only important 'character' is the spectator. In his mind unfolds the whole story which is precisely imagined by him." The verb "imagine" is of course incorrect, while the adverb means nothing. The spectator is *not* imagining the film; he is watching a creation which was made in a precise historic past by a writer, a director, actors, cameramen, etc. Yet to have the spectator or reader involve himself directly and temporally in the act of creation continues to be Robbe-Grillet's goal. He wants "a present which constantly invents itself" with "the reader's creative assistance," participating "in a creation, to invent in his turn the work—and the world—and thus to learn to invent his own life." This is most ambitious. But the ingredients of the formula keep varying. For instance, in praising Raymond Roussel, Robbe-Grillet admires the author's "*investigation* which destroys, in the writing itself, its own object." Elsewhere: "The work must seem necessary but necessary for nothing; its architecture is without use; its strength is untried." And again: "The genuine writer has nothing to say. He has only a way of speaking. He must create a world but starting from nothing, from the dust. . . ." It would not seem to be possible, on the one hand, to invent a world that would cause the reader to "invent his own life" while, on the other hand, the world in question is being destroyed as it is being created. Perhaps he means for the reader to turn to dust, gradually, page by page: not the worst of solutions.

No doubt there are those who regard the contradictions in Robbe-Grillet's critical writing as the point to them—rather in the way that the boredom of certain plays or the incompetence of certain pictures are, we are assured, their achievement. Yet it is worrisome to be told that a man can create a world from nothing when that is the one thing he cannot begin to do, simply because, no matter how hard he tries, he cannot dispose of himself. Even if what he writes is no more than nouns and adjectives, who and what he is will subconsciously dictate order. Nothing human is random and it is nonsense to say:

> Art is based on no truth that exists before it; and one may say that it expresses nothing but itself. It creates its own equilibrium and its own meaning. It stands all by itself . . . or else it falls.

Which reminds us of Professor Herzog's plaintive response to the philosophic proposition that modern man at a given moment fell into the quotidian: so where was he standing before the fall? In any case, how can something unique, in Robbe-Grillet's sense, rise or fall or be anything except itself? As for reflecting "no truth that existed before it," this is not possible. The fact that the author is a man "filled with torments and passion" means that all sorts of "truths" are going to occur in the course of the writing. The act of composing prose is a demonstration not only of human will but of desire to reflect truth—particularly if one's instinct is messianic, and Robbe-Grillet is very much in that tradition. Not only does he want man "to invent his own life" (by reading Robbe-Grillet), but he proposes that today's art is "a way of living in the present world, and of participating in the permanent creation of tomorrow's world." It also seems odd that a theory of the novel which demands total existence in a self-devouring present should be concerned at all with the idea of future time since man exists, demonstrably, only in the present—the future tense is a human conceit, on the order of "majestic peaks." As for the use of the adjective "permanent," one suspects that rhetoric, not thought, forced this unfortunate word from the author's unconscious mind.

The ideal work, according to Robbe-Grillet, is

> A text both "dense and irreducible"; so perfect that it does not seem "to have touched," an object so perfect that it would obliterate our tracks. . . . Do we not recognize here the highest ambition of every writer?

Further, the only meaning for the novel is the invention of the world. "In dreams, in memory, as in the sense of sight, our imagination is the organizing force of our life, of *our* world. Each man, in his turn, must reinvent the things around him." Yet, referring to things, he writes a few pages later,

> They refer to no other world. They are the sign of nothing but themselves. And the only contact man can make with them is to imagine them.

But how is one to be loyal to the actual fact of things if they must be reinvented? Either they are *there* or they are not. In any case, by filtering them through the imagination (reinvention), true objectivity is lost, as he himself admits in a further snarling of his argument: "Objectivity in the ordinary sense of the word—total impersonality of observation—is all too obviously an illusion. But freedom of observation should be possible and yet it is not"— because a "continuous fringe of culture (psychology, ethics, metaphysics, etc.) is added to things, giving them a less alien aspect." But he believes that "humanizing" can be kept to a minimum if we try "to construct a world both more solid and more immediate. Let it be first of all by their presence that objects and gestures establish themselves and let this presence continue to prevail over the subjective." Consequently, the task of the New Novel is nothing less than to seek

> new forms for the novel . . . forms capable of expressing (or of creating) new relations between man and the world, to all those who have determined to invent the novel, in other words, to invent man. Such writers know that the systematic repetition of the forms of the past is not only absurd and futile, but that it can even become harmful: blinding us to our real situation in the world today, it keeps us, ultimately, from constructing the world and man of tomorrow.

With the change of a noun or two, this could easily be the coda of an address on American foreign policy, delivered by Professor Arthur Schlesinger, Jr., to the ADA.

Like Robbe-Grillet, Nathalie Sarraute regards Camus's *The Stranger* as a point of departure. She sees the book's immediate predecessors as "the promising art of the cinema" and "the wholesome simplicity of the new American novel." Incidentally, she is quite amusing when she describes just what the effect of these "wholesome" novels was upon the French during the years immediately after the war:

> By transporting the French reader into a foreign universe in which he had no foothold, (they) lulled his wariness, aroused in him the kind of credulous curiosity that travel books inspire, and gave him a delightful impression of escape into an unknown world.

It is reassuring to learn that these works were not regarded with any great seriousness by the French and that Horace McCoy was not, finally, the master they once hailed him. Apparently the American novel was simply a vigorous tonic for an old literature gone stale. Miss Sarraute is, however, sincerely admiring of

Faulkner's ability to involve the reader in his own world. To her the most necessary thing of all is "to dispossess the reader and entice him, at all costs, into the author's territory. To achieve this the device that consists in referring to the leading characters as 'I' constitutes a means." The use of the first person seems to her to be the emblem of modern art. ("Since Impressionism all pictures have been painted in the first person.") And so, just as photography drove painters away from representing nature (ending such ancient arts as that of the miniaturist and the maker of portrait busts), the cinema "garners and perfects what is left of it by the novel." The novel must now go where the camera may not follow. In this new country the reader has been aided by such modern writers as Proust and Joyce; they have so awakened his sensibilities that he is now able to respond to what is beneath the interior monologue, that "immense profusion of sensations, images, sentiments, memories, impulses, little larval actions that no inner language can convey." For her, emphasis falls upon what she calls the sub-conversation, that which is sensed and not said, the hidden counterpoint to the stated theme (obviously a very difficult thing to suggest, much less write, since "no inner language can convey it").

"Bosquet's universe—ours—is a universe of signs," writes Robbe-Grillet. "Everything in it is a sign; and not the sign of something else, something more perfect [*sic*], situated out of reach, but a sign of itself, of that reality which asks only to be revealed." This answer to Baudelaire's *The Salon of 1859* is reasonable (although it is anthropomorphic to suggest that reality *asks* to be revealed). Robbe-Grillet is equally reasonable in his desire for things to be shown, as much as possible, as they are.

> In the future universe of the novel, gestures and objects will be there before being *something;* and they will still be there afterwards, hard, unalterably, eternally present, mocking their own "meaning," that meaning which vainly tries to reduce them to the role of precarious tools, etc.

One agrees with him that the integrity of the nonhuman world should be honored. But what does he mean (that proscribed verb!) when he says that the objects will be *there*, after meaning has attempted to rape them? Does he mean that they will still exist on the page, in some way inviolate in their thing-ness? If he does, surely he is mistaken. What exists on the page is ink; or, if one wishes to give the ink designs their agreed-upon human meaning, letters have been formed to make words in order to suggest things not present. What is on the page are not real things but their word-shadows. Yet even if the things were there, it is most unlikely that they would be so human as to "mock their own meaning." In an eerie way, Robbe-Grillet's highly rhetorical style has a tendency to destroy his arguments even as he makes them; critically, this technique complements ideally the self-obliterating anecdote.

On the question of how to establish the separateness, the autonomy of things, Robbe-Grillet and Miss Sarraute part company. In contemplating her method, she ceases altogether to be "scientific." Instead she alarmingly intones a hymn to words—all words —for they "possess the qualities needed to seize upon, protect and bring out into the open those subterranean movements that are at once impatient and afraid." (Are those subterranean movements really "impatient and afraid"?) For her, words possess suppleness, freedom, iridescent richness of shading, and by their nature they are protected "from suspicion and from minute examination." (In an age of suspicion, to let words off scot-free is an act of singular trust.) Consequently, once words have entered the other person, they swell, explode, and "by virtue of this game of actions and reactions . . . they constitute a most valuable tool for the novelist." Which, as the French say, goes without saying.

But of course words are not at all what she believes they are. All words lie. Or as Professor Frank Kermode put it in *Literary Fiction and Reality*: "Words, thoughts, patterns of word and thought, are enemies of truth, if you identify that with what may be had by phenomenological reductions." Nevertheless, Miss Sarraute likes to think that subterranean movements (tropisms) can be captured by words, which might explain why her attitude toward things is so much more conventional than that of Robbe-Grillet, who writes:

Perhaps Kafka's staircases lead *elsewhere*, but they are *there*, and we look at them step by step following the details of the banisters and the risers.

This is untrue. First, we do not look at the staircases; we look at a number of words arranged upon a page by a conscious human intelligence which would like us to consider, among a thousand other things, the fact of those staircases. Since a primary concern of the human mind is cause and effect, the reader is bound to speculate upon why those staircases have been shown him; also, since staircases are usually built to connect one man-made level with another, the mind will naturally speculate as to what those two levels are like. Only a far-gone schizophrenic (or an LSD tripper) would find entirely absorbing the description of a banister.

Perhaps the most naïve aspect of Robbe-Grillet's theory of fiction is his assumption that words can ever describe with absolute precision anything. At no point does he acknowledge that words are simply fiat for real things; by their nature, words are imprecise and layered with meanings—the signs of things, not the things themselves. Therefore, even if Robbe-Grillet's goal of achieving a total reality for the world of things was desirable, it would not be possible to do it with language, since the author (that man full of torments and passions) is bound to betray his attitude to the sequence of signs he offered us; he has an "interest" in the matter, or else he would not write. Certainly if he means to reinvent man, then he will want to find a way of defining man through human (yes, psychological) relations as well as through a catalog of things observed and gestures coolly noted. Wanting to play God, ambition is bound to dictate the order of words, and so the subjective will prevail just as it does in the traditional novel. To follow Robbe-Grillet's theory to its logical terminus, the only sort of book which might be said to be *not* a collection of signs of absent things but the actual things themselves would be a collection of ink, paper, cardboard, glue, and typeface, to be assembled or not by the reader-spectator. If this be too heavy a joke, then the ambitious writer must devise a new language which might give the appearance of maintaining the autonomy of things, since the words, new-minted, will possess a minimum of associations of a subjective or anthropomorphic sort. No existing language will be of any use to him, unless it be that of the Trobriand Islanders: those happy people have no words for "why" or "because"; for them, things just happen. Needless to say, they do not write novels or speculate on the nature of things.

The philosophic origins of the New Novel can be found (like most things French) in Descartes, whose dualism was the reflection of a split between the subjective and the objective, between the irrational and the rational, between the physical and the metaphysical. In the last century Auguste Comte, accepting this dualism, conceived of a logical empiricism which would emphasize the "purely" objective at the expense of the subjective or metaphysical. An optimist who believed in human progress, Comte saw history as an evolution toward a better society. For him the age of religion and metaphysics ended with the French Revolution. Since that time the human race was living in what he termed "the age of science," and he was confident that the methods of the positive sciences would enrich and transform human life. At last things were coming into their own. But not until the twentieth century did the methods of science entirely overwhelm the arts of the traditional humanists. To the scientific-minded, all things, including human personality, must in time yield their secrets to orderly experiment. Meanwhile, only that which is verifiable is to be taken seriously; emotive meaning must yield to cognitive meaning. Since the opacity of human character has so far defeated all objective attempts at illumination, the New Novelists prefer, as much as possible, to replace the human with objects closely observed and simple gestures noted but not explained.

In many ways, the New Novel appears to be approaching the "pure" state of music. In fact, there are many like Miss Sontag who look forward to "a kind of total structuring" of the novel, analogous to music. This is an old dream of the novelist. Nearly half a century ago, Joyce wrote (in a letter to his brother), "Why should not a modern literature be as unsparing and as direct as song?" Why not indeed? And again, why? The answer to the second "why" is easy enough. In the age of science, the objective is preferred to the subjective. Since human behavior is notoriously irrational and mysterious, it can be demonstrated only in the most impressionistic and unscientific way; it yields few secrets to objective analysis. Mathematics, on the other hand, is rational and verifiable, and music is a form of mathematics. Therefore, if one were to eliminate as much as possible the human from the novel, one might, through "a kind of total structuring," come close to the state of mathematics or music—in short, achieve that perfect irreducible artifact Robbe-Grillet dreams of.

The dates of Miss Sarraute's essays range from 1947 to 1956, those of Robbe-Grillet from 1955 to 1963. To categorize in the French manner, it might be said that their views are particularly representative of the fifties, a period in which the traditional-minded (among whom they must be counted) still believed it possible to salvage the novel—or anything—by new techniques. With a certain grimness, they experimented. But though some of their books are good (even very good) and some are bad, they did not make a "new" novel, if only because art forms do not evolve —in literature at least—from the top down. Despite Robbe-Grillet's tendency to self-congratulation ("Although these descriptions—motionless arguments or fragments of scene—have acted on the readers in a satisfactory fashion, the judgment many specialists make of them remains pejorative"), there is not much in what he has so far written that will interest anyone except the specialist. It is, however, a convention of the avant-garde that to be in advance of the majority is to be "right." But the New Novelists are not in advance of anyone. Their works derive from what they believe to be a need for experiment and the imposition of certain of the methods of science upon the making of novels. Fair enough. Yet in this they resemble everyone, since to have a liking for the new is to be with the dull majority. In the arts, the obviously experimental is almost never denounced *because* it is new: if anything, our taste-makers tend to be altogether too permissive in the presence of what looks to be an experiment, as anyone who reads New York art criticism knows. There is not much likelihood that Robbe-Grillet will be able to reinvent man as a result of his exercises in prose. Rather he himself is in the process of being reinvented (along with the rest of us) by the new world in which we are living.

At the moment, advance culture scouts are reporting with a certain awe that those men and women who were brought up as television-watchers respond, predictably, to pictures that move and talk but not at all to prose fictions; and though fashion might dictate the presence of an occasional irreducible artifact in a room, no one is about to be reinvented by it. Yet the old avant-garde continues worriedly to putter with form.

Surveying the literary output for 1965, Miss Sontag found it "hard to think of any one book (in English) that exemplifies in a *central* way the possibilities for enlarging and complicating the forms of prose literature." This desire to "enlarge" and "complicate" the novel has an air of madness to it. Why not minimize and simplify? One suspects that out of desperation she is picking verbs at random. But then, like so many at present, she has a taste for the random. Referring to William Burroughs's resolutely random work *The Soft Machine,* she writes: "In the end, the voices come together and sound what is to my mind the most serious, urgent and original voice in American letters to be heard for many years." It is, however, the point to Mr. Burroughs's method that the voices *don't* come together: he is essentially a sport who is (blessedly) not serious, not urgent, and original only in the sense that no other American writer has been so relentlessly ill-humored in his send-up of the serious. He is the Grand Guy Grand of American letters. But whether or not Miss Sontag is right or wrong in her analyses of specific works and general trends, there is something old-fashioned and touching in her assumption (shared with the New Novelists) that if only we all try hard enough in a "really serious" way, we can come up with the better novel. This attitude reflects not so much the spirit of art as it does that of Detroit.

No one today can predict what games post-Gutenberg man will want to play. The only certainty is that his mind will work differently from ours; just as ours works differently from that of pre-Gutenberg man, as Miss Frances Yates demonstrated so dramatically in *The Art of Memory.* Perhaps there will be more Happenings in the future. Perhaps the random will take the place of the calculated. Perhaps the ephemeral will be preferred to the permanent: we stop in time, so why should works of art endure? Also, as the shadow of atomic catastrophe continues to fall across our merry games, the ephemeral will necessarily be valued to the extent it gives pleasure in the present and makes no pretense of having a future life. Since nothing will survive the firewind, the ashes of one thing will be very like those of another, and so what matters excellence?

One interesting result of today's passion for the immediate and the casual has been the decline, in all the arts, of the idea of technical virtuosity as being in any way desirable. The culture (*kitsch* as well as camp) enjoys singers who sing no better than the average listener, actors who do not act yet are, in Andy Warhol's happy phrase, "super-stars," painters whose effects are too easily achieved, writers whose swift flow of words across the page is not submitted to the rigors of grammar or shaped by conscious thought. There is a general Zen-ish sense of why bother? If a natural fall of pebbles can "say" as much as any shaping of paint on canvas or cutting of stone, why go to the trouble of recording what is there for all to see? In any case, if the world should become, as predicted, a village united by an electronic buzzing, our ideas of what is art will seem as curious to those gregarious villagers as the works of what we used to call the Dark Ages appear to us.

Regardless of what games men in the future will want to play, the matter of fiction seems to be closed. Reading skills—as the educationalists say—continue to decline with each new generation. Novel reading is not a pastime of the young now being educated, nor, for that matter, is it a preoccupation of any but a very few of those who came of age in the last warm years of linear type's hegemony. It is possible that fashion may from time to time bring back a book or produce a book which arouses something like general interest (Miss Sontag darkly suspects that "the nineteenth-century novel has a much better chance for a comeback than verse drama, the sonnet, or landscape painting"). Yet it is literature itself which seems on the verge of obsolescence, and not so much because the new people will prefer watching to reading as because the language in which books are written has become corrupt from misuse.

In fact, George Steiner believes that there is a definite possibility that "The political inhumanity of the twentieth century and certain elements in the technological mass-society which has followed on the erosion of European bourgeois values have done injury to language. . . ." He even goes so far as to suggest that for now at least silence may be a virtue for the writer—when

> language simply ceases, and the motion of spirit gives no further outward manifestation of its being. The poet enters into silence. Here the word borders not on radiance or music, but on night.

Although Mr. Steiner does not himself take this romantic position ("I am not saying that writers should stop writing. This would be fatuous"), he does propose silence as a proud alternative for those who have lived at the time of Belsen and of Vietnam, and have witnessed the perversion of so many words by publicists and political clowns. The credibility gap is now an abyss, separating even the most honorable words from their ancient meanings. Fortunately, ways of communication are now changing, and though none of us understands exactly what is happening, language is bound to be affected.

But no matter what happens to language, the novel is not apt to be revived by electronics. The portentous theorizings of the New Novelists are of no more use to us than the self-conscious avant-gardism of those who are forever trying to figure out what the next "really serious" thing will be when it is plain that there is not going to be a next serious thing in the novel. Our lovely vulgar and most human art is at an end, if not the end. Yet that is no reason not to want to practice it, or even to read it. In any case, rather like priests who have forgotten the meaning of the prayers they chant, we shall go on for quite a long time talking of books and writing books, pretending all the while not to notice that the church is empty and the parishioners have gone else-where to attend other gods, perhaps in silence or with new words.

Encounter,
December 1967

The Hacks of Academe

*T*he *Theory of the Novel: New Essays,* edited by John Halperin. The two articles arouse suspicion. *The* theory? *The* novel? Since there is no such thing as the novel, how can there be a single theory? Or is the editor some sort of monist? Blinkered hedgehog in wild fox country? The jacket identifies Mr. Halperin as "Associate Professor and Director of Graduate Studies in the Department of English at the University of Southern California." This is true academic weight. "He is also the author of *The Language of Meditation: Four Studies in Nineteenth-Century Fiction* and *Egoism and Self-Discovery in the Victorian Novel.*" Well, meditation if not language is big in Southern California, where many an avocado tree shades its smogbound Zen master, while the Victorian novel continues to be a growth industry in academe. Eagerly, one turns to Professor Halperin's "A Critical Introduction" to nineteen essays by as many professors of English. Most are American; most teach school in the land of the creative writing course.

"Christ left home at twelve." Professor Halperin's first sentence is startlingly resonant, to use an adjective much favored by the contributors, who also like "mythopoeic," "parameter" (al-most always misused), "existential" (often misused), "linear," "schematic" and "spatial." Professor Halperin tells us that dur-ing the lifetime of Nazareth's gift to the joy of nations,

> poetry's age . . . was in the thousands of years and drama's in the hundreds. It was not until a millennium and a half later that the gestation period of the novel began. Thus it is not surprising, three quarters of the way through the twentieth century, that we find ourselves with a growing but still relatively small body of critical *theory* pertaining to the novel . . .

This is sweet innocence; also, ignorance. Two very good novels *(Satyricon, Golden Ass)* were written by near-contemporaries of the gentle Nazarene. Later, during the so-called long "gestation," other cultures were lightened (as William Faulkner would put it) of novels as distinguished as the Lady Murasaki's *Tale of Genji* (c. A.D. 1005).

But Professor Halperin is not very interested in novels. Rather:

> It is the purpose of the present volume to reflect and hopefully to deal with some of the more radical issues of contemporary novel-theory. . . . This collection, containing original essays of theoretical cast written especially for this volume by some of the most distin-guished critics of our time, hopefully will be a major addition to the growing corpus of theoretical approaches to fiction.

Professor Halperin has not an easy way with our rich language. Nevertheless, one opens his book in the hope that the prose of "some of the most distinguished critics of our time" will be better than his own. Certainly the great names are all here: Meir Stern-berg, Robert Bernard Martin, Irving H. Buchen, Alan Warren Friedman, Max F. Schulz, Alice R. Kaminsky, George Levine, John W. Loofourow, Marvin Mudrick, Walter F. Wright, Robert B. Heilman, Richard Harter Fogle, Dorothea Krook. Also Leon Edel, Leslie A. Fiedler, Walter Allen and Frank Kermode. *Un sac mixte*, as Bouvard might have said to Pécuchet.

Professor Halperin quotes approvingly Barthes's

> Flaubert . . . finally established Literature as an object, through promoting literary labour to the status of a value; form became the end-product of craftsmanship, like a piece of pottery or a jewel

. . . [The] whole of Literature, from Flaubert to the present day, became the problematics of language.

Professor Halperin adds his own gloss.

Modern theoretical novel-criticism . . . is occupied less with the novel as a mimetic and moral performance than with the novel as an autonomous creation independent of or at least not wholly dependent on the real world. The world of the autonomous novel may inevitably resemble our own, but it is not created as a conscious representation of anything outside itself.

American professors of English have never had an easy time with French theoreticians of the novel (close scrutiny of the quotation from Barthes reveals that it was taken from an English not an American translation). Nevertheless, despite various hedges like "may inevitably," Professor Halperin has recklessly enrolled himself in the school of Paris (class of '56). As a result, he believes that the autonomous novel "is not created as a conscious representation of anything outside itself." Aside from the presumption of pretending to know what any writer has in mind (is he inevitably but not consciously describing or mimicking the real world?), it is naïve to assume that a man-made novel can ever resemble a meteor fallen from outer space, a perfectly autonomous artifact whose *raison d'être* is "with the relationships among the various structural elements within the work of fiction itself" rather than "between reader and text." Apparently the novel is no longer what James conceived it, a story told, in Professor Halperin's happy phrase, from "the limited perspective of a single sentient consciousness." And so, in dubious battle, unconscious sentiencies clash in the English departments of the West with insentient consciousnesses.

The first essay is called "What is Exposition?" This subject plainly troubles Professor Meir Sternberg. At a loss for the right words, he resorts to graphics. An inverted "V" occupies the top of one page. At the foot of the left leg is the word "introduction"; then "exciting force"; then "rise." The apex of the inverted "V" is labeled "climax." Partway down the right leg is the word "fall," while at the base occurs the somber word "catastrophe." This treasure-seeker's map to tragedy is something called "Freytag's pyramid," which the eponymous architect set up in the desert of novel-theory to show how "time-honored" exposition works in tragedy.

Professor Sternberg then adds his own markings to the sand. "Suppose an author wishes to compose a narrative which is to consist of three motifs: a1, a2, a3. These motifs, arranged in an order in which a2 follows a1 in a time and a3 follows a2, will form the *fabula* of his story." The sequence of numbered a's is then arranged vertically on the page, and casts almost as minatory a shadow as Freytag's pyramid. Later Professor Sternberg assembles a positively Cheopsean structure with such parallel headings as "story," "*fabula*," "plot," "*sujet*," a monster Rosetta stone with which to confound strawman Freytag. The resulting *agon* (or duel or *lutte*) in the desert is very elaborate and not easy to follow. Occasionally there is a simple sentence like: "A work of fiction presents characters in action during a certain period of time." But, by and large, sentences are as elaborate as the ideas that they wish to express are simple. And so, as the sun sinks behind the last tautology, our guide sums up: "As my definition of it clearly implies, exposition is a time problem *par excellence.*" (Instructor's note: Transpose "it" and "exposition.")

Further on in the Sahelian wilderness we meet Professor Irving H. Buchen. At first, one is charmed: "Critics may need novels to be critics but novels do not need critics to be novels." This is fine stuff. The pathetic fallacy is at last able to define for us that mysterious entity "the living novel." Professor Buchen likes his literature lean.

> Almost all novelistic failures, especially significant ones, are the result of crushing richness. Plenitude swelled to bursting Fielding's *Tom Jones*, deluged Conrad's *Nostromo*, over-refined Proust's sensibility, and transformed Joyce in *Finnegans Wake* into a self parodist.

Solution? "The key to the artistry of the novel is managing fecundity." The late Margaret Sanger could not have put it better.

Although Professor Buchen's "The Aesthetics of the Supra-Novel" deals only in the obvious, his footnotes are often interesting. Occasionally a shy aphorism gleams like a scarab in the sand. "The novel is not a given form; it is given to be formed." Pondering the vast amount of "novel-theory" written for classrooms, he notes that this process of over-explicating texts produces new novelists who, like the re-issue of older novelists, seemed to be buttressed both in front and in back. Finally, virtually every facet of the novel has been subjected to structural, stylistic, formalistic, epistemological processing. Aside from some outstanding seminal pieces, what is instructive about the entire theoretical enterprise is that it has created a Frankenstein.

I assume that he means the monster and not the baron. In any case, relieved of those confining "parameters" of "novel-theory" (also known as "book-chat"), Professor Buchen's footnotes betray glimmers of true intelligence.

In general, Professor Halperin's novel-theorists have nothing very urgent or interesting to say about literature. Why then do they write when they have nothing to say? Because the ambitious teacher can only rise in the academic bureaucracy by writing at complicated length about writing that has already been much written about. The result of all this book-chat cannot interest anyone who knows literature while those who would like to learn something about books can only be mystified and discouraged by these commentaries. Certainly it is no accident that the number of students taking English courses has been in decline for some years. But that is beside the point. What matters is that the efforts of the teachers now under review add up to at least a half millennium of academic tenure.

Although The Novel is not defined by Professor Halperin's colleagues, some interesting things are said about novels. Professor Frank Kermode's "Novel and Narrative" is characteristically elegant. In fact, so fine-meshed is his prose that one often has to reread whole pages but then, as Kant instructs us, "comprehension is only a knowledge adequate to our intention." Kermode is particularly good on the virtues and demerits of Roland Barthes; no doubt, because he has actually read Barthes and not relied upon the odd quotation picked up here and there in translation. Kermode tends to pluralism and he is unimpressed by the so-called great divide between the mimetic fiction of the past and the autonomous fiction of the present. "It seems doubtful, then, whether we need to speak of some great divide—a strict historical *coupure*—between the old and new." Minor complaint: I do wish Kermode would not feel obliged always to drag in the foreign word whose meaning is no different from the English equivalent. Also, my heart sinks every time he fashions a critical category and then announces firmly: "I shall call it, hermeneutic activity." As for the great divide:

> There are differences of emphasis, certainly, as to what it is to read; and there are, within the narratives themselves, rearrangement of emphasis and interest. Perhaps, as metacritics often allege, these are to be attributed to a major shift in our structures of thought; but although this may be an efficient cause of the mutation of interests it does not appear that the object of those interests—narrative— imitates the shift.

Phrased like a lawyer and, to my mind, demonstrably true. Nevertheless, the other "most distinguished critics" seem to believe that there has indeed been at least a gap or split or *coupure* between old and new writing, requiring, if not a critical bridge, an academic's bandage.

Professor Leon Edel chats amiably about "Novel and Camera," reminding us that Robbe-Grillet's reliance on the close-shot in his novels might have something to do with his early training as an agronomist where the use of a microscope is essential. Professor Edel notes that the audience for the novel is dwindling while the audience for films, television, comic books continues to grow; he echoes Saul Bellow:

> Perhaps we have had too many novels. People no longer seem to need them. On the other hand, pictorial biographies—real pictures of real lives—exist in abundance, and there will be more of these in the coming year. The camera is ubiquitous.

In "Realism Reconsidered," Professor George Levine has a number of intelligent things to say about writing. Although limited by a certain conceit about his own place in time ("Reality has become problematic in ways the Victorians could only barely imagine"), he is aware that the word "reality" is protean: even the French ex-agronomist wants to be absolutely realistic. Buttressed by Auerbach, Gombrich and Frye, Professor Levine's meditation on realism in the novel is not only sensible but his sentences are rather better than those of his fellow most-distinguished critics. There is a plainness reminiscent of Edmund Wilson. Possibly because:

My bias, then, is historical . . . . What is interesting here is that at one point in European history writers should have become so self-conscious about truth-telling in art [which I take to imply the growth of doubt about art in society] that they were led to raise truth-telling to the level of doctrine and to imply that previous literatures had not been telling it.

Then Levine states the profound truth that "fiction is fiction," ruling out Truth if not truth. Or as Calvin Coolidge said in a not too dissimilar context: "In public life it is sometimes necessary in order to appear really natural to be actually artificial."

"The Death and Rebirth of the Novel." The confident ring of the title could only have been sounded by America's liveliest full-time professor and seducer of the *Zeitgeist* (no proper English equivalent), Leslie A. Fiedler. A redskin most at home in white clown makeup, Fiedler has given many splendid performances over the years. From a secure heterosexual base, he has turned a bright amused eye on the classic American *goyim* and finds them not only homoerotic to a man (or person as they say nowadays) but given to guilty pleasures with injuns like Queequeg, with niggers like Jim. As far as I know, Fiedler has yet to finger an American-Jewish author as a would-be reveler in the savage Arcadia of Sodom-America, but then that hedge of burning bushes no doubt keeps pure the American Jewish writer/person.

Fiedler reminds us that for a "century or more" the leading novelists and a good many critics have forgotten "that at its most authentic the novel is a form of popular art." But he shares the academic delusion that the novel was invented in the middle of the eighteenth century by "that extraordinary anti-elitist genius" Samuel Richardson, who launched "the first successful form of Pop Art." For Fiedler, Richardson reflects little of what preceded him (the epic, the ballad) but he made possible a great deal that has come since: "the comic strip, the comic book, cinema, TV." After the Second World War, the appearance of mass-production paperback books in the supermarkets of the West was insurance against the main line of the novel becoming elitist, for "the machine-produced commodity novel is, therefore, dream literature, mythic literature, as surely as any tale told over the tribal fire." Consequently, "form and content, in the traditional sense, are secondary, optional if not irrelevant—since it is, in the first instance, primordial images and archetypal narrative structures that the novel is called on to provide." Fiedler believes that dream-literature *(Pickwick Papers, Valley of the Dolls)* is peculiarly "immune to formalist criticism." Further, "it sometimes seems as if all such novels want to metamorphose into movies . . . a kind of chrysalis yearning to be a butterfly."

Certainly Pop narratives reveal the society's literally vulgar daydreams. Over and over again occur and recur the sex lives and the murders of various Kennedys, the sphinx-like loneliness of Greta Garbo, the disintegration of Judy Garland or, closer to the heart of academe, the crack-up of Scott Fitzgerald in Hollywood, the principal factory of this century's proto-myths. Until recently no Art Novelist (Fiedler's phrase) would go near a subject as melodramatic as the collapse of a film star or the murder of a president. Contemporary practitioners of the Art Novel ("beginning with, perhaps, Flaubert, and reaching a climax in the work of Proust, Mann and Joyce") are doggedly at work creating "fiction intended not for the market-place but the library and classroom; or its sub-variety, the Avant Garde Novel, which foresees immediate contempt followed eventually by an even securer status in future Museums of Literary Culture."

> To put it as bluntly as possible, it is incumbent on all who write fiction or criticism in the disappearing twentieth century to realize that the Art Novel or Avant-Garde Novel is in the process of being abandoned wherever fiction remains most alive, which means that that sub-genre of the novel is dying if not dead.

Although Fiedler's funeral oration ought to alarm those teachers who require a certain quantity of serious "novel writing" so that they can practice "novel criticism," I suspect that they will, secretly, agree with him. If all the Art Novels have been written, then no one need ever run the risk of missing the point to something new. After all, a lot can still be written about the old Modern masterpieces.

As always, Fiedler makes some good sense. He can actually see what is in front of him and this is what makes him such a useful figure. Briskly, he names four present-day practitioners of the Art Novel of yesteryear: Bellow, Updike, Moravia, Robbe-Grillet. This is an odd grouping, but one sees what he means. Then he gives two examples of what he calls, approvingly, "the Anti-art Art Novel." One is Nabokov's *Pale Fire.* The other is John Barth's

Giles Goat-Boy: "a strange pair of books really"—note the first sign of unease—

> the former not quite American and the latter absolutely provincial American. Yet they have in common a way of using typical devices of the Modernist Art Novel, like irony, parody, travesty, exhibitionistic allusion, redundant erudition, and dogged experimentalism, not to extend the possibilities of the form but to destroy it.

This is nonsense. Professor (Emeritus) Nabokov's bright clever works are very much in the elitist Art-Novel tradition. It is true that the Black Swan of Lac Léman makes fun of American academics and their ghastly explications, but his own pretty constructions are meant to last forever. They are not autonomous artifacts designed to "self-destruct."

Giles Goat-Boy is a very bad prose-work by Professor John Barth. Certainly the book is not, as Fiedler claims,

> a comic novel, a satire intended to mock everything which comes before it . . . it is itself it mocks, along with the writer capable of producing one more example of so obsolescent a form, and especially us who are foolish enough to be reading it. It is as if the Art Novel, aware that it must die, has determined to die laughing.

With that, Professor Fiedler goes over the side of Huck's raft. Whatever Professor Barth's gifts, humor, irony, wit are entirely lacking from his ambitious, garrulous, jocose productions. If this is the Anti-art Art Novel, then I predict that it will soon be superseded by the Anti-Anti-art Art Novel, which will doubtless prove to be our moribund friend the Art Novel. I suspect that the works of Professor Barth are written not so much to be read as to be taught. If this is the case then, according to Fiedler's own definition, they are Art Novels. Certainly they are not destined for the mass marketplace where daydreams of sex and of money, of movie stars and of murdered presidents are not apt to be displaced by a leaden narrative whose burden is (oh, wit, oh, irony) the universe is the university is the universe.

Happily, Fiedler soon abandons the highlands of culture for those lowlands where thrive science fiction and the Western, two genres that appear to reflect the night mind of the race. Fiedler mentions with approval some recent "neo-Pop Novels." *Little Big*

Man excites him and he is soon back on his familiar warpath as white skin confronts redskin. Yet why the "neo" in front of Pop? Surely what used to be called "commercial fiction" has never ceased to reflect the dreams and prejudices of those still able to read. Fiedler does not quite deal with this. He goes off at a tangent. "At the moment of the rebirth of the novel, all order and distinction seem lost, as High Art and Low merge into each other, as books become films . . . ." Fiedler ends with an analysis of a novel turned into film called *Drive, He Said*, and he suggests that "therapeutic" madness may be the next chapter in our collective dreaming: injuns, niggers, subversives . . . or something.

Rebirth of the novel? That seems unlikely. The University-novel tends to be stillborn, suitable only for classroom biopsy. The Public-novel continues to be written but the audience for it is drifting away. Those brought up on the passive pleasures of films and television find the act of reading anything at all difficult and unrewarding. Ambitious novelists are poignantly aware of the general decline in what Professor Halperin would call "reading skills." Much of Mr. Donald Barthelme's latest novel, *The Dead Father*, is written in a kind of numbing baby talk reminiscent of the "see Jane run" primary school textbooks. Of course Mr. Barthelme means to be ironic. Of course he knows his book is not very interesting to read, but then life is not very interesting to live either. Hopefully, as Professor Halperin would say, the book will self-destruct once it has been ritually praised wherever English is taught but not learned.

Obviously what Fiedler calls the Art Novel is in more trouble than the Pop novel. Movies still need larvae to metamorphose into moths. The Anti-art Art Novel does not exist despite the nervous attempts of teachers to find a way of making the novel if not news, really and truly new. I think it unlikely that Barthes, Barth and Barthelme will ever produce that unified field theory of Art-Novel writing and theory so long dreamed of by students of Freytag's pyramid.

Meanwhile, the caravans bark, and the dogs move on. Last December the Modern Language Association met in San Francisco. According to a reliable authority, the most advanced of the young bureaucrats of literature were all reading and praising the works of Burroughs. Not William, Edgar Rice.

Times Literary Supplement,
February 20, 1976

American Plastic:
The Matter of Fiction

The New Novel is close to forty years old. Although forty is young for an American presidential candidate or a Chinese buried egg, it is very old indeed for a literary movement, particularly a French literary movement. But then what, recently, *has* one heard of the New Novel, whose official *vernissage* occurred in 1938 with Nathalie Sarraute's publication of *Tropismes?* The answer is not much directly from the founders but a good deal indirectly, for, with characteristic torpor, America's Departments of English have begun slowly, slowly to absorb the stern aesthetics of Sarraute and Robbe-Grillet, not so much through the actual writing of these masters as through their most brilliant interpreter, the witty, meta-camp sign-master and analyst of *le degré zéro de l'écriture* Roland Barthes, whose amused and amusing saurian face peers like some near-sighted chameleon from the back of a half-dozen slim volumes now being laboriously read in Academe.

Barthes has also had a significant (or signifying) effect on a number of American writers, among them Mr. Donald Barthelme. Two years ago Mr. Barthelme was quoted as saying that the only American writers worth reading are John Barth, Grace Paley, William Gass, and Thomas Pynchon.* Dutifully, I have read all the writers on Mr. Barthelme's list, and presently I will make my report on them. But first, a look at M. Barthes.

For over twenty years Barthes has been a fascinating high critic who writes with equal verve about Charlie Chaplin, detergents, Marx, toys, Balzac, structuralism, and semiology. He has also put the theory of the New Novelists rather better than they have themselves, a considerable achievement since it is as theoreticians and not as practitioners that these writers excel. Unlike Sarraute, Robbe-Grillet, and Butor, Professor Barthes is much too clever actually to write novels himself, assuming that such things exist, new or old, full of signs or not, with or without sequential narratives. Rather, Barthes has remained a commentator and a theoretician, and he is often pleasurable to read though never blissful, to appropriate his own terminology.

Unlike the weather, theories of the novel tend to travel from east to west. But then, as we have always heard (sometimes from the French themselves), the French mind is addicted to the postulating of elaborate systems in order to explain everything, while the Anglo-American mind tends to shy away from unified-field theories. We chart our courses point to point; they sight from the stars. The fact that neither really gets much of anywhere doesn't mean that we haven't all had some nice outings over the years.

Nine years ago I wrote an exhaustive and, no doubt, exhausting account of the theory or theories of the French New Novel.† Rejected by the American literary paper for which I had written it (subject not all that interesting), I was obliged to publish in England at the CIA's expense. Things have changed since 1967. Today one can hardly pick up a Serious literary review without noting at least one obligatory reference to Barthes, or look at any list of those novelists currently admired by American English departments without realizing that although none of these writers approaches zero degree, quite a few are on the chilly side. This is not such a bad thing. Twice, by the way, I have used the word "thing" in this paragraph. I grow suspicious, as one ought to be

---

*I am told that Mr. Barthelme later, sensibly, denied having made such an exclusive pronouncement.
† See p. 65.

in zero-land, of all *things* and their shadows, words.

Barthes's American admirers are particularly fascinated by semiology, a quasi-science of signs first postulated by Ferdinand de Saussure in his *Course in General Linguistics* (1916). For some years the school of Paris and its American annex have made much of signs and signification, linguistic and otherwise. Barthes's *Elements of Semiology* (1964) is a key work and not easy to understand. It is full of graphs and theorems as well as definitions and puzzles. Fortunately, Susan Sontag provides a useful preface to the American edition of *Writing Degree Zero*, reminding us that Barthes "simply takes for granted a great deal that we do not." Zero degree writing is that colorless "white" writing (first defined and named by Sartre in his description of Camus's *L'Étranger*). It is a language in which, among other things and no-things, metaphor and anthropomorphizing are eliminated. According to Sontag, Barthes is reasonable enough to admit that this kind of writing is but "*one* solution to the disintegration of literary language."

As for semiology or the "science" of signs, Barthes concedes that "this term, *sign*, which is found in very different vocabularies . . . is for these very reasons very ambiguous." He categorizes various uses of the word "from the Gospels to Cybernetics." I should like to give him a use of the word he seems not to know. The word for "sign" in Sanskrit is "lingam," which also means "phallus," the holy emblem of our Lord Shiva.

In *S/Z* (1970) Barthes took "Sarrasine," a Balzac short story, and subjected it to a line-by-line, even a word-by-word analysis. In the course of this assault, Barthes makes a distinction between what he calls the "readerly text" and the "writerly text" (I am using Mr. Richard Miller's translation of these phrases). Barthes believes that "the goal of literary work (of literature as work) is to make the reader no longer a consumer, but a producer of the text. Our literature is characterized by the pitiless divorce . . . between the producer of the text and its user, between its owner and its customer, between its author and its reader. This reader is thereby plunged into a kind of idleness—he is intransitive; he is, in short, *serious*. Opposite the writerly text, then, is its counter-value, its negative, reactive value: what can be read but not written: the *readerly*. We call any readerly text a classic text." Then "the writerly is the novelistic without the novel, poetry without the poem. . . . But the readerly texts? They are products (and not productions), they make up the mass of our literature. How [to] differentiate this mass once again?"

Barthes believes that this can be done through *"interpretation* (in the Nietzschean sense of the word)." He has a passion, incidentally, for lizardlike dodges from the direct statement by invoking some great reverberating name as an adjective, causing the reader's brow to contract. But then the lunges and dodges are pretty much the matter as well as the manner of Barthes's technique as he goes to work on Balzac's short story of a man who falls in love with a famous Italian singer who turns out to be not the beautiful woman of his dreams but a castrated Neapolitan boy.

I do not intend to deal with Barthes's "interpretation" of the text. It is a very elaborate and close reading in a style that seems willfully complicated. I say willfully because the text of itself is a plain and readerly one in no need of this sort of assistance, not that Barthes wants to assist either text or reader. Rather he means to make for his own delectation or bliss a writerly text of his own. I hope that he has succeeded.

Like so many of today's academic critics, Barthes resorts to formulas, diagrams; the result, no doubt, of teaching in classrooms equipped with blackboards and chalk. Envious of the half-erased theorems—the prestigious *signs*—of the physicists, English teachers now compete by chalking up theorems and theories of their own, words having failed them yet again.

Fair stood the wind for America. For twenty years from the east have come these thoughts, words, signs. Let us now look and see what our own writers have made of so much exciting heavy weather, particularly the writers Mr. Donald Barthelme has named. Do they show signs of the French Pox?

Two years ago, I had read some of Gass, tried and failed to read Barth and Pynchon. I had never read Mr. Barthelme and I had never heard of Grace Paley. I have now made my way through the collected published works of the listed writers as well as through Mr. Barthelme's own enormous output. I was greatly helped in my journey through these texts by Mr. Joe David Bellamy's *The New Fiction,* a volume containing interviews with most of the principals and their peers.

Over the years I have seen but not read Donald Barthelme's short stories in *The New Yorker.* I suppose I was put off by the pictures. Barthelme's texts are usually decorated with perspective drawings, ominous faces, funny-looking odds and ends. Let the prose do it, I would think severely, and turn the page, looking for S.J. Perelman. I was not aware that I was *not* reading one who is described in *The New Fiction* as, "according to Philip Stevick . . . 'the most imitated fictionist in the United States today.' " Mr. Stevick is plainly authority to the interviewer, who then gets Barthelme to say a number of intelligent things about the life of a "fictionist" today. Mr. Barthelme tells us that his father was "a 'modern' architect." Incidentally, it is now the fashion to put quotes around any statement or word that might be challenged. This means that the questionable word or statement was not meant literally but ironically or "ironically." Another way of saying, "Don't hit me. I didn't really 'mean' it." As son of a School of Barnstone architect, Barthelme came naturally by those perspective drawings that so annoyed (and still annoy) me. He has worked as an editor and "I enjoy editing and enjoy doing layout-problems of design. I could very cheerfully be a typographer."

Barthelme's first book, *Come Back, Dr. Caligari*, contains short stories written between 1961 and 1964. This was the period during which Sarraute and Robbe-Grillet and Barthes were being translated into English. Although Robbe-Grillet's *For a New Novel* was not translated until 1965, Nathalie Sarraute's *Tropismes* was translated in 1963 as were such essential novels as *Le Planétarium*, *Fruits d'or*, *Jalousie*, and *Le Voyeur*. I note the fact of translation only because Barthelme admits to our common "American lack-of-language." Most American and English writers know foreign literature only through translation. This is bad enough when it comes to literature but peculiarly dangerous when it comes to theory. One might put the case that without a French education there is no way of comprehending, say, Roland Barthes (Sontag suggests as much). One can only take a piece here, a piece there, relate it to the tradition that one knows, and hope for the best. There is comfort, however, in knowing that the French do not get the point to us either.

The stories in *Come Back, Dr. Caligari* are fairly random affairs. Barthelme often indulges in a chilling heterosexual camp that is, nevertheless, quite a bit warmer than zero degree centigrade. There are funny names and cute names. Miss Mandible. Numerous non sequiturs. Dialogue in the manner not only of Ionesco but of Terry Southern (another Texas master). One can read any number of Barthelme's lines with a certain low-keyed pleasure.

But then silliness stops the eye cold. " 'You're supposed to be curing a ham.' 'The ham died,' she said." The Marx Brothers could get a big laugh on this exchange because they would already have given us a dozen other gags in as many minutes. Unhappily one small gag on its own shrivels and dies. " '*You* may not be interested in absurdity,' she said firmly, 'but absurdity is interested in *you.*' "

Three years later came *Snow White*. This fiction was billed by the publisher as "a perverse fairy tale." The book is composed of fairly short passages. Quotation marks are used to enclose dialogue and there are the usual number of "he saids," and "she replieds." This is an important point. *Truly* new writing eliminates quotation marks and "he saids." Barthelme is still cooking on a warm stove. The seven dwarfs are indistinguishable from one another and from the heroine. But the somewhat plodding tone of this work holds the attention rather better than did any of those fragments in the first volume. Yet Barthelme is compelled always to go for the easy twist. "Those cruel words remain locked in his lack of heart." Also, he writes about the writing he is writing:

> We like books that have a lot of *dreck* in them, matter which presents itself as not wholly relevant (or indeed at all relevant) but which, carefully attended to, can supply a kind of "sense" of what is going on. This kind of "sense" is not to be obtained by reading between the lines (for there is nothing there, in those white spaces) but by reading the lines themselves. . . .

Roland Barthes, his mark.

Unspeakable Practices, Unnatural Acts (1968) contains fifteen pieces mostly published in *The New Yorker*. Occasionally the text is broken with headlines in the Brechtian manner. With film subtitles. With lists. One list called *Italian Novel* names sixteen Italian writers "she" was reading. Most are fashionable; some are good; but the premier Sciascia has been omitted. *What can this mean?*

Many proper names from *real* life appear in these texts. Paul Goodman, J. B. Priestley, Julia Ward Howe, Anthony Powell, Godard. Also *Time, Newsweek*, the Museum of Modern Art. Curiously enough those names that are already invested with an *a priori* reality help the texts which, as usual, maunder, talking to themselves, keeping a dull eye out for the odd joke as the author tries not to be himself a maker of dreck but an arranger of dreck.

The most successful of the lot is "Robert Kennedy Saved from Drowning." The reader brings to the story an altogether too vivid memory of the subject. We learn from the interview in Bellamy's book that, though the story "is, like, made up," Barthelme did use a remark that he heard Kennedy make about a geometric painter (" 'Well, at least we know he has a ruler' " . . . high wit from Camelot). Yet the parts that are not, like, made up are shrewd and amusing and truthful (relatively, of course). Also, the see-Jane-run style is highly suited to a parody of a contemporary politician on the make as he calculates his inanities and holds back his truths (relative—and relatives, too) and rage. Mr. William Gass takes an opposite view of this story. "Here Barthelme's method fails; for the idea is to *use* dreck, not write about it." But surely one can do both. Or neither. Or one. Or the other. But then Mr. Gass thinks that Barthelme at his best "has the art to make a treasure out of trash. . . ."

Throughout Barthelme's work one notes various *hommages* to this writer or that (who lives at Montreux? and where will one hear the ultimate message *Trink?*); some are a bit too close. For instance, the famous opening scene of Beckett's *Molloy* in which a father is carrying his son becomes in "A Picture History of the War": "Kellerman, gigantic with gin, runs through the park at noon with his naked father slung under one arm."

City Life (1970). Fourteen short stories, much as before except that now Barthelme is very deep into fiction's R and D (Research and Development) as opposed to the old-fashioned R and R (Rest and Recuperation). There are, galore, graphics. Big black squares occupy the center of white pages. Elaborate studies in perspective. Lots of funny old pictures. There are wide white margins, nice margins, too. There are pages of questions and answers (q and a). Father returns. In fact, the first paragraph of the first story is: "An aristocrat was riding down the street in his carriage. He ran over my father."

It must be said that America's most imitated young writer is also not only the most imitable but one of the most imitative. *Hommage* to Robbe-Grillet:

> Or a long sentence moving at a certain pace down the page aiming for the bottom—if not the bottom of this page then of some other

> page—where it can rest, or stop for a moment to think about the questions raised by its own (temporary) existence, which ends when the page is turned, or the sentence falls out of the mind that holds it (temporarily) in some kind of an embrace

and so on for eight whole pages with *not one full stop,* only a breaking off of the text, which is called "Sentence." The only development in "Sentence" is that what looks to be Robbe-Grillet at work in the first lines turns gradually (temporarily) into something like Raymond Roussel. Not quite zero degree: at the frozen pole no sentence ever thinks or even "thinks."

Sadness (1972). More stories. More graphics. The pictures are getting better all the time. There is a good one of a volcano in eruption. The prose . . . as before. Simple sentences. "Any writer in the country can write a beautiful sentence," Barthelme has declared. But he does not want to be like any writer in the country: "I'm very interested in awkwardness: sentences that are awkward in a particular way." What is "beauty," one wonders, suspicious of words. What, for that matter, is "awkward" or "particular"? But we do know all about sentences and occasionally among the various tributes to European modern masters (in translation), certain themes (or words) reoccur. One is the father. Of that more later. Also, drunkenness. In fact, alcohol runs like a torrent through most of the writers I have been reading. From Barthelme to Pynchon there is a sense of booziness, nausea, hangover.

> I say: "I'm forty. I have bad eyes. An enlarged liver."
> "That's the alcohol," he says.
> "Yes," I say.
> "You're very much like your father, there."

The only pages to hold me were autobiographical. Early dust-jacket pictures of Barthelme show an amiable-looking young man upon whose full upper lip there is a slight shadow at the beginning of the lip's bow. The dust jacket of *Sadness* shows a bearded man with what appears to be a harelip. Barthelme explains that he has had an operation for a "basal-cell malignancy" on his upper lip. True graphics, ultimately, are not old drawings of volcanoes or of perspective but of the author's actual face on the various dust jackets, aging in a definitely serial way with, in

Barthelme's case, the drama of an operation thrown in, very much in the R and R tradition, and interesting for the reader though no doubt traumatizing for the author.

Guilty Pleasures (1974). This writer cannot stop making sentences. I have stopped reading a lot of them. I feel guilty. It is not pleasurable to feel guilty about not reading every one of those sentences. I do like the pictures more and more. In this volume there are more than thirty, pictures. In the prose I spotted *hommages* to Calvino, Borges, early Ionesco. I am now saving myself for *The Dead Father*, the big one, as they say on Publisher's Row, the first big novel, long awaited, even heralded.

In *The Pleasure of the Text*, published just before *The Dead Father* (and by the same American publisher), Roland Barthes observes: "Death of the Father would deprive literature of many of its pleasures. If there is no longer a Father, why tell stories? Doesn't every narrative lead back to Oedipus? Isn't storytelling always a way of searching for one's origin. . . . As fiction, Oedipus was at least good for something: to make good novels. . . ." Apparently Barthelme took the hint. In *The Dead Father* a number of people are lugging about the huge remains of something called The Dead Father. Only this monster is not very dead because he talks quite a bit. The people want to bury him but he is not all that eager to be buried. Barthelme ends his book by deliberately burying the eponymous hero and, perhaps, fiction too. All of this is very ambitious.

Barthelme's narrative is reasonably sequential if lacking in urgency. There is, as always, Beckett: "said Julie, let us proceed. / They proceeded." Within the book is A Manual for Sons, written in a splendid run-on style quite at odds with the most imitated imitable writing that surrounds this unexpectedly fine burst of good writing on the nature of fathers, sons. For the record: there are no quotation marks. And no pictures. There is one diagram of a *placement;* but it is not much fun.

I am not sure that my progress through all these dull little sentences has been entirely justified by A Manual for Sons, but there is no doubt that beneath the mannerisms, the infantile chic, the ill-digested culture of an alien world, Barthelme does have a talent for, of all things in this era, writing. Shall I quote an example? I think not. Meanwhile, Barthelme himself says, "I have trouble reading, in these days. I would rather drink, talk or listen to music. . . . I now listen to rock constantly." Yes.

I can only assume that Grace Paley is a friend of Mr. Barthelme because she does not belong to what a certain Hack of Academe named Harry T. Moore likes, mistakenly, to call a *galère*. Paley is a plain short-story writer of the R and R school, and I got a good deal of pleasure from reading her two collections of short stories, *The Little Disturbances of Man* (with the nice subtitle: "Stories of Men and Women at Love") and *Enormous Changes at the Last Minute*. She works from something very like life . . . I mean "life"; she has an extraordinary ear for the way people sound. She do the ethnics in different voices. Although she tends, at times, to the plain-Jane or see-Jane-run kind of writing, her prose has such a natural energy that one is not distracted, a sign of good writing if not of a blissful text (she is close to boiling, in any case, and will never freeze).

With William Gass we are back in R and D country. I read Gass's first novel *Omensetter's Luck* in 1966 and found much to admire in it. Gass's essays are often eerily good. At his best, he can inhabit a subject in a way that no other critic now writing can do (see, in particular, his commentaries on Gertrude Stein). He seems not to have enjoyed being interviewed in Bellamy's collection, and his tone is unusually truculent (of New York quality lit. types: "I snub them"). It should be noted that of the writers admired by Barthelme only William Gass is an intellectual in the usual sense (I put no quotes around the words "intellectual," "usual," or "sense"). Gass's mind is not only first-rate but far too complex to settle for the easy effects of, say, Mr. Barthelme. But then: "As a student of philosophy, I've put in a great deal of time on the nature of language and belong, rather vaguely, to a school of linguistic philosophy which is extremely skeptical about the nature of language itself."

Gass has a complaint about Barth, Borges, and Beckett: "occasionally their fictions, conceived as establishing a metaphorical relationship between the reader and the world they are creating, leave the reader too passive." This is fair comment, though open to the question: just what is passive in this context? Ought the reader to be dancing about the room? blood pressure elevated? adrenaline flowing as he and the text battle one another? But then Gass shifts ground in his next sentence but one: "I have little patience with the 'creative reader.'" In other words the ideal reader is active but not creative. Quotation marks are now in order to protect these adjectives from becoming meaningless.

"I rarely read fiction and generally don't enjoy it." Gass is as one with the other R and D writers of fiction today. Although they do not read with any pleasure what anyone else is doing, they would like, naturally, to be themselves read with pleasure . . . by whom? Perhaps a college of writerly texts, grave as cardinals.

Gass himself is a curious case. Essentially, he is a traditional prose writer, capable of all sorts of virtuoso effects on the inner ear as well as on the reading eye. Yet he appears to have fallen victim to the R and D mentality. Speaking of a work in progress, "I hope that it will be really original in form and in effect, although mere originality is not what I'm after." This is worthy of Jimmy Carter.

> Fiction has traditionally and characteristically borrowed its form from letters, journals, diaries, autobiographies, histories, travelogues, news stories, backyard gossip, etc. It has simply *pretended* to be one or other of them. The history of fiction is in part a record of the efforts of its authors to create for fiction its own forms. Poetry has its own. It didn't borrow the ode from somebody. Now the novel is imagined news, imagined psychological or sociological case studies, imagined history . . . feigned, I should say, not imagined. As Rilke shattered the journal form with *Malte,* and Joyce created his own for *Ulysses* and *Finnegan,* I should like to create mine.

There seems to me to be a good deal wrong not only logically but aesthetically and historically with this analysis. First, poetry has never *had* its form. The origins of the ode are ancient but it was once created if not by a single ambitious schoolteacher, then by a number of poets roving like Terence's rose down the centuries. Certainly in this century poetry has gone off in as many directions as the novel, an art form whose tutelary deity is Proteus. The more like something else the novel is, the more like its true self it is. And since we do not *have* it, we can go on making it. Finally, whether or not a work of art is feigned or imagined is irrelevant if the art is good.

Like many good books, *Omensetter's Luck* is not easy to describe. What one comes away with is the agreeable memory of a flow of language that ranges from demotic Midwest ("I just up and screams at him—thump thump thump, he'd been going, die die die—I yell . . .") to incantatory ("For knowledge, for good and evil, would Eve have set her will against her Father's? Ah, Horatio . . ."). In his interview the author tells us that he knows nothing of the setting (an Ohio river town); that everything is made up. He also confesses, "I haven't the dramatic imagination at all. Even my characters tend to turn away from one another and talk to the void. This, along with my inability to narrate, is my most serious defect (I think) as a writer and incidentally as a person."

The stories in *In the Heart of the Heart of the Country* seem to me to be more adventurous and often more successful than the novel. "The Pedersen Kid" is beautiful work. In a curious way the look of those short sentences on pages uncluttered with quotation marks gives the text a visual purity and coldness that perfectly complements the subject of the story, and compels the reader to know the icy winter at the country's heart. In most of these stories the prevailing image is winter.

> Billy closes his door and carries coal or wood to his fire and closes his eyes, and there's simply no way of knowing how lonely and empty he is or whether he's as vacant and barren and loveless as the rest of us are—here in the heart of the country.

At actual zero degree, Gass, perversely, blazes with energy.

The title story is the most interesting of the collection. Despite a sign or two that the French virus may have struck: "as I write this page, it is eleven days since I have seen the sun," the whole of the story (told in fragments) is a satisfying description of the world the narrator finds himself in, and he makes art of the quotidian:

> My window is a grave, and all that lies within it's dead. No snow is falling. There's no haze. It's not still, not silent. Its images are not an animal that waits, for movement is no demonstration.

What is art?

Art is energy shaped by intelligence. The energy that the text of *Madame Bovary* generates for the right reader is equal to that which sustains the consumer of *Rebecca*. The ordering intelligence of each writer is, of course, different in kind and intention. Gass's problem as an artist is not so much his inability to come up with some brand-new Henry Ford-type invention that will prove to be a breakthrough in world fiction (this is never going to happen) as what he calls his weak point—a lack of dramatic gift —which is nothing more than low or rather intermittent energy. He can write a dozen passages in which the words pile up without effect. Then, suddenly, the current, as it were, turns on again and the text comes to beautiful life (in a manner of speaking of course . . . who does not like a living novel? particularly one that is literate).

> I have seen the sea slack, life bubble through a body without a trace, its spheres impervious as soda's.

For a dozen years I have been trying to read *The Sot-Weed Factor.* I have never entirely completed this astonishingly dull book but I have read most of John Barth's published work and I feel that I have done him, I hope, justice. There is a black cloth on my head as I write.

First, it should be noted that Barth like Gass, is a professional schoolteacher. He is a professor of English *and* Creative Writing. He is extremely knowledgeable about what is going on in R and D land and he is certainly eager to make his contribution. Interviewed, Barth notes "the inescapable fact that literature—because it's made of the common stuff of language—seems more refractory to change in general than the other arts." He makes the obligatory reference to the music of John Cage. Then he adds, sensibly, that "the permanent changes in fiction from generation to generation more often have been, and are more likely to be, modifications of sensibility and attitude rather than dramatic innovations in form and technique."

Barth mentions his own favorite writers. Apparently "Borges, Beckett and Nabokov, among the living grand masters (and writers like Italo Calvino, Robbe-Grillet, John Hawkes, William Gass, Donald Barthelme)—*have* experimented with form and technique and even with the *means* of fiction, working with graphics and tapes and things. . . ." What these writers have in common (excepting Robbe-Grillet) "is a more or less fantastical, or as Borges would say, 'irrealist,' view of reality. . . ." Barth thinks—hopes—that this sort of writing will characterize the seventies.

What is "irrealism"? Something that cannot be realized. This is a curious goal for a writer though it is by no means an unfamil-

iar terminus for many an ambitious work. Further, Barth believes that realism is "a kind of aberration in the history of literature." I am not exactly sure what he means by realism. After all,
the Greek myths that he likes to play around with were once a
"reality" to those who used them as stuff for narrative. But then
Barth broods. "Perhaps we should *accept* the fact that writing and
reading are essentially linear activities and devote our attention
as writers to those aspects of experience that can best be rendered
linearly—with words that go left to right across the page; subjects, verbs and objects; punctuation!" He ends with the rather
plaintive, "The trick, I guess, in any of the arts at this hour of the
world, is to have it both ways." How true!

The Floating Opera (1956) and *The End of the Road* (1958) are two
novels of a kind and that kind is strictly R and R, and fairly
superior R and R at that. The author tells us that they were
written in his twenty-fourth year, and a good year it was for him.
Publishers meddled with the ending of the first novel. He has
since revised the book and that is the version I read. It is written
in first person demotic (Eastern shore of Maryland, Barth's place
of origin). The style is garrulous but not unattractive. "I was just
thirty-seven then, and as was my practice, I greeted the new day
with a slug of Sherbrook from the quart on my window sill. I've
a quart sitting there now, but it's not the same one. . . ."

There is a tendency to put too much in, recalling Barthes's
"The Prattle of Meaning" *(S/Z)*: certain storytellers

> impose a dense plenitude of meaning or, if one prefers, a certain
> redundancy, a kind of semantic prattle typical of the archaic—or
> infantile—era of modern discourse, marked by the excessive fear of
> failing to communicate meaning (its basis); while, in reaction, in our
> latest—or "new" novels,

the action or event is set forth "without accompanying it with its
signification."

Certainly Barth began as an old-fashioned writer who wanted
us to know all about the adulteries, money-hassling, and boozing
on what sounded like a very real Eastern Shore of a very real
Maryland, as lacking in bears as the seacoast of Illyria: "Charley
was Charley Parks, an attorney whose office was next door
to ours. He was an old friend and poker partner of mine, and
currently we were on opposite sides in a complicated litiga-
tion. . . ."

In 1960 Barth published *The Sot-Weed Factor*. The paperback edition is adorned with the following quotation from *The New York Times Book Review:* "Outrageously funny, villainously slanderous. . . . The book is a brass-knuckled satire of humanity at large. . . ." I am usually quick, even eager, to respond to the outrageously funny, the villainously slanderous . . . in short, to *The New York Times* itself. But as I read on and on, I could not so much as summon up a smile at the lazy jokes and the horrendous pastiche of what Barth takes to be eighteenth-century English (" ' 'Tis not that which distresses me; 'tis Andrew's notion that I had vicious designs on the girl. 'Sheart, if anything be improbable, 'tis. . .' "). I stopped at page 412 with 407 pages yet to go. The sentences would not stop unfurling; as Peter Handke puts it in *Kaspar:* "Every sentence helps you along: you get over every object with a sentence: a sentence helps you get over an object when you can't really get over it, so that you really get over it," etc.

To read Barth on the subject of his own work and then to read the work itself is a puzzling business. He talks a good deal of sense. He is obviously intelligent. Yet he tells us that when he turned from the R and R of his first two novels to the megalo-R and R of *The Sot-Weed Factor*, he moved from "a merely comic mode to a variety of farce, which frees your hands even more than comedy does." Certainly there are comic aspects to the first two books. But the ponderous jocosity of the third book is neither farce nor satire nor much of anything except English-teacher-writing at a pretty low level. I can only assume that the book's admirers are as ignorant of the eighteenth century as the author (or, to be fair, the author's imagination) and that neither author nor admiring reader has a sense of humor, a fact duly noted about Americans in general—and their serious ponderous novelists in particular—by many peoples in other lands. It still takes a lot of civilization gone slightly high to make a wit.

Giles Goat-Boy arrived on the scene in 1966. Another 800 pages of ambitious schoolteacher-writing: a book to be taught rather than read. I shall not try to encapsulate it here, other than to say that the central metaphor is the universe is the university is the universe. I suspect that this will prove to be one of the essential American university novels and to dismiss it is to dismiss those departments of English that have made such a book possible. The writing is more than usually clumsy. A verse play has been included. "*Agnora:* for Pete's sake, simmer down, boys. Don't you think/I've been a dean's wife long enough to stink/my public image up?"

Barth thinks that the word "human" is a noun; he also thinks that Giles is pronounced with a hard "g" as in "guile" instead of a soft "g" as in "giant." But then the unlearned learned teachers of English are the new barbarians, serenely restoring the Dark Ages.

By 1968 Barth was responding to the French New Novel. *Lost in the Funhouse* is the result. A collection (or, as he calls it, a "series") of "Fiction for Print, Tape, Live Voice." Barth is not about to miss a trick now that he has moved into R and D country. The first of the series, "Night-Sea Journey," should—or could—be on tape. This is the first-person narrative of a sperm heading, it would appear, toward an ovum, though some of its eschatological musings suggest that a blow-job may be in progress. Woody Allen has dealt more rigorously with this theme.

The "story" "Lost in the Funhouse" is most writerly and self-conscious; it chats with the author who chats with it and with us. "Description of physical appearance and mannerisms is one of several standard methods of characterization used by writers of fiction." Thus Barth distances the reader from the text. A boy goes to the funhouse and. . . . "The more closely an author identifies with the narrator, literally or metaphorically, the less advisable it is, as a rule, to use the first-person narrative viewpoint." Some of this schoolteacherly commentary is amusing. But the ultimate effect is one of an ambitious but somewhat uneasy writer out to do something brand-new in a territory already inhabited by, among other texts that can read and write, the sinister *Locus Solus,* the immor(t)al *Tlooth* and the dexterous *A Nest of Ninnies.*

It is seldom wise for a born R and R writer to make himself over into an R and D writer unless he has something truly formidable and new to show us. Barth just has books. And sentences. And a fairly clear idea of just how far up the creek he is without a paddle. "I believe literature's not likely ever to manage abstraction successfully, like sculpture for example, is that a fact, what a time to bring up that subject. . . ." What a time! And what is the subject, Alice? Incidentally, Barth always uses quotation marks and "he saids."

In 1972 Barth published three long stories in a volume called *Chimera.* Two of the stories are based on Greek myths, for are they not, as admirers of Jung declare, part of the racial memory, the common stock of all our dreams and narratives? Well, no, they are not. The Greek myths are just barely relevant to those Mediterranean people who still live in a landscape where the *anima* of a lost world has not yet been entirely covered with cement. The myths are useful but not essential to those brought up on the classics, the generation to which Dr. Jung (and T.S. Eliot) belonged; and of course they are necessary to anyone who would like to understand those works of literature in which myth plays a part. Otherwise they are of no real use to Americans born in this century. For us Oedipus is not the doomed king of Thebes but Dr. Freud's depressing protagonist, who bears no relation at all to the numinous figure that Sophocles and Euripides portrayed. Thebes is another country, where we may not dwell.

Joyce's *Ulysses* is often regarded as a successful attempt to use Greek myth to shore up a contemporary narrative. But it is plain to most noncreative readers that the myth does not work at all in Joyce's creation and were it not for his glorious blarney and fine naturalistic gifts, the book's classical structure alone could not have supported the novel. Since Joyce, alas, the incorporation of Greek myth into modern narrative has been irresistible to those who have difficulty composing narrative, and no Greek. These ambitious writers simply want to give unearned resonance to their tales of adultery on the Eastern Shore of Maryland, of misbehavior in faculty rooms, of massive occlusions in the heart of the country. But the results are deeply irritating to those who have some sense of the classical world and puzzling, I would think, to those taking English courses where the novel is supposed to have started with Richardson.

Barth has browsed through Robert Graves's *The Greek Myths* (and gives due acknowledgment to that brilliantly eccentric custodian of the old world). At random, I would guess, Barth selected the story of Bellerophon (tamer of Pegasus) for modernizing; also, more to his point, Perseus, the slayer of Medusa. The first story is taken from Arabian mythology, a narrative called "Dunyaza-diad," as told by the "kid sister of Scheherazade." It should also be noted that two of the stories in *Lost in the Funhouse* were wacky versions of certain well-known highjinks in old Mycenae.

The kid sister of Scheherazade is a gabby co-ed who mentions with awe the academic gifts of her sister "Sherry," "an undergraduate arts-and-sciences major at Banu Sasan University. Besides being Homecoming Queen, valedictorian-elect, and a four-letter varsity athlete. . . . Every graduate department in the East was after her with fellowships." This unbearable cuteness has a sinister side. Since Barth's experience of literature and the world is entirely that of a schoolteacher, he appears to take it for granted that the prevailing metaphor for his own life (and why not all life itself?) is the university. There is also an underlying acceptance of the fact that since no one is ever going to read him except undergraduates in American universities, he had better take into account that their reading skills are somewhat underdeveloped, their knowledge of the way society works vague, and their culture thin.

Barth's *Hamlet* would no doubt begin, "Well, I guess flunking out of Rutgers is no big deal when I got this family up in Wilmington where we make these plastics that, like, kill people but I'm changing all that or I was going to up until my mother went and married this asshole uncle of mine. . . ." Perhaps this is the only way to get the classics into young television-shrunk minds. But the exercise debases both classic and young minds. Of course Barth is no fool. He is often quick to jump in and forestall criticism. Sherry's kid sister remarks: "currently, however, the only readers of artful fiction were critics, other writers, and unwilling students who, left to themselves, preferred music and pictures to words."

Sherry is helped in her literary efforts to think up 1001 stories by a genie who is, like so many of Barth's male protagonists, a *thoroughly good person:* his policy "was to share beds with no woman who did not reciprocate his feelings." For a United Statesman (posing as an Arabian genie), this is true heterosexual maturity. In case we missed Barth's first testimonial to the genie's niceness, we are later told that "he was no more tempted to infidelity than to incest or pederasty." I guess this makes him about the best genie on campus. Between Genie and Sherry there is a lot of talk about the nature of fiction, which is of course the only reason for writing university fiction. There is not a glimmer of intelligence in this jaunty tale.

Barth was born and grew up a traditional cracker-barrelly sort of American writer, very much in the mainstream—a stream by no means polluted or at an end. But he chose not to continue in the vein that was most natural to him. Obviously he has read a good deal about Novel Theory. He has the standard American passion not only to be original but to be great, and this means creating one of Richard Poirier's "worlds elsewhere": an alternative imaginative structure to the mess that we have made of our portion of the Western hemisphere. Aware of French theories about literature (but ignorant of the culture that has produced those theories), superficially acquainted with Greek myth, deeply involved in the academic life of the American university, Barth is exactly the sort of writer our departments of English were bound, sooner or later, to produce. Since he is a writer with no great gift for language either demotic or mandarin, Barth's narratives tend to lack energy; and the currently fashionable technique of stopping to take a look at the story as it is being told simply draws attention to the meagerness of what is there.

I am obliged to remark upon the sense of suffocation one experiences reading so much bad writing. As the weary eyes flick from sentence to sentence, one starts *willing* the author to be good. Either I have become shell-shocked by overexposure to the rockets' red glare and bombs bursting in air or Barth has managed a decent narrative in "Perseid." As usual, the language is jangling everyday speech: "Just then I'd've swapped Mycenae for a cold draught and a spot of shade to dip it in. . . ." The gods and demigods are straight from Thorne Smith, who ought to be regarded, in A.H. Harry T. Moore's *galère.* as the American Dante. But the story of the middle-aged Perseus and his problems of erection (and love) with a young girl seems at times authentic, even true . . . despite Barth's unremitting jocosity: " 'Were you always psychosexually weak, or is that Andromeda's doing?' "

In some way, the writers' interviews are more revealing about the state of fiction than the books they write. The twelve writers interviewed for Joe David Bellamy's book often sound truculent; also, uneasy. For instance, John Gardner (whose *Grendel* I much admired) is very truculent, but then Mr. Barthelme is on record as not admiring him; this cannot help but hurt. Gardner is as much his own man as anyone can be who teaches school and wants to get good reviews from his fellow teachers in *The New York Times Book Review.* Yet he dares to say of *The Sot-Weed Factor:* "nothing but a big joke. It's a philosophical joke; it might even be argued that it's a philosophical advance. But it ain't like Victor Hugo." It also ain't an advance of any kind. Although Gardner is myth-minded, he is much more intuitive and authentic than the usual academic browser in Robert Graves's compendium. Gardner also knows where proto-myths are to be found: Walt Disney's work, for one.

Gardner tells us that "most writers today are academicians: they have writing or teaching jobs with universities. In the last ten years the tone of university life and of intellectuals' responses to the world have changed. During the Cold War there was a great deal of fear and cynicism on account of the Bomb." Gardner then makes the astonishing suggestion that when the other Americans (those somewhat unreal millions condemned to live off-campus) turned against the Vietnam war (after eight years of defeat), the mood changed in the universities as the academicians realized that "the people around you are all working hard to make the world better." A startling observation. In any case, the writers of University or U-novels will now become more life-affirming than they were in the sad sixties; "notable exceptions are writers who very carefully stay out of the mainstream and therefore can't be influenced by the general feeling of people around them."

At first I thought Gardner was joking. But I was wrong. He really believes that the mainstream of the world is the American university and that a writer outside this warm and social-meliorizing ambience will fall prey to old-fashioned cynicism and hardness of heart. For instance, "Pynchon stays out of universities. He doesn't know what chemists and physicists are doing; he knows only the pedantry of chemistry and physics. When good chemists and physicists talk about, say, the possibility of extraterrestrial life, they agree that for life to be evolved beyond our stage, creators on other planets must have reached decisions we now face." Removed from the academic mainstream and its extraterrestrial connections, Pynchon's *Gravity's Rainbow* is just an apocalyptic "whine."

Fortunately, Gardner's imagination is fabulous; otherwise, he would be fully exposed in his work as being not only *not* in the mainstream of American society but perfectly irrelevant in his academic *cul de sac*. Yet if he is right that most contemporary writers are also teaching school and listening in on warm-hearted life-enhancing physicists and chemists as they talk of their peers on other planets, then literature has indeed had its day and there will be no more books except those that teachers write to teach.

Although Barthelme has mentioned Pynchon as one of the writers he admires, neither Gass nor Barth refers to him and

Gardner thinks him a "whiner" because he no longer spawns in the mainstream of Academe. I daresay that it will come as news to these relatively young writers that American literature, such as it is, has never been the work of schoolteachers. Admittedly, each year it is harder and harder for a writer to make a living from writing, and many writers must find the temptation to teach overwhelming. Nevertheless, those of us who emerged in the forties (Roosevelt's children) regarded the university (as did our predecessors) as a kind of skid row far worse than a seven-year writer's contract at Columbia (the studio, not the university). Except for Saul Bellow, I can think of no important novelist who has taught on a regular basis throughout a career.

I find it admirable that of the nonacademics Pynchon did not follow the usual lazy course of going for tenure as did so many writers—no, "writers"—of his generation. He is thirty-nine years old and attended Cornell (took a class from former Professor V. Nabokov); he is eminently *academebile*. The fact that he has got out into the world (somewhere) is to his credit. Certainly he has not, it would seem, missed a trick; and he never whines.

Pynchon's first novel, *V.*, was published in 1963. There is some similarity to other R and D works. Cute names abound. Benny Profane, Dewey Gland, Rachel Owlglass. Booze flows through scene after scene involving members of a gang known as The Whole Sick Crew. The writing is standard American. "Kilroy was possibly the only objective onlooker in Valletta that night. Common legend had it he'd been born in the U.S. right before the war, on a fence or latrine wall." Above this passage is a reproduction of the classic Kilroy sketch; below this passage there is a broken-line Kilroy. These are the only graphics in a long book that also contains the usual quotation marks and "he saids." All in all, a naturalistic rendering of an essentially surrealist or perhaps irrealist subject, depending on one's apprehension of the work.

Benny Profane is described as "a schlemihl and human yo-yo." He is a former sailor. On Christmas Eve 1955 he is in Norfolk, Virginia. He goes into a bar, "his old tin can's tavern on East Main Street." People with funny names sing songs at each other (lyrics provided in full by the author) and everyone drinks a lot. There is vomiting. Scene with a girl: "What sort of Catholic was she? Profane, who was only half Catholic (mother Jewish), whose morality was fragmentary (being derived from experience and

not much of it). . . ." Profane is "girl-shy" and fat. " 'If I was
God . . .' " begins a fantasy. Definitely a clue to the state of mind
of the creator of the three books I have been reading.

A shift from Profane to "Young Stencil, the world adventurer"
and the mystery woman V. Elliptical conversation (1946) between
a margravine and Stencil (whose father Sidney was in the British
foreign office; he died in Malta "while investigating the June
Disturbances"). They sit on a terrace overlooking the Mediterranean. "Perhaps they may have felt like the last two gods." Reference to an entry in father's journal, " 'There is more behind and
inside V. than any of us had suspected. Not who, but what: what
is she.' " Stencil pursues the idea of V. A quest: "in the tradition
of *The Golden Bough* or *The White Goddess.*"

From various references to Henry Adams and to physics in
Pynchon's work, I take it that he has been influenced by Henry
Adams's theory of history as set forth in *The Education of Henry
Adams* and in the posthumously published "The Rule of Phase
Applied to History." For Adams, a given human society in time
was an organism like any other in the universe and he favored
Clausius's speculation that "the entropy of the universe tends to
a maximum" (an early Pynchon short story is called "Entropy").

Maximum entropy is that state at which no heat/energy enters
or leaves a given system. But nothing known is constant. The
Second Law of Thermodynamics appears to be absolute: everything in time loses energy to something else and, finally, drops
to zero (centigrade) and dies or, perhaps, ceases to be matter as
it was and becomes anti-matter. Question: to anti-matter are we
anti-anti-matter or no matter at all?

I have little competence in the other of Lord Snow's celebrated
two cultures. Like so many other writers I flunked physics. But
I know my Adams and I can grasp general principles (without
understanding how they have been arrived at); in any case, to
make literature, a small amount of theory is enough to provide
commanding metaphors. Pynchon's use of physics is exhilarating
and as an artist he appears to be gaining more energy than he is
losing. Unlike the zero writers, he is usually at the boil. From
Adams he has not only appropriated the image of history as
Dynamo but the attractive image of the Virgin. Now armed with
these concepts he embarks in *V.* on a quest, a classic form of
narrative, and the result is mixed, to say the least.

To my ear, the prose is pretty bad, full of all the rattle and buzz that were in the air when the author was growing up, an era in which only the television commercial was demonically acquiring energy, leaked to it by a declining Western civilization. Happily, Pynchon is unaffected by the French disease, except for one passage: "Let me describe the room. The room measures 17 by 11 1/2 feet by 7 feet. The walls are lathe and plaster. . . . The room is oriented so that its diagonals fall NNE/SSW, and NW/SE." As another ex-seaman, I appreciate Pynchon's ability to box the compass, something no French ice-cream vendor could ever do. With this satisfying send-up, Pynchon abandons the New Novel for his own worlds and anti-worlds.

The quest for V. (the Virgin? or nothing much?) takes Stencil to Valletta, capital of Malta, a matriarchal island, we are told, where manhood must identify itself with the massive rock. There are clues. False scents. Faust is on the scene. And Profane is also in Malta. The prose is very close to that of the comic books of the fifties:

> "Thirteen of us rule the world in secret."
>
> "Yes, yes. Stencil went out of his way to bring Profane here. He should have been more careful; he wasn't. Is it really his own extermination he's after?"
>
> Maijstral turned smiling to him. Gestured behind his back at the ramparts of Valletta. "Ask her," he whispered. "Ask the rock."

Energy nicely maintained; controlling intelligence uneven.

With *The Crying of Lot 49* (1966) Pynchon returns to the quest, to conspiracy. Cute names like Genghis Cohen, an ancient Hollywood joke. Bad grammar: "San Narciso lay further south," "some whirlwind rotating too slow for her heated skin." A lot of booze. Homophobia. Mysteries. It would appear that most of the courses Pynchon took at Cornell are being used: first-year physics, psychology, Jacobean tragedy—but then his art is no doubt derived "from experience and not much of that."

This time the grail is an alternative postal service. Haunting the narrative is the noble house of Thurn and Taxis (the wife of a descendant was a literary agent in the United States: known to Pynchon? Also, Rilke's patroness was a princess of that house). Jokes: " 'I was in the little boys' room,' he said. 'The men's room was full.' " There are numerous images of paranoia, the lurking "they" who dominate the phantom postal service of the Tristero (sometimes spelled Trystero), a mirror-alternative in earlier times to the Thurn and Taxis postal monopoly."While the Pony Express is defying deserts, savages and sidewinders, Tristero's giving its employees crash courses in Siouan and Athapascan dialects. Disguised as Indians their messengers mosey westward. Reach the coast every time, zero attrition rate, not a scratch on them. The entire emphasis now toward silence, impersonation, opposition masquerading as allegiance.' " Well, Joyce also chose exile, cunning, silence, but eschewed allegiance's mask. Lot 49 has been cried. Who will bid?

Gravity's Rainbow (1973) contains close to 900 densely printed pages. For a year I have been reading in and at the text. Naturally, I am impressed that a clear-cut majority of the departments of English throughout North America believe this to be the perfect teachers' novel. I am sure that they are right. Certainly no young writer's book has been so praised since Colin Wilson's *The Outsider.*

The first section of *Gravity's Rainbow* is called "Beyond the Zero." Plainly a challenge not only to *l'écriture blanche* but to proud entropy itself. Pynchon has now aimed himself at antimatter, at what takes place beyond, beneath the zero of freezing, and death. This is superbly ambitious and throughout the text energy hums like a . . . well, dynamo.

The narrative begins during the Second War, in London. Although Pynchon works hard for verisimilitude and fills his pages with period jabber, anachronisms occasionally jar (there were no "Skinnerites" in that happy time of mass death). The controlling image is that of the V-2, a guided missile developed by the Germans and used toward the end of the war (has Pynchon finally found V.? and is she a bomb?). There is an interesting epigraph from Werner von Braun: "Nature does not know extinction; all it knows is transformation." Braun believes "in the continuity of our spiritual existence after death." So much then for zero degree. This quasi-Hindu sentiment is beguiling and comforting and, no doubt, as concerns matter, true: in time or phases, energy is always lost but matter continues in new arrangements. Personally, I find it somber indeed to think that individual personality goes on and on beyond zero, time. But I am in a minority: this generation of Americans is god-hungry and craves reassurance of personal immortality. If Pynchon can provide it, he will be as a god—rather his intention, I would guess.

It is curious to read a work that excites the imagination but disturbs the aesthetic sense. A British critic no longer in fashion recently made the entirely unfashionable observation that prose has everywhere declined in quality as a result of mass education. To compare Pynchon with Joyce, say, is to compare a kindergartener to a graduate student (the permanent majority of the culturally inadequate will promptly respond that the kindergartener *sees* more clearly than the graduate student and that his incompetence with language is a sign of innocence not ignorance and hence grace). Pynchon's prose rattles on and on, broken by occasional lengthy songs every bit as bad, lyrically, as those of Bob Dylan.

> *Light-up, and-shine, you—in-candescent Bulb Ba-bies!*
> *Looks-like ya got ra-bies*
> *Just lay there foamin' and a-screamin' like a buncha little demons,*
> *I'm deliv'rin' unto you a king-dom of roa-ches. . . .*

England. Germany. Past. Present. War. Science. Telltale images of approaching . . . deity? Two characters with hangovers "are wasted gods urging on a tardy glacier." Of sandbags at a door, "provisional pyramids erected to gratify curious gods' offspring." And "slicks of nighttime vomit, pale yellow, clear as the fluids of gods." Under deity, sex is central to this work of transformation. A character's erections achieve a mysterious symbiosis with the V-2s. A sadist abuses a young man and woman. "Every true god must be both organizer and destroyer." A character declaims: " 'If only S and M could be established universally, at the family level, the state would wither away.' " This is a nice joke (although I thought S and M was already universal at the family level). " 'Submit, Gottfried. Give it all up. See where she takes you. Think of the first time I fucked you. . . . Your little rosebud bloomed.' " Hard to believe that it is close to a decade since that pretty moss tea-rose was first forced, as it were, in my greenhouse.

Eventually, the text exhausts patience and energy. In fact, I suspect that the energy expended in reading *Gravity's Rainbow* is, for anyone, rather greater than that expended by Pynchon in the actual writing. This is entropy with a vengeance. The writer's text is ablaze with the heat/energy that his readers have lost to him. Yet the result of this exchange is neither a readerly nor a writerly text but an uneasy combination of both. Energy and intelligence are not in balance, and the writer fails in his ambition to be a god of creation. Yet his ambition and his failure are very much in the cranky, solipsistic American vein, and though I doubt if anyone will ever want to read all of this book, it will certainly be taught for a very long (delta) time: "approaching zero, eternally approaching, the slices of time growing thinner and thinner, a succession of rooms each with walls more silver, transparent, as the pure light of the zero comes nearer. . . ." Everything is running down. We shall freeze. Then what? A film by Stanley Kubrick?

Richard Poirier is more satisfied than I with Pynchon's latest work. For one thing, he is awed by the use of science. Approvingly, he quotes Wordsworth's hope that the poet would one day "be ready to follow the steps of the Man of science, not only in those general indirect effects, but he will be at his side, carrying sensation into the midst of science itself." Pynchon would appear to fulfill Wordsworth's reverie. He is as immersed in contemporary physics and cybernetics as Henry Adams was in the scientific theories of *his* day. But the scientific aspects of Pynchon's work will eventually become as out-of-date as those of Henry Adams. Science changes: one day we are monists, the next day pluralists. Proofs are always being disproven by other proofs. At the end, there are only words and their arrangement.

Poirier compares Pynchon to the Faulkner of *Absalom, Absalom* and finds both likeness and a significant difference, for "this genius of our day is shaped by thermodynamics and the media, by Captain Marvel rather than by Colonel Sartoris." This is no doubt a true description, but is the result as good? or good? What I find to be tedious and random in Pynchon's list-making, Poirier sees as so many

> Dreiserian catalogues of the waste materials of our world that only by remaining resolutely on the periphery, without ever intruding himself into the plotting that emanates from his material, only then can he see what most humanly matters.

"Matter," a verb. "Matter," a noun. The matter of fiction has been expanded by Pynchon's ascent from zero degree (writing as well as centigrade); nevertheless, entropy is sovereign. That which gains energy/heat does so at the expense of that which is losing energy/heat to it. At the end there is only the cold and no sublunary creatures will ever know what songs the quasars sing in their dark pits of anti-matter.

I cannot help but feel a certain depression after reading Mr. Barthelme's chosen writers. I realize that language changes from generation to generation. But it does not, necessarily, improve. The meager rattling prose of all these writers, excepting Gass, depresses me. Beautiful sentences are not easy to write, despite Mr. Barthelme's demur. Since beauty is relative only to intention, there are doubtless those who find beauty in the pages of books where I find "a flocculent appearance, something opaque, creamy and curdled, something powerless ever to achieve the triumphant smoothness of Nature. But what best reveals it for what it is is the sound it gives, at once hollow and flat; its noise is its undoing, as are its colors, for it seems capable of retaining only the most chemical-looking ones. Of yellow, red and green, it keeps only the aggressive quality. . . ." What is "it"? The work of the new American formalists? No, "it" is plastic, as described by Barthes in *Mythologies*.

The division between what I have elsewhere called the Public-novel and the University-novel is now too great to be bridged by any but the occasional writer who is able to appeal, first to one side, then to the other, fulfilling the expectations (more or less) of each. I find it hard to take seriously the novel that is written to be taught, nor can I see how the American university can provide a base for the making of "new" writing when the American university is, at best, culturally and intellectually conservative and, at worst, reactionary.

Academics tell me that I am wrong. They assure me that if it were not for them, the young would never read the Public-novels of even the recent past (Faulkner, Fitzgerald). If this is true, then I would prefer for these works decently to die rather than to become teaching-tools, artifacts stinking of formaldehyde in a classroom (original annotated text with six essays by the author and eight critical articles examining the parameters of the author's vision). But the academic bureaucracy, unlike the novel, will not wither away, and the future is dark for literature. Certainly the young in general are not going to take up reading when they have such easy alternatives as television, movies, rock. The occasional student who might have an interest in reading will not survive a course in English, unless of course he himself intends to become an academic bureaucrat.

As for Thomas Pynchon, one can applaud his deliberate ascent from Academe into that dangerous rainbow sky in which he will make his parabola and fall as gravity pulls him back to where he started, to Academe, to zero, or to (my first graphic, ever) ◯ .

The New York Review of Books,
July 15, 1974

Two

The Matter of Fact

Some Memories of the Glorious Bird and an Earlier Self

"I particularly like New York on hot summer nights when all the . . . uh, superfluous people are off the streets." Those were, I think, the first words Tennessee addressed to me; then the foggy blue eyes blinked, and a nervous chuckle filled the moment's silence before I said whatever I said.

Curtain rising. The place: an apartment at the American Academy in Rome. Occasion: a party for some newly arrived Americans, among them Frederic Prokosch, Samuel Barber. The month: March 1948. The day: halcyon. What else could a March day be in the golden age?

I am pleased that I can remember so clearly my first meeting with the Glorious Bird, as I almost immediately called him for reasons long since forgotten (premonition, perhaps, of the eventual take-off and flight of youth's sweet bird?). Usually, I forget first meetings, excepting always those solemn audiences granted by the old and famous when I was young and green. I recall vividly every detail of André Gide's conversation and appearance, including the dark velvet beret he wore in his study at 1 bis

rue Vaneau. I recall even more vividly my visits to George Santayana in his cell at the Convent of the Blue Nuns. All these
audiences, meetings, introductions took place in that *anno mirabi-
lis* 1948, a year that proved to be the exact midpoint between the
end of the Second World War and the beginning of what looks
to be a permanent cold war. At the time, of course, none of us
knew where history had placed us.

At that first meeting I thought Tennessee every bit as ancient
as Gide and Santayana. After all, I was twenty-two. He was
thirty-seven; but claimed to be thirty-three on the sensible
ground that the four years he had spent working for a shoe
company did not count. Now he was the most celebrated American playwright. *A Streetcar Named Desire* was still running in New
York when we met that evening in a flat overlooking what was,
in those days, a quiet city where hardly anyone was superfluous
unless it was us, the first group of American writers and artists
to arrive in Rome after the war.

In 1946 and 1947 Europe was still out-of-bounds for foreigners.
But by 1948 the Italians had begun to pull themselves together,
demonstrating once more their astonishing ability to cope with
disaster which is so perfectly balanced by their absolute inability
to deal with success.

Rome was strange to all of us. For one thing, Italy had been
sealed off not only by war but by Fascism. Since the early thirties
few English or American artists knew Italy well. Those who did
included mad Ezra, gentle Max, spurious B.B. and, of course, the
Anglo-American historian Harold (now Sir Harold) Acton, in
stately residence at Florence. By 1948 Acton had written su-
premely well about both the Bourbons of Naples and the later
Medici of Florence; unfortunately, he was—is—prone to the
writing of memoirs. And so, wanting no doubt to flesh out yet
another chapter in the ongoing story of a long and marvelously
uninteresting life, Acton came down to Rome to look at the new
invaders. What he believed he saw and heard, he subsequently
published in a little volume called *More Memoirs of an Aesthete*, a
work to be cherished for its quite remarkable number of unaes-
thetic misprints and mispellings.

"After the First World War American writers and artists had
emigrated to Paris; now they pitched upon Rome." So Acton
begins. "According to Stendhal, the climate was enough to glad-
den anybody, but this was not the reason: one of them explained

to me that it was the facility of finding taxis, and very little of Rome can be seen from a taxi. Classical and Romantic Rome was no more to them than a picturesque background. Tennessee Williams, Victor [he means Frederic] Prokosch and Gore Vidal created a bohemian annexe to the American Academy. . . ." Liking Rome for its many taxis is splendid stuff and I wish I had said it. Certainly whoever did was putting Acton on, since the charm of Rome—1948—was the lack of automobiles of any kind. But Acton is just getting into stride. More to come.

Toward the end of March Tennessee gave a party to inaugurate his new flat in the Via Aurora (in the golden age even the street names were apt). Somehow or other, Acton got himself invited to the party. I remember him floating like some large pale fish through the crowded room; from time to time, he would make a sudden lunge at this or that promising bit of bait while Tennessee, he tells us, "wandered as a lost soul among the guests he assembled in an apartment which might have been in New York. . . . Neither he nor any of the group I met with him spoke Italian, yet he had a typically Neapolitan protégé who could speak no English."

At this time Tennessee and I had been in Rome for only a few weeks and French, not Italian, was the second language of the reasonably well-educated American of that era. On the other hand, Prokosch knew Italian, German, and French; he also bore with becoming grace the heavy weight of a Yale doctorate in Middle English. But to Acton the author of *The Asiatics*, the translator of Hölderlin and Louise Labé was just another barbarian whose works "fell short of his perfervid imagination, [he] had the dark good looks of an advertiser of razor blades. . . ." Happily, "Gore Vidal, the youngest in age, aggressively handsome in a clean-limbed sophomore style, had success written all over him. . . . His candour was engaging but he was slightly on the defensive, as if he anticipated an attack on his writings or his virtue." Well, the young G.V. wasn't so dumb: seeing the old one-two plainly in the middle distance, he kept sensibly out of reach.

"A pudgy, taciturn, moustached little man without any obvious distinction." Thus Acton describes Tennessee. He then zeroes in on the "protégé" from Naples, a young man whom Acton calls "Pierino." Acton tells us that Pierino had many complaints about Tennessee and his friends, mostly due to the language barrier. The boy was also eager to go to America. Acton

tried to discourage him. Even so, Pierino was enthralled. " 'You
are the first *galantuomo* who has spoken to me this evening.' "
After making a date to see the *galantuomo* later on that evening,
Pierino split. Acton then told Tennessee, "as tactfully as I could,
that his young protégé felt neglected. . . . [Tennessee] rubbed his
chin thoughtfully and said nothing, a little perplexed. There was
something innocently childish about his expression." It does not
occur to the memoirist that Tennessee might have been alarmed
at his strange guest's bad manners. "Evidently he was not aware
that Pierino wanted to be taken to America and I have wondered
since whether he took him there, for that was my last meeting
with Tennessee Williams." It must be said that Acton managed
to extract quite a lot of copy out of a single meeting. To put his
mind at rest, Tennessee did take Pierino to America and Pierino
is now a married man and doing, as they say, well.

"This trifling episode illustrated the casual yet condescending
attitude of certain foreigners towards the young Italians they
cultivated on account of their Latin charm without any interest
in their character, aspirations or desires." This sentiment or sentimentality could be put just as well the other way around and
with far more accuracy. Italian trade has never had much interest
in the character, aspirations or desires of those to whom they rent
their ass. When Acton meditates upon The Italian Boy, a sweet
and sickly hypocrisy clouds his usually sharp prose and we are
in E. M. Forsterland where the lower orders (male) are wor-
shiped, and entirely misunderstood. But magnum of sour grapes
to one side, Acton is by no means inaccurate. Certainly he got
right Tennessee's indifference to place, art, history. The Bird
seldom reads a book and the only history he knows is his own;
he depends, finally, on a romantic genius to get him through life.
Above all, he is a survivor, never more so than now in what he
calls his "crocodile years."

I picked up Tennessee's *Memoirs* with a certain apprehension.
I looked myself up in the Index; read the entries and found some
errors, none grave. I started to read; was startled by the technique
he had chosen. Some years ago, Tennessee told me that he had
been reading (that is to say, looking at) my "memoir in the form
of a novel" *Two Sisters*. In this book I alternated sections describing certain events in 1948 with my everyday life while writing the
book. Memory sections I called *Then*. The day-by-day descriptions I called *Now*. At the time Tennessee found *Two Sisters* inter-

esting because he figured in it. He must also have found it technically interesting because he has serenely appropriated my form
and has now no doubt forgotten just how the idea first came to
him to describe the day-to-day life of a famous beleaguered playwright acting in an off-Broadway production of the failing play
Small Craft Warnings while, in alternating sections, he recalls the
early days not only of Tennessee Williams but of one Thomas
Lanier Williams, who bears only a faint familial resemblance to
the playwright we all know from a thousand and one altogether
too candid interviews.

There is a foreword and, like all forewords, it is meant to
disarm. Unfortunately, it armed me to the teeth. During the 1973
tryout of a play in New Haven, Tennessee was asked to address
some Yale drama students. Incidentally, the style of the foreword
is unusually seductive, the old master at his most beguiling: self-
pity and self-serving kept in exquisite balance by the finest comic
style since S. L. Clemens.

"I found myself entering (through a door marked EXIT) an
auditorium considerably smaller than the Shubert but containing
a more than proportionately small audience. I would say roughly
about two-score and ten, not including a large black dog which
was resting in the lap of a male student in the front row. . . . The
young faces before me were uniformly inexpressive of any kind
of emotional reaction to my entrance. . . ." I am surprised that
Tennessee was surprised. The arrogance and self-satisfaction of
drama students throughout Academe are among the few con-
stants in a changing world. Any student who has read Sophocles
in translation is, demonstrably, superior to Tennessee Williams
in the untidy flesh. These dummies reflect of course the proud
mediocrity of their teachers, who range, magisterially, through
something called "world drama" where evolution works only
backward. Teachers and taught are to be avoided.

"I am not much good at disguising my feelings, and after a few
moments I abandoned all pretense of feeling less dejection than
I felt." The jokes did not work. So "I heard myself describing an
encounter, then quite recent, with a fellow playwright in the Oak
Room Bar at Manhattan's Plaza Hotel." It was with "my old
friend Gore Vidal. I had embraced him warmly. However, Mr.
Vidal is not a gentleman to be disarmed by a cordial embrace, and
when, in response to his perfunctory inquiries about the progress
of rehearsals . . . I told him . . . all seemed a dream come true after

many precedent nightmares, he smiled at me with a sort of rueful benevolence and said 'Well, Bird, it won't do much good, I'm afraid, you've had too much bad personal exposure for anything to help you much anymore.'

"Well, then, for the first time, I could see a flicker of interest in the young faces before me. It may have been the magic word Vidal or it may have been his prophecy of my professional doom." Asked if the prognosis was accurate, Tennessee looked at the black dog and said, "Ask the dog."

An unsettling anecdote. I have no memory of the Plaza meeting. I am also prone, when dining late, to suffer from what Dorothy Parker used grimly to refer to as "the frankies," or straight talk for the other person's good like frankly-that-child-would-not-have-been-born-mongoloid-if-you-hadn't. . . . An eyewitness, however, assures me that I did not say what Tennessee attributes to me. Yet his paranoia always has some basis in reality. I have an uncomfortable feeling that I was probably thinking what I did not say and what he later thought I did say. When it comes to something unspoken, the Bird has a sharp ear.

It is hard now to realize what a bad time of it Tennessee used to have from the American press. During the forties and fifties the anti-fag battalions were everywhere on the march. From the high lands of *Partisan Review* to the middle ground of *Time* magazine, envenomed attacks on real or suspected fags never let up. A *Time* cover story on Auden was killed when the managing editor of the day was told that Auden was a fag. From 1945 to 1961 *Time* attacked with unusual ferocity everything produced or published by Tennessee Williams. "Fetid swamp" was the phrase most used to describe his work. But, in *Time*, as well as in time, all things will come to pass. The Bird is now a beloved institution.

Today, at sixty-four, Tennessee has the same voracious appetite for work and for applause that he had at twenty-four. More so, I would suspect, since glory is a drug more addictive than any other as heroes have known from Achilles on (Donald Wyndham's *roman à clef* about Tennessee bore the apt title *The Hero Continues*). But fashions in the theater change. The superstar of the forties and fifties fell on bad times, and that is the burden of these memoirs. In sharp detail we are told how the hero came into being. Less sharply, Tennessee describes the bad days when the booze and the pills caused him to hallucinate; to slip out of a world quite bad enough as it is into nightmare land. "I said to my friend Gore, 'I slept through the sixties,' and he said, 'You didn't miss a thing.' " Tennessee often quotes this exchange. But he leaves out the accompanying caveat: "If you missed the sixties, Bird, God knows what you are going to do with the seventies."

But of course life is not divided into good and bad decades; it is simply living. For a writer, life is, again simply, writing and in these memoirs the old magician can still create a world. But since it is hardly news to the Bird that we are for the night, the world he shows us is no longer the Romantic's lost Eden but Prospero's island where, at sunset, magicians often enjoy revealing the sources of their rude magic, the tricks of a trade.

Not that a magician is honor-bound to tell the whole truth. For instance: "I want to admit to you that I undertook this memoir for mercenary reasons. It is actually the first piece of work, in the line of writing, that I have undertaken for material profit." The sniffy tone is very much that of St. Theresa scrubbing floors. Actually, Tennessee is one of the richest of living writers. After all, a successful play will earn its author a million or more dollars and Tennessee has written quite a few successful plays. Also, thirteen of his works have been made into films.

Why the poor-mouthing? Because it has always been the Bird's tactic to appear in public flapping what looks to be a pathetically broken wing. By arousing universal pity, he hopes to escape predators. In the old days before a play opened on Broadway, the author would be asked to write a piece for the Sunday *New York Times* drama section. Tennessee's pieces were always thrilling; sometimes horrendous. He would reveal how that very morning he had coughed up blood with his sputum. But, valiantly, he had gone on writing, knowing the new play would be his last work, ever . . . By the time the Bird had finished working us over, only Louis Kronenberger at *Time* had the heart to attack him.

But now that Tennessee's physical and mental health are good (he would deny this instantly; "I have had, in recent days, a series of palpitations of the variety known as terminal"), only the cry of poverty will, he thinks, act as lightning conductor and insure him a good press for the *Memoirs*. Certainly he did not write this book for the $50,000 advance. As always, fame is the spur. Incidentally, he has forgotten that in the past he *did* write for money when he was under contract to MGM and worked on a film called *Marriage Is a Private Affair*, starring Lana Turner and James Craig (unless of course Tennessee now sees in this movie that awesome

moral grandeur first detected by the film critic Myra Breckinridge).

The *Memoirs* start briskly. Tennessee is a guest at a country
house in Wiltshire near Stonehenge. On the grounds of the estate
is a "stone which didn't quite make it to Henge." He looks himself up in *Who's Who*. Broods on his past; shifts back and forth in
time. *Now* and *Then*. The early days are fascinating to read about
even though the Williams family is already known to every
playgoer not only from *The Glass Menagerie* but also from the
many other plays and stories in which appear, inexorably, Rose
the Sister, Edwina the Mother, Dakin the Brother, Cornelius the
Father, Reverend Dakin the Grandfather, as well as various other
relatives now identified for the first time. He also tells us how he
was hooked by the theater when some St. Louis amateurs put on
a play he had written. "I knew that writing was my life, and its
failure would be my death. . . ."

I have never known any writer with the exception of the artis-
tically gifted and humanly appalling Carson McCullers who
cared so much about the opinion of those condemned to write for
newspapers. Uneasily confronting a truly remarkable hunger for
absolute praise and total notice, Tennessee admits that, when
being interviewed, he instinctively "hams it up in order to provide 'good copy.' The reason? I guess a need to convince the
world that I do indeed still exist and to make this fact a matter
of public interest and amusement." Fair enough, Bird. But leave
your old friends out.

"This book is a sort of catharsis of puritanical guilt feelings, I
suppose. 'All good art is an indiscretion.' Well, I can't assure you
that this book will be art, but it is bound to be an indiscretion,
since it deals with my adult life. . . .

"Of course I could devote this whole book to a discussion of the
art of drama, but wouldn't that be a bore?

"It would bore me to extinction, I'm afraid, and it would be a
very, very short book, about three sentences to the page with
extremely wide margins. The plays speak for themselves."

A wise choice: the plays do speak for themselves and Tennessee's mind is not, to say the least, at home with theory. Most
beautifully, the plays speak for themselves. Not only does
Tennessee have a marvelous comedic sense but his gloriously
outrageous dramatic effects can be enormously satisfying. He
makes poetic (without quotes) the speech of those half-educated

would-be genteel folk who still maintain their babble in his head. Only on those rare occasions when he tries to depict educated or upper-class people does he falter. Somewhat reproachfully, he told me that he had been forced several times to use a dictionary while reading *Two Sisters.*

What, I asked, was one of the words you had to look up? "Solipsistic," he said. Tennessee's vocabulary has never been large (I note that he still thinks "eclectic" means "esoteric"). But then he is not the sort of writer who sees words on the page; rather he hears them in his head and when he is plugged into the right character, the wrong word never sounds.

"Life that winter in Rome: a golden dream, and I don't just mean Raffaello (Acton's "Pierino") and the mimosa and total freedom of life. Stop there: What I do mean is the total freedom of life and Raffaello and the mimosa. . . ." That season we were, all of us, symbolically, out of jail. Free of poverty and hack work, Tennessee had metamorphosed into the Glorious Bird while I had left behind me three years in the wartime army and a near-fatal bout with hepatitis. So it was, at the beginning of that golden dream, we met.

Tennessee's version: "[Gore] had just published a best-seller, called *The City and the Pillar,* which was one of the first homosexual novels of consequence. I had not read it but I knew that it had made the best-seller lists and that it dealt with a 'forbidden subject.' " Later, Tennessee actually read the book (the only novel of mine he has ever been able to get through) and said, "You know you spoiled it with that ending. You didn't know what a good book you had." Fair comment.

"Gore was a handsome kid, about twenty-four [*sic*], and I was quite taken by his wit as well as his appearance." Incidentally, I am mesmerized by the tributes to my beauty that keep cropping up in the memoirs of the period. At the time nobody reliable thought to tell me. In fact, it was my impression that I was not making out as well as most people because, with characteristic malice, Nature had allowed Guy Madison and not me to look like Guy Madison.

"We found that we had interests in common and we spent a lot of time together. Please don't imagine that I am suggesting that there was a romance." I don't remember whether or not I ever told Tennessee that I had actually seen but not met him the previous year. He was following me up Fifth Avenue while I, in turn, was stalking yet another quarry. I recognized him: he wore a blue bow tie with white polka dots. In no mood for literary encounters, I gave him a scowl and he abandoned the chase just north of Rockefeller Center. I don't recall how my own pursuit ended. We walked a lot in the golden age.

"I believe we also went to Florence that season and were entertained by that marvelous old aesthete Berenson." No, that was someone else. "And then one afternoon Gore took me to the Convent of the Blue Nuns to meet the great philosopher and essayist, by then an octogenarian and semi-invalid, Santayana." I had to drag Tennessee to meet Santayana. Neither had heard of the other. But Tennessee did stare at the old man with great interest. Afterward, the Bird remarked, "Did you notice how he said 'in the days when I had secretaries, *young men?*' "

In the *Memoirs* Tennessee tells us a great deal about his sex life, which is one way of saying nothing about oneself. Details of this body and that body tend to blur on the page as they do in life. Tennessee did not get around to his first homosexual affair until he was well into his twenties, by which time he had achieved several mature as well as sexually meaningful and life-enhancing heterosexual relationships. Except he wasn't really all that enhanced by these "mature" relationships. Lust for the male set his nerves to jangling. Why was he such a late-developer? Well, this was close to half a century ago, and Tennessee was the product of that Southern puritan environment where all sex was sin and unnatural sex was peculiarly horrible.

I think that the marked difference between my attitude toward sex and that of Tennessee made each of us somewhat startling to the other. I never had the slightest guilt or anxiety about what I always took to be a normal human appetite. He was—and is— guilt-ridden, and although he tells us that he believes in no after-life, he is still too much the puritan not to believe in sin. At some deep level Tennessee truly believes that the homosexualist is wrong and that the heterosexualist is right. Given this all-pervading sense of guilt, he is drawn in both life and work to the idea of expiation, of death.

Tennessee tells of his affair with a dancer named Kip. But Kip left him; got married; died young. Then Tennessee was drawn to a pseudonymous lover in New Orleans; that affair ended in drink and violence. For a number of years Tennessee lived with an Italo-American, Frank Merlo. Eventually they fell out. They were reunited when Frank was dying of cancer. Frank's last days were sufficiently horrifying to satisfy any puritan's uneasy conscience while, simultaneously, justifying the romantic's extreme vision of the world: "I shall but love thee better after death."

The other line running through Tennessee's emotional life is what I call the Monster Women. Surrogate mothers one might say if Tennessee's own mother, Miss Edwina, were not so implacably in this world, even as I write these lines. Currently convinced that the blacks signal to one another during the long St. Louis nights by clanging the lids of the trash cans, Miss Edwina is every inch the Amanda of *The Glass Menagerie*. In fact, so powerful is Tennessee's creation that in the presence of Miss Edwina one does not listen to her but only to what he has made of her.

"I had forty gentlemen callers that day," she says complacently. We are having dinner in the restaurant of the Robert Clay Hotel in Miami. Delicately she holds a fork with a shrimp on it. Fork and shrimp proceed slowly to her mouth while Tennessee and I stare, hypnotized not only by the constant flow of conversation but by the never-eaten shrimp for just as she is about to take the first bite, yet another anecdote wells up from deep inside her . . . ah, *solipsistic* brain and the fork returns to the plate, the shrimp untouched. "Tom, remember when that little dog took the hat with the plume and ran all 'round the yard . . .?" This is also from *The Glass Menagerie*. Tennessee nervously clears his throat. Again the shrimp slowly rises to the wide straight mouth which resembles nothing so much as the opening to a miniature letter box— one designed for engraved invitations only. But once again the shrimp does not arrive. "Tom, do you remember . . .?"

Tennessee clears his throat again. *"Mother, eat your shrimp."*

"Why," counters Miss Edwina, "do you keep making that funny sound in your throat?"

"Because, Mother, when you destroy someone's life you must expect certain nervous disabilities."

Yet Tennessee went on adding even more grotesque ladies than Miss Edwina to his life. I could never take any of them from Carson McCullers to Jane Bowles to Anna Magnani. Yes, yes, yes, they were superb talents all. Part of the artistic heritage of the twentieth century. I concede their talent, their glory, their charm —for Tennessee but not for me. Carson spoke only of her work. Of its greatness. The lugubrious Southern singsong voice never stopped: "Did ya see muh lovely play? Did ya lahk muh lovely

play? Am Ah gonna win the Pew-litzuh prahzz?" Jane ("the finest
writer of fiction we have in the States") Bowles was more original. She thought and talked a good deal about food and made
powerful scenes in restaurants. The best that one could say of
Magnani was that she liked dogs. When Marlon Brando agreed
to act with her in the film of Tennessee's *Orpheus Descending,* he
warned, "When I do a scene with her, I'm going to carry a rock
in each hand."

I don't know what Tennessee gets from the Monster Women,
but if they give him solace nothing else matters. Certainly he has
a huge appetite for the grotesque not only in art but in life. In
fact, he is dogged by the grotesque. Once, in the airport at Miami,
we were stopped by a plump middle-aged man who had known
Tennessee whom he called Tom from the old days in St. Louis.
The man seemed perfectly ordinary. He talked to Tennessee
about friends they had in common. Then I noticed that the man
was carrying a large string bag containing two roast turkeys and
a half dozen loaves of bread. "What," I asked, "is that?" The man
gave us a knowing wink. "Well, I got me two roast turkeys in
there. And also these loaves of bread *because you know about the food
in Miami.*" Then he was gone. It would seem that the true artist
need never search for a subject; the subject always knows where
to find him.

It is curious how friends actually regard one another—or think
they do—when memoir-time rolls around, and the boneyard
beckons. A figure of some consequence in our far-off golden age
was the composer-novelist Paul Bowles. From time to time over
the years, Tennessee has bestowed a number of Walter Winchell-
ish Orchids on Paul as well as on Jane (I fear that a lifetime on
Broadway has somewhat corrupted the Bird's everyday speech
and prose although nothing, happily, can affect the authenticity
of those voices in his head). Certainly Bowles was an early hero
of Tennessee's.

But now let us see what Bowles makes of Tennessee in *his*
memoir *Without Stopping.* "One morning when we were getting
ready to leave for the beach" (this was Acapulco, 1940), "someone
arrived at the door and asked to see me. It was a round-faced,
sun-burned young man in a big floppy sombrero and a striped
sailor sweater, who said his name was Tennessee Williams, that
he was a playwright, and that Lawrence Langner of the Theatre
Guild had told him to look me up. I asked him to come in and

installed him in a hammock, explaining that we had to hurry to the beach with friends. I brought him books and magazines and rum and coke, and told him to ask the servants for sandwiches if he got hungry. Then we left. Seven hours later we got back to the house and found our visitor lying contentedly in the hammock, reading. We saw him again each day until he left."

Paul Bowles used to quote Virgil Thomson's advice to a young music critic: Never intrude your personal opinions when you write music criticism. "The words that you use to describe what you've heard will be the criticism." Bowles on Tennessee demonstrates a mastery of the unsaid. Needless to say, Tennessee read what Bowles had written about him. Now watch the Bird as he strikes . . .

"It was there in Acapulco that summer that I first met Jane and Paul Bowles. They were staying at a pension in town and Paul was, as ever, upset about the diet and his stomach. The one evening that we spent together that summer was given over almost entirely to the question of what he could eat in Acapulco that he could digest, and poor little Janie kept saying, 'Oh, Bubbles, if you'd just stick to cornflakes and fresh fruit!' and so on and so on. None of her suggestions relieved his dyspeptic humor.

"I thought them a very odd and charming couple." I think I give Tennessee that round, on points. But Bowles's prose still remains the perfect model for judgment by indirection even though, like Tennessee, he occasionally gets the facts wrong. Bowles writes: "Gore had just played a practical joke on Tennessee and Truman Capote which he recounted to me in dialect, as it were. He had called Tennessee on the telephone and, being a stupendous mimic, had made himself into Truman for the occasion. Then, complete with a snigger, he induced Tennessee to make uncomplimentary remarks about Gore's writing."

This is a curious variation on the actual story. A number of times I would ring Tennessee, using Capote's voice. The game was to see how long it would take him to figure out that it was not Capote. One day I rang and spoke to what I thought was Tennessee. But it was Frank Merlo, newly installed in the flat. I had not got beyond my imitable whine, "This is *Tru*man," when Frank began to attack Tennessee. I broke the connection. Frank never knew whether or not I had repeated his complaints to Tennessee. I did not. But years later I did tell Bowles the story.

Back to 1948: "In those days Truman was about the best com-

panion you could want," writes Tennessee. "He had not turned
bitchy. Well, he had not turned *maliciously* bitchy. But he was full
of fantasies and mischief." That summer Capote arrived in Paris
where Tennessee and I were staying at the Hôtel de l'Université
("A raffish hotel but it suited Gore and me perfectly as there was
no objection to young callers"), and Capote would keep us en-
tranced with mischievous fantasies about the great. Apparently,
the very sight of him was enough to cause lifelong heterosexual
men to tumble out of unsuspected closets. When Capote refused
to surrender his virtue to the drunken Errol Flynn, "Errol threw
all my suitcases out of the window of the Beverly Wilshire Hotel!" I should note here that the young Capote was no less attractive in his person then than he is today.

When Tennessee and I would exchange glances during these
stories, Capote would redouble his efforts. Did we know that
Albert Camus was in love with him? Yes, Camus! Madly in love.
Recently Capote's biographer told me that the Capote-Camus
connection might well prove to be a key chapter. No doubt it will
also provide a startling footnote to the life story of Camus, a man
known until now as a womanizer. Then Capote showed us a gold
and amethyst ring. "From André Gide," he sighed. Happily, I
was able to check that one out. A few days later I called on Gide
in the company of my English publisher. "How," I asked in my
best Phillips Exeter French, "did you find Truman Capote?"
"Who?" Gide asked. I suspect that it was then, in the fabulous
summer of '48, that the nonfiction novel was born.

To return again to 1948, I have a bit more to report on that
season.

"Frankie and I had been out late one evening and when we
returned to the apartment the transom on the front door was
open and from within came the voice of Truman Capote, shrill
with agitation. . . . In the apartment were Truman, Gore Vidal,
and a female policeman. . . . It seemed that Truman and Gore, still
on friendly terms at this point, had got a bit drunk together and
had climbed in through the transom of the apartment to wait for
me and Frankie."

Before this story petrifies into literary history, let me amend
the record. Tennessee, an actress, and I came back to Tennessee's
flat to find Capote and a friend in the clutches of the law. They
had indeed been caught entering the flat. But by the time we
arrived, Capote had matters well under control. Plainclothes-

woman and plainclothesman were listening bug-eyed to Capote, who was telling them *every*thing about the private lives of Mr. and Mrs. Charles Chaplin.

Tennessee's asides on the various personages who have come his way are often amusing, sometimes revelatory. He describes a hilarious dinner with the Russian performer Yevtushenko, who saw fit to lecture Tennessee on commercialism, sexual perversion, and the responsibilities of art while swilling expensive wine. Tennessee admired Dylan Thomas until he actually met him and received "this put-down: 'How does it feel to make all that Hollywood money?' " There was also the snub from Sartre. Tennessee gave a party at the Hôtel de l'Université, hoping that Sartre would come. Instead the Master sat a few blocks away at a café, and for several hours he made a point of *not* coming to the party despite the pleas of various emissaries.

Tennessee omits to mention a splendid lunch given us at the Grand Véfour by Jean Cocteau, who wanted the French rights to *A Streetcar Named Desire* for Jean Marais to act in. I came along as translator. Marais looked beautiful but sleepy. Cocteau was characteristically brilliant. He spoke no English but since he could manage an occasional "th" sound as well as the final "g," he often gave the impression that he was speaking English. Tennessee knew no French. He also had no clear idea just who Cocteau was, while Cocteau knew nothing about Tennessee except that he had written a popular American play with a splendid part in it for his lover Marais. Between Tennessee's solemn analyses of the play and Cocteau's rhetoric about theater (the long arms flailed like semaphores denoting some dangerous last junction), no one made any sense at all except Marais who broke his long silence to ask, apropos the character Stanley Kowalski, "Will I have to use a Polish accent?"

Although Marais and Cocteau broke up soon afterward, Cocteau did the play without Marais. Cocteau's adaptation was, apparently, a gorgeous mess. Naked black youths writhed through beaded curtains while Arletty, miscast as Blanche, struck attitudes among peacock feathers.

The situation of a practicing playwright in the United States is not a happy one, to understate (or bowles) the matter. Broadway is more and more an abandoned parcel of real estate. Except for a native farce or two and a handful of "serious" plays imported from the British Isles, Broadway is noted chiefly for large and usually bad musicals. During the theater season of 1947–48 there were 43 straight plays running on Broadway. In 1974–75 there were 18, mostly imported. Adventurous plays are now done off-Broadway and sometimes off-off . . . where our memoirist ended up as a performer in *Small Craft Warnings.*

Unique among writers, the American playwright must depend upon the praise of journalists who seldom know very much about anything save the prejudices of their employers. With the collapse of a half dozen newspapers in the last third of a century, the success of a play now depends almost entirely upon the good will of the critic for *The New York Times.* The current reviewer is an amiable and enthusiastic Englishman who knows a good deal about ballet but not so much about the social and political nuances of his adopted land. Yet at sixty-four Tennessee Williams is still trying to curry favor with the press. Of *Small Craft Warnings,* "Clive Barnes" (in *The New York Times*) "was cautiously respectful. With the exception of Leonard Harris, I disregard TV reviews. I suppose they were generally negative."

Then Tennessee has second thoughts. And a new paragraph: "To say that I disregard TV reviews is hardly the total truth. How could I disregard any review which determines the life or death of a production?" How indeed? Yet after thirty years of meaningless praise and equally meaningless abuse, it is no wonder that Tennessee is a bit batty. On those rare occasions when Tennessee's literary peers have got around to looking at his work, the result has been depressing: witness, Mary McCarthy's piece "A Streetcar Named Success."

There have been complaints that these *Memoirs* tell us too much about Tennessee's sex life and too little about his art. Personally, I find the candor about his sex life interesting if not illuminating. At the worst, it will feed that homophobia which is too much a part of the national psyche. Yet perhaps it is better to write this sort of thing oneself rather than leave it to others to invent.

Recently that venerable vendor of book-chat Alfred Kazin wrote, "Vidal gets more literary mileage out of his sex life than anyone since Oscar Wilde and Jean Cocteau." This struck me as breathtakingly wrong. First, neither Wilde nor Cocteau ever exploited his sex life for "mileage." Each was reticent in public. Eventually the law revealed the private life of the first, while friends (and an ambiguous sort of unsigned memoir) revealed the life of the second. The book-chat writer does mention the admittedly too many interviews I've lately given to magazines like *Playboy* where sex is always a Solemn and Sacred subject and where I, too, am Solemn but never personal. As evidence of my seeking mileage he quotes the rather lame " 'In youth I never missed a trick . . . I tried everything . . . I could no more go to bed with somebody whose work I admired than I could . . . well, make love to a mirror. Fame in others switches off desire.' " Not, I would say, the most prurient of giveaway lines. Except in *Two Sisters,* a memoir done with mirrors, I have not used myself as a subject for private analysis on the ground that since we live in a time where the personality of the writer is everything and what he writes is nothing, only a fool would aid the enemy by helping to trivialize life, work.

A columnist reports that Tennessee was obliged to cut his *Memoirs* in half because of the "filth." I hope that we are given that other half one day; and I doubt that there will be much "filth," only indiscretions which ought to be interesting. After all, Tennessee has known or come across a great many of our time's movers and shakers. I say "come across" because for a long period he was . . . well, inattentive. Sometimes the stupefying combination of Nembutal and vodka (now abandoned) addled him. I was present when Edna Ferber (yes, Edna Ferber) came over to our table at a restaurant and introduced herself. With considerable charm, she told Tennessee how much she admired him. He listened to her with eyes that had narrowed to what Miss Ferber would have described as "mere slits." As she walked away, the Bird hissed, "Why is that woman attacking me?"

Tennessee is the sort of writer who does not develop; he simply continues. By the time he was an adolescent he had his themes. Constantly he plays and replays the same small but brilliant set of cards. I am not aware that any new information (or feeling?) has got through to him in the twenty-eight years since our Roman spring. In consequence, we have drifted apart. "Gore no longer receives me," said the Bird to one of his innumerable interviewers; and he put this down to my allegedly glamorous social life. But the reason for the drifting apart is nothing more than difference of temperament. I am a compulsive learner of new things while the Bird's occasional and sporadic responses to the world outside the proscenium arch have not been fortunate. "Castro was, after all, a gentleman," he announced after an amiable meeting with the dictator. Tell that to the proscribed fags of Cuba.

Tennessee's much publicized conversion to Roman Catholicism took place during the time of his great confusion. Shortly after the Bird was received into the arms of Mother Church, a Jesuit priest rang him up and asked if he would like an audience with the Pope? a meeting with the head of the Jesuit order? Oh yes. Yes! Tennessee was delighted. The next morning the priest arrived to take Tennessee to the Vatican where, presumably, the Pope was waiting on tenterhooks to examine the Church's latest haul. Unfortunately, Tennessee had forgotten all about the audience. He would have to beg off, he said; he was just not up to the Pope that day. The priest was stunned. The Pope's reaction has not been recorded.

The Jesuits, however, are made of tougher material. The secretary of the Black Pope rang to say that since a cocktail party had been arranged, Mr. Williams was going to be there, or else. The Bird was present. Almost immediately, he began to ham it up about God. Now if there is anything a Jesuit likes less than chat of God, it is having to listen to the religious enthusiasm of a layman. Trying to deflect Tennessee from what was fast turning into a Billy Graham exhortation about God and goodness, one of the Jesuits asked, "How do you start to write a play, Mr. Williams?" The Bird barely paused in his glorious ascent. "I start," he said sharply, "with a sentence." He then told the assembled members of the Society of Jesus that ever since becoming a Roman Catholic, he had felt a divine presence constantly with him. The Jesuits shifted uneasily at this. Like the old trouper he is, the Bird then paused abruptly in midflight in order to see just what effect he was having. After a moment of embarrassed silence, one of the Jesuits asked, timidly, "Is this presence a *warm* presence?"

"There is," said the Bird firmly, "no temperature."

But despite the "conversion," Tennessee now writes, "I am unable to believe that there is anything but permanent oblivion after death. . . . For me, what is there but to feel beneath me the steadily rising current of mortality and to summon from my blood whatever courage is native to it, and once there was a great deal." As he ends the *Memoirs,* he thinks back upon Hart Crane, whose legend has always haunted him. But though a romantic, Tennessee is no Crane. For one thing, it is too late to choose an abrupt death at sea. For another, art is too beguiling and difficult: "life is made up of moment-to-moment occurrences in the nerves and the perceptions, and try as you may, you can't commit them to the actualities of your own history."

But Tennessee continues to try. Now he has invited the world to take a close look at him, more or less as he is (the lighting of course has been carefully arranged, and he is not one to confuse an Entrance with an Exit). The result should be gratifying. The Glorious Bird is not only recognized but applauded in the streets. When he came to sign copies of the *Memoirs* in a large Manhattan bookstore, nearly a thousand copies were sold and the store had to be shut because of overcrowding. The resemblance to the latter days of Judy Garland would be disquieting were it not for the happy fact that since Tennessee cannot now die young he will probably not die at all (his grandfather lived for almost a century). In any case, artists who continue to find exhilarating the puzzles art proposes never grow bored and so have no need of death.

As for life? Well, that is a hard matter. But it was always a hard matter for those of us born with a sense of the transiency of these borrowed atoms that make up our corporeal being.

"I need," Tennessee writes with sudden poignancy, "somebody to laugh with." Well, don't we all, Bird? Anyway, be happy that your art has proved to be one of those stones that really did make it to Henge, enabling future magicians to gauge from its crafty placement not only the dour winter solstice of our last days but the summer solstice, too—the golden dream, the mimosa, the total freedom, and all that lovely time unspent now spent.

The New York Review of Books
February 5, 1976

Contagious Self-Love

The Seventh Earl of Longford and I appeared together on British television. As the Seventh Earl was introduced to the viewers, he swung around in his chair and looked at himself in the television monitor; it was plain that he was ravished by what he saw. And I? In those few seconds I was depraved and corrupted by the sort of blind self-love that is so communicable that one is transformed. I was—am—like Onan on a peak in Darien; the prurient theater of my mind, hopelessly dominated by the fact of the Seventh Earl who made me love him as he loves him.

In front of me now is the Seventh Earl's third volume of memoirs. On the dust jacket there is a photograph *in color* of the Seventh Earl's head. He looks mighty pleased with himself—as well he ought. Beneath the picture, the words *The Grain of Wheat, an Autobiography, Frank Longford*. That's all: a vivid contrast to the Seventh Earl's billing on the slender paperback *Humility*. The title *Humility* was hardly visible, modest mauve on black, while the author's name was in stark white *Frank Pakenham, Earl of*

Longford. But no matter how Frank wants to be known, I find his ruling passion perfectly irresistible.

In the present volume Frank brings us up to date. He admits right off to being an intellectual and a quotation from A. J. Cronin early on convinced me that the contents of Frank's mind are well worth a detour. As he says, "my special kind of brain is well above average in literature." After all, he produced "*Peace by Ordeal,* still the standard book on the Anglo-Irish Treaty of 1931"; as for his biography of De Valera, "Sales were highly satisfactory . . . and the English reviews were very pleasing." Frank tells us that his college was Christchurch, "certainly the most aristocratic college in the world." Frank's war was not much good; he was "invalided out with a nervous breakdown" in May 1940. But Frank turned his misfortune to tremendous advantage:

> with prisoners, ex-prisoners, outcasts generally and all those who hesitate to show their faces abroad, I have had one unfailing and unforeseen point of contact. I can say and mean and be believed— "I also have been humiliated." The gulf is bridged as if by magic. If my sense of compassion has been strengthened and activated from any human experience, it is from my own infirmities and the indignities I have myself undergone.

Like Henry James, Frank does not spell out those infirmities and indignities. We can only guess at his anguish. But he does share his triumphs with us: "according to the *Economist,* I was an enormously successful amateur banker." When Leader of the House of Lords, Frank spoke on Rhodesia and "Harold Wilson and other leaders crowded in to listen. Next day, Harold Wilson congratulated me in front of the Cabinet." Later, "when I resigned I was overwhelmed with letters . . . referring in glowing terms to my leadership." And why not? On one occasion, when Leader, *Frank spoke from the back benches!* "I can't find that a Leader of the House had ever previously done what I did."

Frank had his downs as well as his ups in politics. He was not heeded as often as he ought to have been. He might "have swayed the issue" on devaluation, but didn't. Serenely he records that Harold Wilson is supposed to have noted, "Frank Longford quite useless. Mental age of 12." Frank takes this very well (after all, any *bright* 12-year-old is perfectly able to lead the Lords). But he does hope that in future Harold "will avoid such indiscretions." Anyway, "nothing in any membership of the Wilson Government became me so well—it was said at the time—as the manner of my leaving it." He left it on a Point of Principle. He "most treasures" a letter he got from someone mysteriously called "Bobbity Salisbury." Truly great men like Clem Attlee thought the world of Frank who also

> treasures more than one of his letters running like this: "My dear Frank, I will look into the point you mentioned as soon as possible. Yours ever, Clem."

Yet for all the wonderful letters and compliments from his peers, "I felt, and still feel, that I was largely wasted in the Cabinet." But, Frank, that's the point isn't it? To be humiliated in order that you may be able to grow as a human being, to learn compassion so that you can help us outcasts across that awful gulf.

Frank writes a lot about sinners (loves them, hates the sin). He got to know the gangster brothers Kray: "talking to me that afternoon, I am sure that they had made a resolution: never again." He befriended Ian Brady and Myra Hindley, of the Moors murders fame: "their agony is never far from my mind." Frank admits that he is sometimes criticized for his Christian treatment of murderers: "psychologists and other men assess my motives as they wish." But Frank is, simply, good. There is no other word. Best of all, he wants us to share with him through his many testaments his many good actions. That's why he writes books and appears on television programs. By reading Frank and looking at Frank people will want to be as good as he is. Of course he can be stern. Although Frank doesn't want to put homosexualists in jail, he doesn't want people to forget that "homosexual conduct . . . remains wrongful." Pornography, on the other hand, is not only wrongful but must be rooted out and the makers and dispensers of it punished.

Frank reports on his still unfinished crusade against pornography. All in all, he has been having a super time even though he is a bit miffed that the press has not so far acknowledged that "I had an experience of inquiries which no one in politics could equal." Unfortunately, "these rather striking qualifications . . . were never mentioned." But more fortunately,

> I was featured in the *Evening Standard* as "British worthy No. 4," my predecessors being the Duke of Norfolk, the Archbishop of Canterbury and Mick Jagger. I was interviewed times without num-

ber and was chosen by the *Sunday Times* as the most caricatured figure of 1972 . . . My citation as "Man of the Year" referred to me as Crusader Extraordinary.

Then came The Garter, "a clear reminder that I was not without recognition." And so, gartered as well as belted, on to Copenhagen. TV cameras. Strippers. Porn. Jesus. Love. Compassion. Outrage. Filth. Human decency. Where will it end, Frank?

I think I know, because Frank let a bit of the cat's whisker out of the bag when he quoted a journalist who wrote:

> Lord Longford is clearly a good man. If he is not actually a saint, he is certainly the most saintly member of the Upper Chamber, and I do not overlook the Bishops.

That's it. After the humiliation of the bad war, the failed career in politics, the eccentric attempt to regulate England's morals, now comes the halo, the nimbus, the mandala the translation to Paradise by special arrangement with Telstar. And so at God's right hand, forever and ever stands the Seventh Earl of Longford, peering happily into an eternal television monitor. Pray for us, Saint Frank. Intercede for us, and teach us to love ourselves as you loved you.

New Statesman
March 8, 1974

The Four Generations
of the Adams Family

T he Inventors of the United States decided that there would
be no hereditary titles in God's country. Although the
Inventors were hostile to the idea of democracy and believed
profoundly in the sacredness of property and the necessary dignity of those who owned it, they did not like the idea of king,
duke, marquess, earl. Such a system of hereditary nobility was
liable to produce aristocrats who tended to mix in politics (like
the egregious Lord North) instead of politically responsible
burghers.

But the Inventors were practical men and the federal constitution that they assembled in 1787 was an exquisite machine that,
with a repair here and a twist there, has gone on protecting the
property of the worthy for two hundred years while protecting
in the Bill of Rights (that sublime afterthought) certain freedoms
of speech and assembly which are still unknown even now to that
irritable fount of America's political and actual being, old
Europe. The Inventors understood human greed and self-interest. Combining brutal cynicism with a Puritan sense of virtue,

they used those essential drives to power the machinery of the state.

Certainly none wanted to change the way people were. "As to political reformation in Europe or elsewhere," wrote conservative Inventor John Jay in 1796, "I confess that . . . I do not amuse myself with dreams about an age of reason. I am content that little men should be as free as big ones and have and enjoy the same rights, but nothing strikes me as more absurd than projects to stretch little men into big ones, or shrink big men into little ones. . . . We must take men and measures as they are, and act accordingly." That is the very voice of the American Inventors: conservative, commonsensical, and just—within (as opposed to the age of) reason.

At the Constitutional Convention in Philadelphia a few romantics fought a losing battle to make Washington king and to create a peerage using the odd title "margrave." The matter was then settled, the Inventors thought, once and for all. Government would be by the best people in order to forward the best interests of the country's owners. They might have invented the word "meritocracy" had they not had the same prejudice against neologisms that they had against new men.

But although America's "best" people were not to have titles, they did have names; they also acquired fortunes which they passed on to sons and to grandsons and to great-grandsons. As a result, the history of the American republic is the history of certain families, of names that are now every bit as awesome as titles.

First among the country's political families are the Adamses. In four successive generations the Adams family produced not only two presidents but a number of startlingly brilliant men and women, culminating in the country's only major historian, Henry Adams, the bright light of the fourth and the last splendid generation that ended with the death of Henry's brother Brooks Adams in 1927.

To try to understand the Adamses one must begin by placing them. The first Adams to come to America was a copy-hold farmer in Somerset, on land belonging to the Lord of the Manor of Barton St. David. For reasons unknown, this Henry Adams, with wife and nine children, emigrated to Boston in 1636. Possible sign of character? Of proto-Puritanism? Most English emigrants of that period preferred the balmy West Indies to the cold arduousness of New England.

Ten years later, Adams died, leaving a comfortable property. The next two generations produced dim but increasingly prosperous farmers. In the third generation, church deacon John Adams performed that obligatory act of all families destined to distinguish themselves. He committed hypergamy by marrying Susanna Boylston of Brookline, Massachusetts. The Boylstons were distinguished physicians and for an Adams to consort with a Boylston was very much a step up in that little world. Their first child was John Adams (born October 30, 1735); and with him the family entered history, remaining at the center of national and sometimes world affairs for nearly two centuries.

John Adams was a small plump man, fierce of face and brusque of manner, and very much unlike everyone else. Although he was a true child of the bleak New England countryside and mind, he was a good deal more complicated than any of the other Inventors, saving Jefferson. Adams kept, intermittently, a diary; he composed some chaotic fragments of autobiography; and he copied out most of his letters. Adams thought a very great deal about himself and of himself, and much of his worrying is now available in the many yards of microfilm that record his papers.

At the age of forty-four John Adams scrutinized his own character: "There is a Feebleness and a Languor in my Nature. My Mind and Body both partake of this Weakness." Like so many valetudinarians, John Adams suffered good health until the age of ninety-one. "By my Physical Constitution I am but an ordinary Man. The Times alone have destined me to Fame—and even these have not been able to give me much." Note the irritability; the sense that fate—or something—does not properly value him. This will be one of the family's important recurring motifs. "Yet some great Events, some cutting Expressions, some mean Hypocrisies, have at Times, thrown this Assemblage of Sloth, Sleep, and littleness into Rage a little like a Lion."

John Adams could not be better described. He was indeed born at the right time and in the right place, and at great moments he was more than a little like a lion. But he was also a Puritan. He worried about his vanity. When his legal career started to flourish, he wrote, "What is the end and purpose of my studies, journeys, labours . . .? Am I grasping at money or scheming for power? Am I planning the illustration of my family or the welfare of my country? These are great questions. . . . Which of these lies nearest my heart?"

The answer of course is that all these things can dwell in

reasonable harmony within the same great bosom. But only a
New England Puritan would fret so. Certainly one does not find
in Franklin, Jefferson or Washington any of the cold-eyed self-
scrutiny that the first and all the subsequent Adamses turned
upon themselves. Happily, the Adamses were not uncritical of
others. In fact, a certain censoriousness is very much the family
style. John Adams managed to quarrel hugely with Franklin,
Jefferson, and, disastrously, with the co-leader of his own party
Alexander Hamilton. He was also wary of the cold, self-loving,
and self-satisfied grandeur of his predecessor in the office of first
magistrate, George Washington.

In the New England slang of the day, Adams was "saucy." He
was also prone to nervous breakdowns ("my Fidgets"). Peter
Shaw* writes that "Adams suffered from a constantly rising temper at *anticipated* enmity. But when attacked directly he rarely
took offense." Despising popularity, Adams required universal
applause for his good works. Yet laurel wreaths tended to give
him headaches for "Good Treatment makes me think I am admired, beloved and my own Vanity will be indulged in me. So
I dismiss my Gard and grow weak, silly, vain, conceited, ostenta-
tious. But a Check, a frown, a sneer, a Sarcasm . . . makes me more
careful and considerate." Or, as Mr. Shaw puts it, "The truth was
that from the beginning he courted not popularity but un-
popularity as a mark of distinction."

The facts of John Adams's early career are unremarkable. He
attended Harvard; studied law; was admitted to the bar in 1758 at
Boston. Had the English Ministry not managed entirely to outrage its American colonies, John Adams would be known today,
if at all, as a sharp New England lawyer who kept a diary not so
good as Pepys's. As it was, by the age of thirty-six, he had the
largest law practice in the colony. He owned a house at Braintree
near Boston, and he commuted between the private practice of
law and public life. "Farewell Politicks," he writes time and
again. But with the American Revolution it was farewell to private life for thirty years.

"The year 1765 has been the most remarkable Year of my Life.
That enormous Engine, fabricated by the British Parliament, for
battering down all the Rights and Liberties of America, I mean
the Stamp Act, has raised and spread, thro the whole Continent,

* *The Character of John Adams* (University of North Carolina Press, 1976).

a Spirit that will be recorded to our Honour, with all future Generations."

Adams was one of those chosen to present the objections of the people of Massachusetts to the taxes levied on them by the far-away Ministry at London. When selected by his fellow citizens, Adams wondered how it was that someone "unknown as I am" should have been thrust into history. Obviously some "secret invisible Laws of Nature" were at work. This is to be one of the family's principal themes, ultimately expressed in Henry Adams's theory of history.

Adams enjoyed describing the pathetic departure for Philadelphia of the Massachusetts delegates, "all destitute of Fortune, four poor Pilgrims, proceeded in one coach." Actually they were splendidly accompanied by two armed white servants and four blacks in livery.

But no matter how or why John Adams was chosen by the *Zeitgeist* to lead, he more than any other Inventor prepared the way intellectually and rhetorically for Revolution, as we like to call the slow separation of the colonies from England. "I grounded my Argument on the Invalidity of the Stamp Act, if not being in any sense our Act, having never consented to it." Or, "No taxation without representation." With that mighty line, the United States were born as a political entity and in the two hundred years since that noble genesis the government of our states has blithely taxed other peoples from the far-off Filipinos to the nearby residents of the District of Columbia without for a moment allowing *them* representation.

Adams was a member of the Continental Congress from 1774 to 1778. By seconding the nomination of the Virginian George Washington as commander-in-chief, he ensured Washington's selection. Alas. From that moment on Adams tended to regard Washington rather the way Baron Frankenstein was to regard *his* handiwork. At forty, Adams toyed with the idea of winning glory as a soldier; but decided that he was "too old, and too much worn with fatigues of study in my youth." Yet he was three years younger than Washington; but then Washington had never fatigued himself with books.

In November 1777 Adams was bored with the Congress. But Congress was not bored with Adams. He was sent in February 1778 to France, to join the other American representatives there, chief among them Benjamin Franklin. Adams admitted that

Franklin was "a great genius, a great wit, a great humorist, a great satirist, and a great politician." After all, Adams happened to be none of those things and did not value them. But he did doubt if Franklin was "a great philosopher, a great moralist, and a great statesman . . . " like John Adams.

He also deeply envied Franklin's charm and universal popularity ("I expect soon to see a proposition to name the 18th Century, the Franklinian Age"). He also found Franklin dissipated, lazy, and Frenchified. More in sorrow than in anger, Franklin observed that Adams was "in some things, absolutely out of his senses."

Adams took with him to Europe his ten-year-old son John Quincy, a future diplomat and president. The education of John Quincy Adams was to be the most superb of any of the American presidents, and consequently absolutely crippling. He was too brilliant and too addicted to toil; he knew too many languages, books, nations, political and philosophical systems to be able to preside with any grace or tolerance over the dingy republic of his day. But in late eighteenth-century Europe the boy was wide-eyed and impressionable. The world was his.

In due course, John Adams was chosen to negotiate the peace with England. After seven dreadful years Washington had finally blundered not into a clear-cut American victory over the English but into a situation where a nervous and weary Ministry at London wanted to cut its losses in America. Summarily, the English abandoned their former colonies and went home.

For three successive generations each head of the Adams family was, in a sense, made by England, for each was American minister at London during a crisis and each did his job satisfactorily, if sometimes tactlessly. Or as Sir John Temple noted of John Adams, "He is the most ungracious man I ever saw."

Negotiations with the English themselves were not as difficult for Adams as getting on with his two American co-negotiators Franklin and Jay: "the one malicious, the other, I think honest. . . . Franklin's cunning will be to divide us; to this end he will provoke, he will insinuate, he will intrigue, he will maneuver." As it turned out, Franklin was not all that bad and Jay was brilliant. Meanwhile, the fourteen-year-old John Quincy Adams left the school he was attending at The Hague and went off to be secretary to the American minister at St. Petersburg. The education was proceeding uniquely well. John Quincy now spoke

French, Dutch, German; knew Latin and Greek.

In 1785 John Adams was appointed first American minister to England. By then Adams had been joined by his wife Abigail. In marrying the daughter of the noted Reverend William Smith and the very grand Elizabeth Quincy, Adams had, like his father, committed the obligatory act of hypergamy and his children were now related to *everyone* in Massachusetts.

The sharp-tongued Abigail was a devoted wife and a fine letter writer. Exactly a century ago, Charles Francis Adams edited some three hundred of the letters his grandparents wrote to each other. Now *The Book of Abigail and John** has just been published. This selection of letters between husband and wife is a good deal more lively than the demure 1876 arrangement. While Adams fretted about politics and history, Abigail was the efficient manager of the household and the farm. She had a first-rate mind and resented her own lack of education. In 1776, she wrote wistfully, "I always had a fancy for a closet with a window which I could peculiarly call my own." But she was, like it or not, farm-manager, wife, mother. Although the eldest son John Quincy Adams was, from the beginning, a paragon, the second son Charles took to drink and died at thirty, while a daughter married not too well. But Abigail's principal interest was her prickly husband and their marriage was happy.

Abigail's political judgment was often shrewd. Rightly suspicious of Jefferson and the Virginians, she wondered whether or not these slave owners could truly possess a "passion for Liberty" when they "have been accustomed to deprive their fellow creatures of theirs." Yet she did her best to keep smooth relations between John Adams and Jefferson.

In 1788 Adams returned home where he was much admired for his labors in England. Everyone quoted his prescription for the new republic, "a government of laws and not of men." But like his descendants, Adams could never *not* express himself. In a lengthy treatise on the various American state constitutions, he made it plain that the country ought to be governed by "the rich, the well-born and the able." But the poor, the ill-born, and the incompetent, that is to say the majority, disliked this bold elitism, and Adams was to suffer to the end of his career gibes accusing

---

**Selected Letters of the Adams Family, 1762–1784*, edited by L. H. Butterfield et al. (Harvard University Press, 1975).

him of being in favor of monarchy and aristocracy.

Democracy, Adams believed, was "the most ignoble, unjust and detestable form of government." The other Inventors agreed. But then, early on, they had a great fright. Before the separation from England only men of property could vote in Massachusetts. After independence, only men of property could vote in Massachusetts; but the property qualifications were doubled. A number of former soldiers led by one Daniel Shays revolted. Shays' Rebellion was quickly put down. In the process, the Inventors came to the conclusion that a relatively strong federal constitution was needed to make thirteen loosely allied states into a single nation with the sort of powers that would discourage rebellion and protect property. Carefully, they limited the franchise to some 700,000 propertied adult males. Out of a total population of 3,-250,000, slaves, indentured servants, and convicts comprised nearly a third of the total. The Inventors also devised an Electoral College to choose president and vice president. As expected, George Washington was unanimously elected president while the man who got the second most votes in the College became vice president. On April 21, 1789, John Adams began the first of two terms as vice president.

Adams was much misunderstood during this period. Although he had never been a lover of Demos, he was not in favor of aristocracy. Yet, according to Mr. Shaw, "he forged an enduring reputation as a champion of aristocracy by the manner in which he opposed himself to it: namely by warning that aristocrats were dangerous because superior." Also, he did himself harm when "Apparently unaware of the new prestige of equality, he defended the people while emphasizing their inferiority." Thus was laid the curse upon the house of Adams.

Nicknamed "His Rotundity," Adams presided over the Senate, and waited his turn to replace Washington. That turn almost never came, thanks to Alexander Hamilton. In many ways the most brilliant as well as the most unstable of the Inventors, Hamilton was magically beguiling when he chose to be, particularly with doting older men like George Washington. During the eight years of Washington's presidency, Secretary of the Treasury Hamilton was, in effect, the actual ruler of the United States. Hamilton's preeminence did not please his senior the vice president. Because of an untidy private life, foreign birth, and a personality calculated to make the ill-born froth with Jacobin sentiments, Hamilton was never himself a candidate for president. But he did his best to make Adams's elevation not the natural thing it ought to have been but a complicated near-miss. Adams defeated Jefferson by only three votes.

In 1875, that glorious crook, contender for the presidency, and nobody's fool James G. Blaine was firmly opposed to the idea of nominating for president John Adams's grandson Charles Francis Adams. Blaine was firm: both President John Adams and his son President John Quincy Adams had each managed to kill his party. The Republican party of 1875 might be defeated and still survive, said Blaine, "but if it should win with Adams it would never live again." In one sense, this was very much a bum rap for the Adamses since their parties were, in any case, deteriorating. Yet it is true that their overwhelming *amour-propre* was such that they were hopeless when it came to the greasy art of survival in American politics. Although they were sly enough to rise to the top, they were never sufficiently adhesive to stay there.

John Adams began his presidency in a sour mood. He had nearly been robbed of the office by Hamilton. At the inaugural, Washington got all the attention: "He seemed to enjoy a triumph over me." The man he trusted least, the head of the Republican party, Thomas Jefferson, was vice president. Nevertheless, Adams decided to do his best to transcend faction, and so made the fatal mistake of retaining George Washington's cabinet. This group of second-raters was for the most part loyal to Alexander Hamilton, now practicing law at New York and dreaming of one day leading a great army into Mexico and South America in order to make himself another Bonaparte.

But for Hamilton to raise a great army he needed a war. After much intrigue, Hamilton nearly maneuvered the United States into a war with France (one issue: Talleyrand had suggested that to keep the peace a bribe might be in order; virtuous United Statesmen were outraged). The Republican party under Jefferson was not only pro-French but opposed to standing armies, taxes, and all the accouterments of that nation-state which Hamilton saw as inevitable and desirable. Although Adams did his best to maintain the peace, Hamilton orchestrated the war-scare so skillfully that Adams was obliged to call Washington out of retirement to take charge of a mobilization.

Ever obedient to the beloved Hamilton, Washington insisted that Adams make Hamilton the ranking major-general of the army. Overwhelmed by *force majeure* from Mount Vernon, Adams gave way. Hamilton could now attend cabinet meetings; organize the coming war with France; and plan the eventual conquest of Latin America. But Adams was not without cunning. He continued to play up to the jingoes while quietly preparing an accommodation with France. Shortly before the election of 1800, the president's own minister to France made peace.

Finished as a party leader, Hamilton felt obliged to damage if not destroy Adams. With that creative madness for which he was noted, Hamilton wrote a "secret" attack on the president while, quixotically, proposing that of course he be re-elected. Aaron Burr got a copy of Hamilton's pamphlet and published it, fatally splitting the Federalist party. Even so, had Burr not carried New York State for Jefferson and himself, Adams would have been re-elected. As it was, Adams spent his last days in office at the new and dreadful "city" of Washington, creating Federalist judges. The most significant act of John Adams's presidency was the appointment of John Marshall to be chief justice. More than any other Inventor, the conservative Marshall defined the United States and shaped its Constitution.

During the war-scare, the infamous Alien and Sedition Acts were passed by a panicky Congress, and Adams had the bad sense to sign them. In effect, they suspended freedom of speech "in the national interest," as the Nixonians used to say. Historians have tended to be overwhelmed by this blot on the Adams administration; yet hardly any historian, retrospectively, much minds the fact that the sainted Lincoln suspended habeas corpus during the Civil War. Actually, it was not the high-handed attitude toward civil rights that harmed the Federalists but, as John Quincy Adams wrote, "The [creation of] the army was the first decisive symptom of a schism in the Federal Party itself, which accomplished its final overthrow and that of the administration."

Nevertheless, Adams continued to feel guilty about having signed into law measures designed to curtail free speech and assembly. A decade later he blamed the Alien and Sedition Acts on Hamilton. "Congress, however, adopted both these measures." Then he trims. After all, they were "War measures" and "I knew there was need enough of both, and therefore I consented to them." Abigail was a good deal firmer. Referring to an offensive editor, "In any other Country [he] and all his papers would have been seazd and ought to be here, but Congress are dilly dallying about passing a Bill enabling the President to seize suspisious Persons and their papers."

Refusing to remain in Washington for the inauguration of his successor Thomas Jefferson, Adams went home to Massachusetts where he lived for another twenty-six years, eating too much, reading Cicero, following with delighted apprehension his son's rise in the world. Although he wanted his son to succeed, the Puritan in John Adams insisted that noble failure was the only grace to be longed for. In 1808, he wrote, "Happy will you be if you can be turned out as your Father has been. . . ." But in 1825, John Quincy Adams became the president. His father wrote Jefferson, with whom he had become reconciled, "He appeared to be almost as much your boy as mine."

Summing up his own career, Adams wrote, "I cannot repent of anything I ever did conscientiously and from a sense of duty. I never engaged in public affairs for my own interest, pleasure, envy, jealousy, avarice, or ambition, or even the desire of fame." Excepting "pleasure" and perhaps "avarice," Adams listed his own peculiar faults. Yet he was by no means an opportunist. In fact, he believed that his best act as president was the one that cost him re-election: "I desire no other inscription over my gravestone than: 'Here lies John Adams, who took upon himself the responsibility of the peace with France in the year 1800.'"

In the mantelpiece of the dining room at the White House is carved a line from one of Adams's letters to his wife, "May none but honest and wise men ever rule under this roof."

When John Adams ceased to be president, his son John Quincy Adams was thirty-three years old and the ablest of America's diplomats. In 1791 John Quincy was in London, helping John Jay negotiate a treaty. Although John Quincy was now too grand to stoop to hypergamy, he did manage to bring into the family a new type. Louisa Johnson was the daughter of the American consul general at London. Mr. Johnson was a feckless Marylander married to an Englishwoman. Brought up in Europe, Louisa was "charming, like a Romney portrait," according to her grandson Henry Adams, "but among her many charms that of being a New England woman was not one." Louisa did not take to Boston or Braintree ("Had I stepped into Noah's Ark, I do not think I could have been more utterly astonished"). Happily, the old President took to her. She also made John Quincy a good wife; but then great men seldom make bad marriages.

Nevertheless, in a recent biography of John Quincy Adams,* Marie B. Hecht (who annoyingly refers to her subject as "Johnny") suggests that the marriage must have been rather hard-going for the Europeanized Louisa, who once confided to her son Charles Francis that the Adams men were "peculiarly harsh and severe with their women." Frequent miscarriages, bouts of fainting and illness were to be Louisa's revenge. But her husband never varied from his view that "political subserviency and domestic influence must be the lot of women. . . . " Also, to be fair, he was as hard and severe with himself as he was with others.

John Quincy disliked the idea of holding diplomatic posts under his father. Uncharacteristically, Washington himself wrote to the new president John Adams, expressing the hope "that you will not withhold merited promotion from Mr. John (Quincy) Adams because he is your son." So John Quincy Adams was posted American minister to Prussia 1797–1801. He then returned to Boston ostensibly to practice law but actually to become the president. He served as a commissioner in bankruptcy until removed by President Jefferson (who later, disingenuously, denied any knowledge of this petty act against the son of his predecessor). After service in the Massachusetts state legislature, John Quincy was sent to the United States Senate in 1803. As senator, he showed a complete independence of party, supporting Jefferson's Embargo Act. Consequently "the Republicans trampled upon the Federalists, and the Federalists trampled upon John Quincy Adams."

Personally, John Quincy was esteemed but not much liked. He himself liked neither political party: "between both, I see the impossibility of pursuing the dictates of my own conscience, without sacrificing every prospect, not merely of advancement, but even of retaining that character and reputation I have enjoyed. Yet my own choice is made, and if I cannot hope to give satisfaction to my country, I am at least determined to have the approbation of my own reflections."

But presently John Quincy gave satisfaction both to country and self. After losing his seat in the Senate, he served four years as President Madison's minister to Russia during the War of 1812. Czar Alexander took to John Quincy and kept open Russian ports to American shipping. In 1812 John Quincy Adams was appointed

*John Quincy Adams: A Personal History of an Independent Man (Macmillan, 1972).

one of the commissioners to make peace with England, the meetings to be held at Ghent.

Among the other four commissioners were the brilliant Albert Gallatin, Geneva-born secretary of the treasury to Jefferson, and the rising Kentucky lawyer and quadrennial presidential candidate Henry Clay. They shared the same house in Ghent. Clay wanted to sit up all night and gamble while Adams liked to go to bed at nine; wild oats seem never to have been planted (at least visibly) in the garden of any Adams. John Quincy particularly avoided actresses "because," he writes in old age, "the first woman I ever loved was an actress, but I never spoke to her, and I think I never saw her off the stage. . . . Of all the ungratified longings that I ever suffered, that of being acquainted with her, merely to tell her how much I adored her, was the most intense." At the time this Laura and Petrarch were each fourteen years old. The Puritan must suffer or he is not good.

Clay had been as responsible as any American leader for the 1812 war with England (he particularly wanted to annex Canada); consequently, he was quite willing to prolong the war in order "to make us a warlike people." But John Quincy was not a war-lover; he also knew that the English Ministry was unhappy with a war that could not be won, particularly at a time when not only had Castlereagh managed to antagonize both Russia and Prussia but Lord Liverpool's Government was being much criticized for imposing a property tax in order to prosecute a far-off war. On December 24, 1814, the treaty of Ghent was signed. Two weeks later, a wild Tennessee backwoodsman named Andrew Jackson won a mighty victory over English troops at New Orleans. The fact that the war was already over made the victory no less sweet for the humiliated Americans, and the political star of Jackson was now in the ascendant.

Like his father before him, John Quincy Adams was appointed minister to England. For two years the Adamses lived at Ealing; they were pressed for money, which was just as well for they were not much sought after by London society. For one thing, Americans of any kind were less than the vogue; for another, Adamses can never be in vogue. But John Quincy's eye was as sharp as ever. Of Castlereagh he wrote, "His manner was cold, but not absolutely repulsive." He did enjoy Holland House and what intellectual company came his way. Yet he was eager to go home. He feared expatriation—taking on "an European disposi-

tion" and then, returning home, "a stranger in his own country."
Meanwhile, his son Charles Francis Adams was initiated to the
glories and miseries of the English public school, where being an
American was not a passport to gentle treatment.

For some time John Quincy had been a Republican. As early
as 1802, he wrote his brother Tom: "I concur with you in the
opinion that the cause of federalism is irretrievable." The old
Federalist party had indeed fallen apart. Everyone was now a
Republican of one sort or another. The Western leader of the
party was Henry Clay, closely pressed by Andrew Jackson. John
Quincy himself was not a man of locality: "My system of politics
more and more inclines to strengthen the union and the government." Yet when he heard an American jingo say, as a toast, "Our
country, right or wrong," John Quincy responded severely: "I
disclaim all patriotism incompatible with the principles of eternal justice." As far as we know, it never occurred to any Adams
of the Four Generations that there might be no such thing as
eternal justice. The first Adams believed in the Puritan God. The
second was equally devout (until the very end). In the last generations overt religion vanished almost entirely from their voluminous letters and diaries; nevertheless, the idea of eternal justice,
of moral right, of some essential and binding law to the universe
never ceased to order their lives.

President Monroe appointed John Quincy to be his secretary
of state, at that time the second most important office in the land
and the surest way to the presidency. The eight years that John
Quincy served President Monroe were known as the era "of good
feelings." It was indeed a tribute to John Quincy's pronounced
excellence that he was given the post; for Monroe was a Virginian
and the Virginians had governed the United States from the
beginning: Washington, Jefferson, Madison, and Monroe dominated the nation for thirty-six years with only one break, the four
years that John Adams of Massachusetts was president.

John Quincy was not delighted with cabinet life: "There is a
slowness, want of decision, and a spirit of procrastination in the
President, which perhaps arouses more from his situation than
his personal character." Experiencing flak from the ambitious
Clay and his other rivals for the presidency Jackson and Crawford, John Quincy wrote: "My office . . . makes it for the interest
of all the partisans of the candidates for the next Presidency
. . . to decry me as much as possible." "Always complain, but
superbly explain" could be the Adams family motto.

Although John Quincy was generally admired for his intellectual brilliancy and hard work—certainly he was our best secretary of state—he was filled with the usual Adams misgivings. When he gave a reception, he was certain that no one would come. He was afraid of either talking too much or too little. The ladies of the family worried about his shabby appearance. Watery of eye, tremulous of hand, he grew fat, and flatulent. He feared —but finally dared—to eat a peach. With quiet satisfaction, he confided to his diary: "I am a man of reserved, cold, austere and forbidding manners. . . ." He was prone to such solitary pleasures as swimming in the Potomac River, wearing nothing but a black swimming cap and green goggles. Much of the time he was bored by the politicians he had to deal with. But when he was stimulated intellectually, he could be eloquent.

During this period, General Andrew Jackson was on the rampage in the Spanish Floridas, hanging people right and left, including two Englishmen. Yet John Quincy did his best to defend Jackson (a man of whom Jefferson wrote: Now he is *really* crazy!). In the process Adams helped formulate what is known as the Monroe Doctrine—that no European power may interfere in the Western hemisphere while no American government will interfere in Europe. This proud doctrine is still, theoretically, in force although it ceased to have any meaning when the United States went to war with Germany in 1917.

Jackson's filibuster-capers appealed hugely to the electorate and in 1824, under the system of the Electoral College, Jackson received 99 votes for president; Adams, 84; Crawford, 41; Clay, 37. Since no candidate had the required majority, the election went into the House of Representatives for decision. Rightly, Clay feared Jackson, the hero of New Orleans, more than he did John Quincy. Clay gave his support to John Quincy Adams, who became president in February 1825. Clay was then appointed secretary of state. Everyone cried "Foul," and John Quincy was held to be corrupt by all Jackson men and a good many disinterested worthies as well.

Now, once again, there was a President Adams; and he proved to be every bit as wounded in his *amour-propre,* as bitter as the first Adams who wrote from Massachusetts: "My dear son, Never did I feel so much solemnity as upon this occasion. The multitude of my thoughts, and the intensity of my feelings are too much for a mind, like mine, in its 90th year."

The administration of John Quincy Adams proved to be even

more of a disaster (for him) than that of his father. Jackson and his allies were rightly indignant at losing an election in which Jackson had, after all, got the most votes; they also regarded as corrupt the alliance between John Quincy and Clay. Nor did the new president very much like or understand the country he presided over. For one thing, democracy had made a sudden advance with universal suffrage—that is, any free man over twenty-one could now vote. The rule by "the best" was ended once and for all.

John Quincy saw what was coming but he meant to hold the line, and his first inaugural address was a challenge to the democrats: "While foreign nations, less blessed with that freedom which is power than ourselves" (obligatory gesture to Demos) "are advancing with gigantic strides in the career of public improvements, are we to slumber in our indolence or fold up our arms and proclaim to the world that we are *palsied by the will of our constituents?*" There sounded for the last time *ex cathedra presidentis* the voice of the original Inventors of the nation.

John Quincy had great plans to foster education, science, commerce, civil service reform; but his projects were too rigorous and too unpolitical to be accepted. For instance, the United States had not one astronomical station while in Europe there were 130 "lighthouses of the sky." This happy phrase was received with perfect derision by the mob. It was plain that John Quincy was not suited to lead a quasi-democracy. He was too intelligent, too unyielding, too tactless. He also found hard to bear the inanities of political attack (he was supposed to have supplied a lecherous Russian nobleman with an innocent American girl). Needless to say, Jackson swamped him in the next election. The Jackson slogan was prophetic of the era: "Jackson who can fight, and Adams who can write."

But John Quincy saw the future more clearly than most of the mob-pleasing politicians. Of slavery he wrote privately in 1820, it is "an outrage upon the goodness of God." But at the time he stayed clear of the subject because he saw that any challenge to the slave-owning states would lead to the dissolution of the Union. In 1837, after President Jackson's savage treatment of the Creeks and Cherokees, John Quincy wrote: "We have done more harm to the Indians since our Revolution than had been done to them by the French and English nations before. . . . These are crying sins for which we are answerable before a higher Jurisdiction."

"Three days more, and I shall be restored to private life . . . I go into it with a combination of parties and of public men against my character and reputation such as I believe never before was exhibited. . . . " Pure Adams, the self-pity; but not so far off the mark.

Like his father, John Quincy Adams refused to attend the inaugural of his successor. Back in Massachusetts, he started to put his father's papers in order but this bookish task bored him. He was not cut out for libraries and retirement. To the horror of his son Charles Francis Adams, John Quincy "demeaned" himself and went back to Washington as a mere representative to Congress, where he served in the House until his death seventeen years later. As Emerson rather unexpectedly wrote, "Mr. Adams chose wisely and according to his constitution, when, on leaving the presidency, he went into Congress. He is no literary old gentleman, but a bruiser, and he loves the *mélée.* . . . He is an old *roué* who cannot live on slops, but must have sulphuric acid in his tea."

Certainly John Quincy Adams's most useful period was the last when he was obliged to enter the hurly-burly at something of a disadvantage. For one thing, his voice was weak, his manner tentative: "It is so long since I was in the habit of speaking to a popular assembly, and I am so little qualified by nature for an extemporaneous orator, that I was at the time not a little agitated by the sound of my own voice." But he persisted, fighting and eventually winning the battle to admit those petitions against slavery that the House would not for years entertain. He helped create the Smithsonian Institution. He denounced the American conquest of Mexico which added Texas and California to the empire. Then, in the midst of a debate, he collapsed on the floor of the House; he was taken to the Speaker's chambers. On February 23, 1848, he died. Final words: "This is the last of earth. I am composed."

The Third Generation was on the rise. Charles Francis Adams had commited hypergamy in the sense that he was the first Adams to marry a lot of money in the shape of Abigail Brooks, who, according to one of her children, took a "constitutional and sincere pleasure in the forecast of evil. She delighted in the dark side of anticipation." Four of her sons were to be remarkable in the next generation: John Quincy II, Charles Francis II, Henry, and Brooks. Like all the Adamses the sons were voluminous writers and Henry was a writer of genius even though his brother Charles wrote rather better prose. Their father also wrote copiously or, as his son Charles observed glumly, while writing his father's biography: "He took to diary writing early, and he took to it bad." Mark Twain apologized to William Dean Howells for using "three words where one would answer—a thing I am always trying to guard against. I shall become as slovenly a writer as Charles Francis Adams if I don't look out. . . ."

It is during the Fourth Generation that the high moral style of the early and the puissant Adamses is now tinged with irony, that necessary weapon of the powerless. There was to be no more life at the very top for the family but there were still good, even great things to be done.

Of his father Charles Francis Adams, Henry wrote, "[his] memory was hardly above the average; his mind was not bold like his grandfather's or restless like his father's, or imaginative, or oratorical—still less mathematical; but it worked with singular perfection. . . . Within its range it was a model." The range included diplomacy and the by now inevitable family post of minister at London. Charles Francis was minister during the difficult years 1861–1868 when a powerful movement in England favored the Confederacy for reasons both sentimental and practical. The despised colonies of four-score years before had now become a predatory and dangerous empire, filling up the North American continent and threatening, by its existence, the British Empire. The vision of the United States split into two countries brought roses to many a cheek both on the government and the opposition benches.

Adams went about his work of keeping England neutral with that coolness which had caused a political associate to describe him as "the greatest Iceberg in the Northern Hemisphere." Or as this solemn gelidity himself put it: "My practice has been never to manifest feeling of any kind, either of elation or of depression. In this, some Englishmen have taken occasion to intimate that I have been thought quite successful."

Paradoxically, much of the pro-Southern sentiment in England came from those who abominated the peculiar institution of slavery. Although they disapproved of the slave-holding South, they saw Lincoln as a ruthless despot, trying to hold together by force a union that was constitutionally based on the right of any state to leave that union when it chose. Lincoln was never, to say the least, devoted to the abolition of slavery; and not until the third year of the war to preserve the union did he free the slaves in the

Confederacy (slaves were not freed in those states that had not seceded). Consequently Charles Francis was forced to listen to much sharp criticism from high-minded anti-slave Englishmen while his son Henry (acting as the minister's secretary) was denounced in the street for Lincoln's wickedness by Thackeray.

The chief crisis in Anglo-American relations during Charles Francis's ministry was the *Alabama* affair. The *Alabama* was a formidable warship built at Liverpool for the South. Charles Francis maintained that if the English allowed such a ship to be built and armed, they automatically ceased to be neutral. Foreign Secretary Lord John Russell asked for proof of the ship's ultimate use. When this was provided, the attorney general supported Charles Francis and recommended that the ship be seized. But by then the *Alabama* had sailed. The American minister then proceeded to keep careful count of each ship sunk by the *Alabama* in the course of the war and later saw to it that England paid the bill.

When another ship destined for the Confederacy was ready to go to sea and Lord John seemed unwilling to stop it, Charles Francis played the diplomat's ultimate card: "it would be superfluous in me to point out to your lordship that this is war." Three days later Lord John seized the Southern warships.

Now the focus shifts to the Fourth Generation. Henry Adams in his autobiography writes a good deal about his formative years in London as his father's secretary. Although there is little doubt that Henry inherited the family passion to be the first in the nation, it was already plain to him that the plutocratic-democracy was not apt to take well to one with such an "education." The age of the robber barons was now in full swing. Shysters like Jay Gould and Jim Fisk controlled the economic life of the country, buying and selling members of Congress—and presidents, too. Although Henry's father was, from time to time, mentioned for president, no one ever took very seriously this brilliant, cold man who spoke French better than English.

Of the four sons of Charles Francis only John Quincy II got into elective politics. And failed. Just as he failed to get out from under the weight of the family's intellectual tradition by, among other things, abandoning "the vile family habit of preserving letters."

The second son Charles Francis II was a marvelous scribbler; also, a man of action. After examining in detail the misdeeds of the railroad tycoons (published in a volume called *Chapters of Erie*, with several essays by his brother Henry), he himself became a railroad tycoon and president of the Union Pacific. The next brother, Henry, was to write the finest of American histories as well as one of our few good political novels. The youngest brother, Brooks, was also a writer very much in the Adams (by now) highly pessimistic vein. In fact, it is he who rather gives the game away with the title he chose for a posthumous edition of some of his brother Henry's essays, *The Degradation of the Democratic Dogma.*

I cannot remember when I was not fascinated by Henry Adams. I was brought up in Washington; belonged to a political family; and used often to pass the site of the house where Adams had lived in Lafayette Park, just opposite the White House.

Once I asked Eleanor Roosevelt if she had known Henry Adams, who died in 1918. "Oh, yes! He was such a kind man, so good with the children. They would crawl all over him when he sat in his victoria. He was very . . . tolerant. But," and she frowned, "we did *not* agree politically. I remember the first time we went to his house. My Franklin had just come to Washington" (as assistant secretary of the navy) "and I of course was very shy then and could never get the courage to speak up, particularly with someone so much older. Well, my Franklin made some remark about President Wilson, about how well he was doing. And Mr. Adams just laughed at him and pointed toward the White House and said, 'Young man, it doesn't make the slightest difference who lives in that house, history goes on with or without the president.' Well, I just couldn't keep quiet. 'Mr. Adams,' I said, 'that is a very terrible thing to say to a young man who wants to go into politics and be of use to other people.' Oh, I made quite a speech."

"And what did Mr. Adams say?"

"I can't remember. I think he just laughed at me. We were always good friends."

So the great Adams line ended with a theory of history that eliminated Carlyle's hero and put in its stead something like Hegel's "course of the divine life." Yet one can see from the beginning the family's dependency on fate, on some inscrutable power at work in the universe which raised men up or cut them down, and guided nations. At the beginning this was, plainly, the work of the Puritan God. Later, when that god failed, it was simply energy or "the Dynamo," as Henry Adams called those "secret invisible Laws of Nature" that hurl this petty race through time and spinning space.

There was more than a degree of sourness in Henry's old age; after all, he was living across the park from the White House where grandfather and great-grandfather had presided. As compensation, his beautiful memoir is filled with a good deal of mock humility, confessions of "failure," and a somewhat overwrought irony. "I like [Henry]," wrote Henry James, "but suffer from his monotonous, disappointed pessimism. . . . However, when the poor dear is in London, I don't fail to do what I can." Luckily, the Master never read the diary of Mrs. Henry Adams: "high time Harry James was ordered home by his family." She thought "if he wants to make a lasting literary reputation," he must settle in Cheyenne and "run a hog ranch."

But, politically, Henry Adams was not without influence; his best friend and next-door neighbor was that most literary of secretaries of state John Hay, while Adams himself was always at the center of the capital's intellectual life. Invitations to his house were much sought after; yet he "called on no one and never left a card." Henry James in a short story set in Washington describes a distinguished figure based on Henry Adams. As the character draws up a guest list for a party, he says, finally, wearily: "Well, why not be vulgar? Let us ask the President."

Henry Adams was remarkably prescient about the coming horrors; like his mother he anticipated the worst. Before the First World War, he prophesied the decline of England and France, and the rise of the United States, Russia and Germany. But in the long run, he felt that Germany was too small a power "to swing the club." Ultimately, he saw the world in two blocs: the east dominated by Russia; the west dominated by the United States. He also predicted that should Russia and China ever come together "the result will be a single mass which no amount of force could possibly deflect." He predicted that this great mass would be both socialist and despotic; and its only counterbalance would be an "Atlantic combine," stretching from "the Rocky Mountains on the west to the Elbe on the east." Henry Adams always used what influence he had to try to persuade the various American administrations to bring Russia into our sphere of influence.

The last days of Henry Adams were spent trying to understand the forces that control history. He wanted an equivalent in history to Einstein's never-to-be-found unified field theory. The best Henry Adams could come up with was a chapter of the memoir called "A Dynamic Theory of History"; and it was not enough. Finally, Adams abandoned history altogether. "I don't give a damn what happened," he wrote, "what I want to know is why it happened—never could find out—stopped writing history."

How would John Adams have responded to such despair? In his college diary he copied out *Contemptu Famae, Contemni Virtutem,* which he translated as "A Contempt of Fame generally begets or accompanies a Contempt of Virtue." And then he adds: "Iago makes the reflection that Fame is but breath, but vibrated Air, an empty sound. And I believe Persons of his Character are most inclined to feel and express such an Indifference about fame." No Adams was ever, to himself, truly famous and so all Adamses thought themselves used poorly by fate. But then from the beginning they set themselves intellectual and moral standards that no one could live up to. With Puritan vigor they positively insisted on noble failure in a society that has always been devoted to easy, crass success. So let us, late in the day as it is, praise such famous men.

The New York Review of Books
March 18 and April 1, 1976

President and
Mrs. U.S. Grant

S ome years ago a friend remarked to a brand-new President's
wife (a woman of unique charm, wit, sensibility, and good
grooming) that there was no phrase in our language which so sets
the teeth on edge as "First Lady."

"Oh, how true!" said that lady, after the tiniest of pauses. "I
keep telling the operators at the White House not to call me that,
but they just love saying 'First Lady.' And of course Mrs. E
+ + + + + + + + +r always insisted on being called that."

According to one Ralph Geoffrey Newman, in a note to the
recently published *The Personal Memoirs of Julia Dent Grant*, "the
term 'First Lady' became a popular one after the *Lady in the Land*
. . . December 4, 1911." The phrase was in use, however, as early
as the Ladyhood of Mrs. Rutherford B. ("Lemonade Lucy")
Hayes.

Martha Washington contented herself with the unofficial
(hence seldom omitted) title "Lady" Washington. Mrs. James
Monroe took a crack at regal status, receiving guests on a dais
with something suspiciously like a coronet in her tousled hair.

When twenty-four-year-old Miss Julia Gardiner of Gardiners Island became the doting wife of senior citizen John Tyler, she insisted that his stately arrivals and departures be accompanied by the martial chords of "Hail to the Chief." Mary Todd Lincoln often gave the impression that she thought she was Marie Antoinette.

It is curious that a Johnny-come-fairly-lately republic like the United States should so much want to envelop in majesty those for the most part seedy political hacks quadrennially "chosen" by the people to rule over them. As the world's royalties take to their bicycles—or to their heels—the world's presidents from Giscard to Leone to our own dear sovereign affect the most splendid state.

It would seem to be a rule of history that as the actual power of a state declines, the pageantry increases. Certainly the last days of the Byzantine empire were marked by a court protocol so elaborate and time-consuming that the arrival of the Turks must have been a relief to everyone. Now, as our own imperial republic moves gorgeously into its terminal phase, it is pleasant and useful to contemplate two centuries of American court life, to examine those personages who have lived in the White House and borne those two simple but awful titles "The President," "The First Lady" and, finally, to meditate on that peculiarly American religion, President-worship.

The Eighteenth President Ulysses Simpson Grant and his First Lady Julia Dent Grant are almost at dead center of that solemn cavalcade which has brought us from Washington to Ford, and in the process made a monkey of Darwin. Since 1885 we have had Grant's own memoirs to study; unfortunately, they end with the Civil War and do not deal with his presidency. Now Julia Dent Grant's memoirs have been published for the first time and, as that ubiquitous clone of Parson Weems Mr. Bruce Catton says in his introduction, she comes through these pages as a most "likeable" woman. "No longer is she just Mrs. Grant. Now she has three dimensions."

From her own account Julia Dent Grant does seem to have been a likeable, rather silly woman, enamored of First Ladyhood (and why not?), with a passion for clothes. If photographs are to be trusted (and why should they be when our Parson Weemses never accept as a fact anything that might obscure those figures illuminated by the high noon of Demos?), Julia was short and dumpy, with quite astonishingly crossed eyes. As divinity in the form of First Ladyhood approached, Julia wanted to correct with surgery nature's error but her husband very nicely said that since he had married her with crossed eyes he preferred her to stay the way she was. In any case, whatever the number of Julia's dimensions, she is never anything but Mrs. Grant and one reads her only to find out more about that strange enigmatic figure who proved to be one of our country's best generals and worst presidents.

Grant was as much a puzzle to contemporaries as he is to us now. To Henry Adams, Grant was "pre-intellectual, archaic, and would have seemed so even to the cave-dwellers." Henry Adams's brother had served with Grant in the war and saw him in a somewhat different light. "He is a man of the most exquisite judgment and tact," wrote Charles Francis Adams. But "he might pass well enough for a dumpy and slouchy little subaltern, very fond of smoking." C. F. Adams saw Grant at his best, in the field; H. Adams saw him at his worst, in the White House.

During Grant's first forty years of relative failure, he took to the bottle. When given command in the war, he seems to have pretty much given up the booze (though there was a bad tumble not only off the wagon but off his horse at New Orleans). According to Mr. Bruce Catton, "It was widely believed that [Grant], especially during his career as a soldier, was much too fond of whiskey, and that the cure consisted in bringing Mrs. Grant to camp; in her presence, it was held, he instantly became a teetotaler. . . . This contains hardly a wisp of truth." It never does out there in Parson Weems land where all our presidents were good and some were great and none ever served out his term without visibly growing in the office. One has only to listen to Rabbi Korff to know that this was true even of Richard M. Nixon. Yet there is every evidence that General Grant not only did not grow in office but dramatically shrank.

The last year of Grant's life was the noblest, and the most terrible. Dying of cancer, wiped out financially by a speculator, he was obliged to do what he had always said he had no intention of doing: write his memoirs in order to provide for his widow. He succeeded admirably. The two volumes entitled *Personal Memoirs of U.S. Grant* earned $450,000; and Julia Grant was able to live in comfort for the seventeen years that she survived her husband. Now for the first time we can compare Grant's memoirs with those of his wife.

With the instinct of one who knows what the public wants (or ought to get), Grant devoted only thirty-one pages to his humble youth in Ohio. The prose is Roman—lean, rather flat, and, cumulatively, impressive. Even the condescending Matthew Arnold allowed that Grant had "the high merit of saying clearly in the fewest possible words what had to be said, and saying it, frequently, with shrewd and unexpected turns of expression." There is even a quiet wit that Grant's contemporaries were not often allowed to see: "Boys enjoy the misery of their companies, at least village boys in that day did" (this is known as the Eisenhower qualification: is it taught at West Point? in order to confuse the press?), "and in later life I have found that all adults are not free from this peculiarity."

The next 161 pages are devoted to West Point and to Grant's early career as a professional army officer. Grant's eyes did not fill with tears at the thought of his school days on the banks of the Hudson. In fact, he hated the Academy: "Early in the session of the Congress which met in December, 1839, a bill was discussed abolishing the Military Academy. I saw this as an honorable way to obtain a discharge . . . for I was selfish enough to favor the bill." But the Academy remained, as it does today, impregnable to any Congress.

On graduation, Second Lieutenant Grant was posted to Jefferson Barracks, St. Louis, where, he noted, "too many of the older officers, when they came to command posts, made it a study to think what orders they could publish to annoy their subordinates and render them uncomfortable."

Grant also tells us, rather casually, that "At West Point I had a classmate . . . F.T. Dent, whose family resides some five miles west of Jefferson Barracks . . . ." The sister of the classmate was Julia Dent, aged seventeen. According to Grant, visits to the Dent household were "enjoyable." "We would often take long walks, or go on horseback to visit the neighbors. . . . Sometimes one of the brothers would accompany us, sometimes one of the younger sisters."

In May 1844, when it came time to move on (the administration was preparing an interdiction or incursion of Mexico), Grant writes: "before separating [from Julia] it was definitely understood that at a convenient time we would join our fortunes. . . ." Then Grant went off to his first war. Offhandedly, he gives us what I take to be the key if not to his character to his success: "One of my superstitions had always been when I started to go any where, or to do anything, not to turn back, or stop until the thing intended was accomplished." This defines not only a certain sort of military genius but explains field-commander Grant who would throw wave after wave of troops into battle, counting on superior numbers to shatter the enemy while himself ignoring losses.

When Henry Adams met Grant at the White House, he came away appalled by the torpor, the dullness of the sort of man "always needing stimulants, but for whom action was the highest stimulant—the instinct of fight. Such men were forces of nature, energies of the prime. . . ." This was of course only partly true of Grant. Unlike so many American jingoes, Grant did not like war for its own bloody self or conquest for conquest's sake. Of the administration's chicanery leading up to the invasion of Mexico, he wrote with hard clarity, "I was bitterly opposed to the measure, and to this day regard the war, which resulted, as one of the most unjust ever waged by a stronger against a weaker nation. . . . It was an instance of a republic following the bad example of European monarchies, in not considering justice in their desire to acquire additional territory."

Grant also had a causal sense of history that would have astonished Henry Adams had he got to know the taciturn and corrupted, if not corrupt, president. Of the conquest of Mexico and the annexation of Texas, Grant wrote, "To us it was an empire and of incalculable value; but it might have been obtained by other means. The Southern rebellion was largely the outgrowth of the Mexican War. Nations, like individuals, are punished for their transgressions. We got our punishment in the most sanguinary and expensive war of modern times." If Grant's law still obtains, then the only hope for today's American is emigration.

The Grant of those youthful years seems most engaging (but then we are reading his own account). He says firmly, "I do not believe that I ever would have the courage to fight a duel." He was probably unique among military commanders in disliking dirty stories while "I am not aware of ever having used a profane expletive in my life; but I would have the charity to excuse those who may have done so, if they were in charge of a train of Mexican pack mules. . . ."

Grant saw right through the Mexican war, which "was a political war, and the administration conducting it desired to make party capital of it." Grant was also very much on to the head of the army General Scott, who was "known to have political aspirations, and nothing so popularizes a candidate for high civil positions as military victories." It takes one, as they say, to know another.

Mark Twain published Grant's memoirs posthumously, and one wonders if he might have added a joke or two. Some possible Twainisms: "My regiment lost four commissioned officers, all senior to me, by steamboat explosions during the Mexican war. The Mexicans were not so discriminating. They sometimes picked off my juniors." The cadence of those sentences reveals an expert sense of music-hall timing. When a Mexican priest refused to let Grant use his church during an engagement, Grant threatened the priest with arrest. Immediately, the man "began to see his duty in the same light that I did, and opened the door, though he did not look as if it gave him any special pleasure to do so." But whether or not Twain helped with the jokes, it must be remembered that the glum, often silent, always self-pitying president was capable, when he chose, of the sharp remark. Told that the brilliant but inordinately vain *littérateur* Senator Charles Sumner did not believe in the Bible, Grant said, "That's only because he didn't write it."

The Mexican war ended, and "On the twenty-second of August, 1848, I was married to Miss Julia Dent Grant, the lady of whom I have before spoken." With that Caesarian line, the lady appears no more in the two volumes dedicated to the fighting of the Civil War. Now Julia's memoirs redress the balance.

In old age, Julia put pen to paper and gave her own version of her life and marriage, but for one reason or another she could never get the book published. Now, at last, her memoirs are available, suitably loaded with a plangent introduction by Mr. Catton ("they shared one of the great, romantic, beautiful loves of all American history"), a note by R.G. Newman on "The First Lady as an Author," and a foreword and notes by J.Y. Simon. The notes are excellent and instructive.

In her last years Julia was not above hawking her manuscript to millionaire acquaintances; at one point she offered the manuscript to book-lover Andrew Carnegie for $125,000. Just why the book was never published is obscure. I suspect Julia wanted too much money for it; also, as she wrote in a letter, the first readers of the text thought it *"too* near, *too* close to the private life of the

Genl for the public, and I thought this was just what was wanted." Julia was right; and her artless narrative does give a new dimension (if not entirely the third) to one of the most mysterious (because so simple?) figures in our history.

"My first recollections in life reach back a long way, more than three-score years, and ten now. We, my gentle mother and two little brothers, were on the south end of the front piazza at our old home, White Haven." Julia sets us down firmly in Margaret Mitchell country. "Life seemed one long summer of sunshine, flowers, and smiles to me and to all at that happy home." Mamma came from "a large eastern city," and did not find it easy being "a western pioneer's wife." The darkies were happy as can be (this was slave-holding Missouri) and "I think our people were very happy. At least they were in mamma's time, though the young ones became somewhat demoralized about the beginning of the Rebellion, when all the comforts of slavery passed away forever."

Julia was obviously much indulged. "Coming as I did to the family after the fourth great boy, I was necessarily something of a pet. . . . It was always 'Will little daughter like to do this?' 'No!' Then little daughter did not do it." I suspect that little daughter's alarmingly crossed eyes may have made the family overprotective. She herself seems unaware of any flaw: "Imagine what a pet I was with my three, brave, handsome brothers." She was also indulged in school where she was good in philosophy (what could that have been?), mythology, and history, but "in every other branch I was below the standard, and, worse still, my indifference was very exasperating." Although Julia enjoys referring to herself as "poor little me," she sounds like a pretty tough customer.

Enter Lieutenant Grant. Julia's description of their time together is considerably richer than that of the great commander. "Such delightful rides we all used to take!" So far her account tallies with his. But then, I fear, Julia falls victim to prurience: "As we sat on the piazza alone, he took his class ring from his finger and asked me if I would not wear it. . . . I declined, saying, 'Oh, no, mamma would not approve . . . !'" "I, child that I was, never for a moment thought of him as a lover." He goes. "Oh! how lonely it was without him." "I remember he was kind enough to make a nice little coffin for my canary bird and he painted it yellow. About eight officers attended the funeral of my little pet." When Grant came back to visit, Julia told him "that

I had named one of my new bedstead posts for him." Surely the good taste of the editor might have spared us this pre-Freudian pornography. In any case, after this shocker, Julia was obliged to marry Grant . . . or "Ulys" as she called him.

"Our station at Detroit is one pleasant memory . . . gay parties and dinners, the fêtes champêtres. . . . Our house was very snug and convenient: two sitting rooms, dining room, bedroom, and kitchen all on the first floor." (And all of this on a captain's pay). Julia's especial friend that winter was the wife of Major John H. Gore. Together they gave a fancy dress ball on a Sunday, invoking the wrath of the Sabbatarians. But the girls persisted and Mrs. Gore came as the Sultana of Turkey while "I, after much consideration, decided upon the costume of the ideal tambourine girl. . . . Ulys called me 'Tambourina' for a long time afterwards."

But then Grant left the army; and the descent began. "I was now to commence," he wrote, "at the age of thirty-two, a new struggle for our support." Like most professional army men Grant was fitted for no work of any kind save the presidency and that was not yet in the cards. "My wife had a farm near St. Louis, to which we went, but I had no means to stock it." Nevertheless, "I managed to keep along very well until 1858, when I was attacked by fever and ague." Perhaps he was; he was also attacked by acute alcoholism.

But the innumerable clones of Parson Weems tend to ignore any blemish on our national heroes. And Julia does her part, too. She writes, "I have been both indignant and grieved over the statement of pretended personal acquaintances of Captain Grant at this time to the effect that he was dejected, low-spirited, badly dressed, and even slovenly." "Low-spirited" is a nice euphemism for full of spirits. Julia had the Southern woman's loyalty to kin: protect at all costs and ignore the unpleasant. She even goes beyond her husband's dour record, declaring, "Ulys was really very successful at farming . . . and I was a splendid farmer's wife."

Julia's family loyalty did not extend to Ulys's folks. Although Ulys and the Dent family could do no wrong, the Grants were generally exempted from her benign policy. In fact, Julia loathed them. "I was joyous at the thought of not going to Kentucky, for the Captain's family, with the exception of his mother, did not like me. . . . we were brought up in different schools. They considered me unpardonably extravagant, and I considered them inexcusably the other way and may, unintentionally, have shown my feelings." There were also political disagreements between the two families as the Civil War approached. The Dents were essentially Southern, and Julia "was a Democrat at that time (because my father was). . . . I was very much disturbed in my political sentiments, feeling that the states had a right to go out of the Union if they wished to." But she also thought that the Union should be preserved. "Ulys was much amused at my enthusiasm and said I was a little inconsistent when I talked of states' rights."

With the coming of the Civil War, the lives of the Grants were never again to be private. Rapidly he rose from Illinois colonel (they had moved to Galena) to lieutenant general in command of the Union forces. The victories were splendid. Julia had anxious moments, not to mention innumerable prophetic dreams which she solemnly records.

At one point, separated from the General, "I wept like a deserted child . . . Only once again in my life—when I left the White House—did this feeling of desertion come over me." There were also those unremitting base rumors. Why, "The report went out," on some crucial occasion, "that General Grant was not in the field, that he was at some dance house. The idea! Dear Ulys! so earnest and serious; he never went to a party of any kind, except to take me." Julia's usual euphemism for the drunken bouts was "he was ill." And she always helped him get well.

Grant was not above making fun of her. Julia: "Ulys, I don't like standing stationary washstands, do you?" Ulys: "Yes, I do; why don't you?" Julia: "Well, I don't know." Ulys: "I'll tell you why. You have to go to the stand. It cannot be brought to you."

Midway through the war, some Southern friends were talking of "the Constitution, telling me the action of the government was unconstitutional. Well, I did not know a thing about this dreadful Constitution and told them so. . . . I would not know where to look for it even if I wished to read it. . . . I was dreadfully puzzled about the horrid old Constitution." She even asked her father: "Why don't they make a new Constitution since this is such an enigma—one to suit the time." I suspect Julia was pretty much reflecting her husband's lifelong contempt for a Constitution that he saw put aside in the most casual way by Abraham Lincoln, who found habeas corpus incompatible with national security. But although neither Grant nor Julia was very strong on the Bill of Rights, she at least had a good PR sense. When "General Grant wrote that obnoxious order expelling the Jews from his lines for which he was so severely reprimanded by the federal Congress —the General said deservedly so, as he had no right to make an order against any special sect."

In triumph, Julia came east after Ulys assumed command of the armies. Julia was enchanted by the White House and President Lincoln, in that order. Mrs. Lincoln appears to have been on her worst behavior and Julia has a hard time glossing over a number of difficult moments. On one occasion, Julia plumped herself down beside the First Lady. Outraged, Mrs. Lincoln is alleged to have said, "How dare you be seated, until I invite you?" Julia denies that this ever happened. But she does describe a day in the field when Mrs. Lincoln was upset by a mounted lady who seemed to be trying to ride beside President Lincoln. As one reads, in the vast spaces between the lines of Julia's narrative, it would seem that Mrs. Lincoln went absolutely bananas, "growing more and more indignant and not being able to control her wrath. . . ." But, fortunately, Julia was masterful—"I quietly placed my hand on hers"—and was soothing.

Later, when the presidential yacht was in the James River, close to Grant's headquarters, Julia confesses that "I saw very little of the presidential party now, as Mrs. Lincoln had a good deal of company and seemed to have forgotten us. I felt this deeply and could not understand it. . . . Richmond had fallen; so had Petersburg. All of these places were visited by the President and party, and I, not a hundred yards from them, was not invited to join them."

Despite the dresses, the dreams, the self-serving silly-little-me talk, Julia has a sharp eye for detail; describing Richmond, the last capital of the Confederacy, she writes: "I remember that all the streets near the public buildings were covered with papers— public documents and letters, I suppose. So many of these papers lay on the ground that they reminded me of the forest leaves when summer is gone."

Although Grant ignores such details he is shrewd not only about his colleagues but about his former colleagues, the West Pointers who led the Confederate army. He writes of Jefferson Davis with whom he had served in Mexico: "Mr. Davis had an exalted opinion of his own military genius. . . . On several occasions during the war he came to the relief of the Union army by means of his superior *military genius.*" Grant also makes the

Cromwellian assertion: "It is men who wait to be selected, and not those who seek, from whom we may always expect the most efficient service."

Although never a Lincoln man in politics, Grant came to like the President, and would listen respectfully to Lincoln's strategic proposals, refraining from pointing out their glaring flaws. Grant also took seriously Secretary of War Stanton's injunction never to tell Lincoln his plans in advance because the President is "so kind-hearted, so averse to refusing anything asked of him, that some friend would be sure to get from him all he knew." Lincoln was plainly aware of this defect because he "told me he did not want to know what I proposed to do."

At about this time the press that was to be Grant's constant, lifelong *bête noir* began to get on his nerves. *The New York Times* was a particular offender; grimly, Grant remarked on that portion of the press which "always magnified rebel successes and belittled ours." In fact, "the press was free up to the point of treason."

Grant had great respect for the Confederate army, and in retrospect lauded the Fabian tactics of General J. E. Johnston on the ground that "anything that could have prolonged the war a year beyond the time that it did finally close, would probably have exhausted the North to such an extent that they might then have abandoned the contest and agreed to a separation." Because "the South was a military camp, controlled absolutely by the government with soldiers to back it . . . the war could have been protracted, no matter to what extent the discontent reached. . . ." One suspects that if Grant had been the president, he would have shut down the press, sent Congress home, and made the North an armed camp.

Grant had much the same lifelong problem with the "horrid old Constitution" that Julia had. Magisterially, he writes, "The Constitution was not framed with a view to any such rebellion as that of 1861–5. While it did not authorize rebellion it made no provision against it. Yet the right to resist or suppress rebellion is as inherent as the right of self defense. . . ." Accepting this peculiar view of that intricate document, Grant noted with some satisfaction that "the Constitution was therefore in abeyance for the time being, so far as it in any way affected the progress and termination of the war." During Grant's presidency, the Constitution was simply an annoyance to be circumvented whenever possible. Or as he used to say when he found himself, as president, blocked by mere law: "Let the law be executed."

On that day when lilacs in the dooryard bloomed, Julia was in Washington preparing to go with Grant to Philadelphia. At noon, a peculiar-looking man rapped on her door. " 'Mrs. Lincoln sends me, Madam, with her compliments, to say she will call for you at exactly eight o'clock to go to the theater.' To this, I replied with some feeling (not liking either the looks of the messenger or the message, thinking the former savored of discourtesy and the latter seemed like a command), 'You may return with my compliments to Mrs. Lincoln and say I regret that as General Grant and I intend leaving the city this afternoon, we will not, therefore, be here. . . .'"

It is nice to speculate that if Mrs. Lincoln had asked Julia aboard the yacht that day in the James River, there might never have been a Grant administration. Julia has her own speculation: "I am perfectly sure that he [the messenger], with three others, one of them [John Wilkes] Booth himself, sat opposite me and my party at luncheon."

That night in Philadelphia they heard the news. "I asked, 'This will make Andy Johnson President, will it not?' 'Yes,' the General said, 'and for some reason, I dread the change.' " Nobly, Julia did her duty: "With my heart full of sorrow, I went many times to call on dear heart-broken Mrs. Lincoln, but she could not see me."

After commanding the armies in peacetime and behaving not too well during that impasse between President Johnson and Secretary of War Stanton which led to Johnson's impeachment, Grant was himself elected president. Although, unhappily, Grant's own memoirs stop with the war, Julia's continue gaily, haphazardly, and sometimes nervously through that gilded age at whose center these two odd little creatures presided.

Until our own colorful period, nothing quite like the Grant administration had ever happened to the imperial republic. In eight years almost everyone around Grant was found to be corrupt from his first vice president Colefax to his brother-in-law to his private secretary to his secretary of war to his minister to Great Britain; the list is endless. Yet the people forgave the solemn little man who had preserved the Union and then proposed himself to a grateful nation with the phrase "Let us have peace."

Grant was re-elected president in 1872, despite a split in the

Republican party: the so-called Liberal Republicans supported Horace Greeley as did the regular Democrats. Although the second term was even more scandalous than the first, the Grants were eager for yet a third term. But the country was finally fed up with Grantism. In the centennial summer of 1876, at the Philadelphia exhibition, President Grant had the rare experience of being booed in public. Julia does not mention the booing. But she does remember that the Empress of Brazil was asked to start the famous Corliss engine, while "I, the wife of the President of the United States—I, the wife of General Grant—was there and was not invited to assist at this little ceremony. . . . Of this I am quite sure: if General Grant had known of this intended slight to his wife, the engine never would have moved with his assistance."

Nevertheless, after four years out of office General and Mrs. Grant were again eager to return to the White House, to "the dear old house. . . . Eight happy years I spent there," wrote Julia, "so happy! It still seems as much like home to me as the old farm in Missouri, White Haven." But it looked rather different from the farm or, for that matter, from the way the White House has usually looked. By the time Mrs. Grant had finished her refurbishments, the East Room was divided into three columned sections and filled with furniture of ebony and gold. Julia was highly pleased with her creation; in fact, "I have visited many courts and, I am proud to say, I saw none that excelled in brilliancy the receptions of President Grant."

Except for a disingenuous account of the secretary of war's impeachment (his wife "Puss' Belknap was a favorite of Julia's), the First Lady herself hardly alludes to the scandals of those years. On the other hand, Julia describes in rapturous detail her trip around the world with Ulys. In London dinner was given them by the Duke of Wellington at Apsley House. "This great house was presented to Wellington by the government for the single [*sic*] victory at Waterloo, along with wealth and a noble title which will descend throughout his line. As I sat there, I thought, 'How would it have been if General Grant had been an Englishman—I wonder, I wonder?' "

So did Grant. Constantly. In fact, he became obsessed by the generosity of England to Marlborough and to Wellington and by the niggardliness of the United States to its unique savior. It is possible that Grant's corruption in office stems from this resentment; certainly, he felt that he had every right to take expensive

presents from men who gained thereby favors. Until ruined by
a speculator-friend of his son, Grant seems to have acquired a
fortune; although nowhere near as large as that of the master-
criminal Lyndon Johnson, it was probably larger than that of
another receiver of rich men's gifts, General Eisenhower.

Circling the globe, the vigorous Grant enjoyed sightseeing and
Julia enjoyed shopping. There was culture, too: at Heidelberg
"we remained there all night and listened with pleasure to Wagner or Liszt—I cannot remember which—who performed several
of his own delightful pieces of music for us." (It was Wagner.) "Of
course, we visited the Taj and admired it as everyone does.
. . . Everyone says it is the most beautiful building in the world,
and I suppose it is. Only I think that everyone has not seen the
Capitol at Washington!" It is no accident that General Grant's
favorite book was *Innocents Abroad.* After nearly two years, Mag-
gie and Jiggs completed the grand tour, and came home with
every hope of returning to the "dear old house" in Washington.

A triumphal progress across the States began on the West Coast
(it was Grant's misfortune never to have become what he had
wanted to be ever since his early years in the army, a Californian).
Then they returned to their last official home, Galena, Illinois,
"To Galena, dear Galena, where we were at home again in reality," writes Julia. Then "after a week's rest, we went to Chicago."
The Grants were effete Easterners now, and Galena was no more
than a place from which to regain the heights. "We were at
Galena when the Republican Convention met at Chicago . . . I did
not feel that General Grant would be nominated. . . . The General
would not believe, but I saw it plainly." Julia was right, and
James A. Garfield was nominated and elected.

Galena was promptly abandoned for a handsome house in New
York City's East 66th Street. The Grants' days were halcyon until
that grim moment when Grant cried out while eating a peach: he
thought that something had stung him in the throat. It was cancer. The Grants were broke, and now the General was dying.
Happily, various magnates like the Drexels and the Vanderbilts
were willing to help out. But Grant was too proud for overt
charity. Instead he accepted Mark Twain's offer to write his
memoirs. And so, "General Grant, commander-in-chief of 1,000,-
000 men, General Grant, eight years President of the United
States, was writing, writing of his own grand deeds, recording
them that he might leave a home and independence to his fam-

ily." On July 19, 1885, Grant finished the book, "and on the morning of July the twenty-third, he, my beloved, my all, passed away, and I was alone, alone."

In *Patriotic Gore* Edmund Wilson writes: "It was the age of the audacious confidence man, and Grant was the incurable sucker. He easily fell victim to their [*sic*] trickery and allowed them to betray him into compromising his office because he could not believe that such people existed." This strikes me as all wrong. I think Grant knew exactly what was going on. For instance, when Grant's private secretary General Babcock was indicted for his part in the Whisky Ring, the President, with Nixonian zeal, gave a false deposition attesting to Babcock's character. Then Grant saw to it that the witnesses for the prosecution would not, as originally agreed, be granted exemption for testifying. When this did not inhibit the United States Attorney handling the suit, Grant fired him in mid-case: obstruction of justice in spades.

More to the point, it is simply not possible to read Grant's memoirs without realizing that the author is a man of first-rate intelligence. As president, he made it his policy to be cryptic and taciturn, partly in order not to be bored by the politicians (and from the preening Charles Sumner to the atrocious Roscoe Conkling it was an age of insufferable megalomaniacs, so nicely described by Henry Adams in *Democracy*) and partly not to give the game away. After all, everyone was on the take. Since an ungrateful nation had neglected to give him a Blenheim palace, Grant felt perfectly justified in consorting with such crooks as Jim Fisk and Jay Gould, and profiting from their crimes.

Neither in war nor in peace did Grant respect the "horrid old Constitution." This disrespect led to such bizarre shenanigans as Babcock's deal to buy and annex to the United States the unhappy island of Santo Domingo, the Treasury's money to be divvied up between Babcock and the Dominican president (and, perhaps, Grant, too). Fortunately, Grant was saved from this folly by cabinet and Congress. Later, in his memoirs, he loftily justifies the caper by saying that Santo Domingo would have been a nice place to put the former slaves.

Between Lincoln and Grant the original American republic of states united in free association was jettisoned. From the many states they forged one union, a centralized nation-state devoted to the acquisition of wealth and territory by any means. Piously, they spoke of the need to eliminate slavery but, as Grant remarked to Prince Bismarck, the real struggle *"in the beginning"* was to preserve the Union, and slavery was a secondary issue. It is no accident that although Lincoln was swift to go to war for the Union, he was downright lackadaisical when it came to Emancipation. Much of the sympathy for the South among enlightened Europeans of that day was due to the fierce arbitrariness of Lincoln's policy to deny the states their constitutional rights while refusing to take a firm stand on the moral issue of slavery.

In the last thirty-four years, the republic has become, in many ways, the sort of armed camp that Grant so much esteemed in the South. For both Lincoln and Grant it was *e pluribus unum* no matter what the price in blood or constitutional rights. Now those centrifugal forces they helped to release a century ago are running down and a countervailing force is being felt: *ex uno plures.*

But enough. In this bicentennial year, as the benign spirit of Walt Disney ranges up and down the land, let us look only to what was good in Ulysses S. Grant. Let us forget the corrupted little president and remember only the great general, the kind and exquisitely tactful leader, the Roman figure who, when dying, did his duty and made the last years of his beloved goose of a wife comfortable and happy.

The New York Review of Books
September 18, 1975

West Point

On the table at which I write is a small silver mug with a square handle; it is inscribed to *Eugene L. Vidal, Jr., October 3, 1925*—a gift from the West Point football team to its mascot, which that year was not a mule but me. I drank milk from the cup for a good many years and from the look of the rim did a bit of teething on it, too.

I have no early memory of West Point. Apparently I was born in the cadet hospital on a Saturday morning because my mother had decided to stay on the post and go to a football game. I was delivered not by an obstetrician but by one Major Howard Snyder who happened to be officer of the day at the cadet hospital. Later, as surgeon general of the army, he looked after President Eisenhower ("Just indigestion, Mamie," he was reported to have said when she rang him in the middle of the night with news of the Great Golfer's first tussle with the Reaper. "Give him some bicarbonate"). More than thirty years later I visited General Snyder at his office in the basement of the White House. He recalled my birth; was still angry at my mother for not having gone to a civilian hospital; was most protective of his old friend the President. "Tough South German peasant. There's nothing at all wrong with him, you know, except this really nasty temper. That's what'll kill him." Then the inevitable question, "Why didn't *you* go to the Point?" A member of a West Point family had chosen *not* to join the Long Gray Line. Something wrong there.

At the time of my birth Eugene L. Vidal, *Sr.*, was known as Gene Vidal to the world of jocks—and to just about everybody else in the country for in those days college athletes were like rock stars (Scott Fitzgerald's apostrophe to Princeton's Hobe Baker is plainly tribute to a god). Class of 1918 at West Point, G.V. was an All-American quarterback; he is still regarded as the best all-around athlete in the history of the Academy, moving with equal ease from track to basketball to football to rugby (learned in one afternoon); a master of every sport except the one invented by Abner Doubleday (West Point 1842). "Baseball is the favorite American sport because it's so slow," G.V. used to say. "Any idiot can follow it. And just about any idiot can play it." After graduation, he came back to the Point as football coach; he was also the first instructor in aeronautics.

Shortly after I was born, G.V. resigned from the army (he found it boring) and went into civil aviation. But, as with most West Pointers of his generation, the links between him and the Academy proved to be unbreakable. Although his disposition was ironic, his style deflationary, his eye for the idiocies of the military sharp, he took some pride in being not only a part of the history of the Point but also a sort of icon for those graduates who came to prominence in the Second War.

The Eisenhowers, Groveses, Stratemeyers, Ridgways and Taylors created the American world empire; they also gave us the peacetime draft, a garrison state, and the current military debacle in Southeast Asia. With the best will in the world (and with the blessing of their civilian masters to whom the cold war was good business), these paladins have in the quarter century since Hiroshima wasted lives and money while treating with contempt the institutions of the republic. Now the game is changing—the army, too. Currently the West Pointers are fighting for a permanent draft. Otherwise, they tell us, we will have an "unrepresentative" (i.e., black) military establishment. But these same officers never objected to the prewar army, which was redneck and every bit as dumb as the coming black army because nobody smart (black or white) is going to be an enlisted man in the American army if he can help it.

I was less than a year old when my parents moved into the Washington house of my mother's father, Senator T. P. Gore (where I was put to bed in a bureau drawer). Like a number of high-powered cadets Gene Vidal was hypergamous. Yet, as a boy growing up in Madison, South Dakota, he was not particularly ambitious, as far as one can tell—which is not much: he had no memory for the past, his own or that of the family. He was so vague, in fact, that he was not certain if his middle initial "L" stood for Louis, as he put on my birth certificate, or for Luther. It was Luther. At fourteen I settled the confusion by taking my grandfather's name Gore.

As it turned out, the congressman from South Dakota was ambitious enough for two. After watching G.V. play football at the University of South Dakota, the congressman said, "How would you like an appointment to West Point?" "And where," answered my father with his usual charm and inability to dissemble, "is West Point? And what is there?" He was promptly appointed; thus ended his dream of becoming a barber because barbers seemed to have a lot of free time. Apparently in a town like Madison there was no one very interesting to emulate. Certainly G.V.'s father Felix was no model. Felix had been an engineer on whatever railroad it is that goes through South Dakota; for reasons unknown, he got off at Madison one day and went into the coal business.

Felix's father had been born in Feldkirch, Austria, of Romanic stock (descendants of the Roman legionnaires who settled Rhaetia in the first century).* A hypergamous adventurer and phony MD, Eugen Fidel Vidal married Emma de Traxler Hartmann of Lucerne, Switzerland—an heiress until she married him and got herself disinherited. "A *real* countess," my aunt used to say with wonder. In 1848 the unhappy couple came to Wisconsin where the Gräfin was promptly deserted by her husband. She brought up five children by translating American news stories for German, French, and Italian newspapers. She had every rea-

---

*A certain venerable vendor of American book-chat thought it preposterous that I should claim descent from the Romans. But the Romanic Vidals were originally called Vitalis and from Trieste north to Friuli to Vorarlberg, Roman monuments bear witness to our ubiquitousness.

son to be bitter; and was bitter. I go into all this family history because it has a good deal to do with the kind of men who went to West Point in those days.

Athlete. Lapsed Roman Catholic. The meager prairie background, somewhat confused by a family tradition of exciting wars (the Traxlers and Hartmanns had been professional soldiers for several hundred years). Then West Point and the companionship of men like himself. In the class three years ahead of G.V. were Bradley and Eisenhower (Ike was known as the "Swedish Jew"—my father as "Tony the Wop"); while in the class of 1918 were Mark Clark, Leslie Groves, and Lucius Clay (who once persuaded me to write a speech for his friend President Eisenhower on the virtues—if any—of integration: the speech was not delivered). Among those my father taught was the grand architect of our empire's Syracusan adventure in Southeast Asia, the Alcibiades of counterinsurgency, Maxwell Taylor.

These men had a good deal in common even before they were put into the pressure cooker on the Hudson. Most came from rural backgrounds; from lower-middle-class families; certainly they were not representative of the country's ruling class. In this century our nobles have not encouraged their sons to go to West Point. There were also no blacks at the Academy and few, if any, Jews or Roman Catholics. West Point was a very special sort of place.

According to K. Bruce Galloway and Robert Bowie Johnson, Jr. *(West Point: America's Power Fraternity),** "The Military Academy offers an ideology, not an education, and because of this and the uniform, the graduates find themselves anointed with access to America's ruling elite." The authors take a dark view of the Academy and its graduates, and they tend to see conspiracy where there is often only coincidence. For instance:

> By 1933 President Roosevelt had created the position of Director of Aeronautics . . . and appointed Eugene L. Vidal (W.P. 1918) as first director. Vidal had to deal immediately with the controversy over the place of aviation in—where else?—military affairs. He survived that problem, only to be faced with the airmail scandals of 1933 and 1934. . . . In the years following, West Point control of civil aeronautics lapsed only temporarily.

* Simon and Schuster, 1973.

Actually, it was civil not military aviation that pushed for my father's appointment, while the decision for the army to fly the mail was Roosevelt's. After a series of aerial disasters, Roosevelt turned to my father one evening and said, "Well, brother Vidal, *we* seemed to've made a mistake." Ever a good (if sardonic) soldier, G.V. took the rap for the President. "I liked that 'we' he used."

Galloway and Johnson would be more nearly right if they simply said that all West Pointers tend to look out for one another. In 1943 (aged seventeen) I enlisted as a private in the army and was assigned to a much publicized Training Program, which promptly collapsed. Aware that I was about to be shunted off to an infantry outfit that was soon to contribute a number of half-trained eighteen-year-olds to be butchered on the Rhine, I signaled to the nonexistent but very real West Point Protective Association. I was promptly transferred to the Air Force. I do not in the least regret this use of privilege and would do it again; but privilege comes from the Latin words meaning "private law," and even in a would-be canting democracy like ours there ought to be only public laws.

Duty, Honor, Country. That is the motto of West Point. It is curious that no one until recently seems to have made much of an ominous precedence that makes the nation the third loyalty of our military elite. Duty comes first. But duty to what? Galloway and Johnson are plain: the officer class. Or as a veteran instructor at the Point puts it, "In my system of values West Point comes first, the Army second, and the country comes third."

Honor. Galloway and Johnson are particularly interesting on the origins of West Point's honor system. The Academy's true founding father, Sylvanus Thayer, was a passionate admirer of Bonaparte; he also found good things in the Prussian system. Although the United States did not seem to have much need for an officer caste when he took charge of the Academy in 1817 (of course the British had burned down Washington a few years earlier but that sort of thing doesn't happen very often), Thayer set about creating a four-year hell for the young men sent to him from all over the country. They were kept constantly busy; treated like robots; given an honor system which, simply put, required them to spy on one another.

This sort of system is always diabolic and usually effective, particularly in an environment like West Point where, according to Colonel L.C. West of the Judge Advocate General Corps, "at a tender age, the West Point Cadet learns that military rules are sacred and in time readily accepts them as a substitute for integrity. As he progresses through his military career, the rules remain uppermost in his code of honor. In fact, his 'honor' is entwined with the rules and so long as he obeys the rules, whatever their content, or whatever manner of man or fool may have written them, his honor is sound." This explains the ease with which these self-regarding young men whose honor is, officially, not to lie, cheat or steal (or go to the bars in Highland Falls) can with such ease cover up a massacre like My Lai or, like General Lavelle, falsify bombing reports, invent military victories in order to help one another get decorations and promotions—not to mention take bribes from those large corporations whose manufacture of expensive weaponry absorbs so much of the military budget.

Country. To the West Pointer loyalty to the United States comes after loyalty to the Academy and to himself. Over the years this lack of patriotism has not gone entirely unnoticed. In fact, ever since the Academy was founded there have been critics of Thayer's military elite and its separateness from the rest of the country. According to the third superintendent, Alden Partridge (W.P. 1806), the Academy was "monarchial, corrupt and corrupting . . . a palpable violation of the constitution and laws of the country, and its direct tendency to introduce and build up a privileged order of the very worst class—a military aristocracy—in the United States."

In 1830 Tennessee's show-biz congressman Davy Crockett introduced a bill to shut down the Academy while in 1863 another bill in Congress also proposed abolition. Speaking for the later measure, the radical Republican Senator B.F. Wade of Ohio declared: "I do not believe that there can be found on the whole face of the earth . . . any institution that has turned out as many false, ungrateful men as have emanated from this institution."

For more than a century West Pointers have returned the compliment. They do not like civilians, while their contempt for politicians is as nearly perfect as their ignorance of the institutions of the country that they are required to serve—after duty, that is; after honor. Specifically, my father's generation—the empire-makers—disliked Jews, regarded blacks as low comedy relief, politicians as corrupt, Filipinos as sly . . . still fresh in everyone's memory was the slaughter by the American army of some three million Filipinos at the beginning of the century: the largest experiment in genocide the world was to know until Hitler. The West Pointers regard only one another with true reverence.

The authors of *West Point* are particularly interesting when they discuss what goes on nowadays in the classrooms at the Academy. One of the authors graduated in 1965 and no doubt writes from personal experience. Since the teachers tend to be graduates, they often have no special knowledge of the subject they teach—nor do they need to have because each day's lesson is already prepared for them in "blocs." But then, according to General George A. Lincoln, the Academy's academic guru (and Nixon adviser): "West Point is an under-graduate scholarship school without many scholars or any great motivation for learning as far as a material proportion of each class is concerned." He seems rather pleased by this. Galloway and Johnson are not. They believe that the cadets are taught "the ability to think and reason without really being able to do so."

Boys who go to West Point today do so for a variety of reasons, none having much to do with learning. There is the romantic appeal of the Long Gray Line. There is the cozy appeal of a life in which all important decisions will be made by others. There is the attractive lure of retirement at an early age—not to mention translation to the upper echelons of those corporations which do business with the Pentagon. Simply by stepping on an escalator, the West Pointer can have the sense of duty done, of honor upheld, of country served—and self, too. It is an irresistible package. Yet an instructor at the Academy recently commented (anonymously), "The cadets at West Point are fifth rate." To which the answer must be: they are fifth-rate because that is what the system requires of them. Since they are not different from other American boys their age, their intellectual torpor is due to a system that requires loyalty and obedience above all else—two qualities that flourish most luxuriantly in the ignorant; most dangerously in the fanatic.

It is no surprise that the military elite was delighted by the anti-communist line of their civilian masters. The Truman-Acheson, Eisenhower-Dulles, Kennedy-Johnson-Rusk, Nixon-Kissinger war on commies at home and abroad was thrilling to the military. For one thing the ideals of socialism are anathema to them even though, paradoxically, the West Pointer is entirely cared for by the state from his birth in any army hospital (if he is born into a military family) to taps at government expense in a federal bone-yard. Yet the West Pointer takes this coddling as his due and does not believe that a steel worker, say, ought to enjoy privileges that belong rightfully to the military elite. Retired officers are particularly articulate on this point, and their passionate letters supporting the AMA's stand against socialized medicine are often as not written from government-paid private rooms at Walter Reed.

The cold war also meant vast military appropriations for weapons. One of the few American traditions (almost as venerable as the Warner Brothers Christmas layoff) is the secretary of defense's annual warning to Congress at budget time. Since his last request for money, the diabolical Reds are once again about to pass us—or have passed us—in atomic warheads, cutlery, missiles, saddles, disposable tissues. Distraught, Congress immediately responds to this threat with as many billions of dollars as the military feel they need to defend freedom and human dignity for all men everywhere regardless of color or creed—with the small proviso that important military installations and contracts be located in those areas whose representatives enjoy seniority in Congress.

In this fashion, more than a third of the nation's federal income has been spent for more than a generation in order that the congressmen who give the generals the money they ask for will then be re-elected with money given *them* by the corporations that were awarded federal money by generals who, when they retire, will go to work for those same corporations. Beautifully, both nation and self are served because the commies are rats, aren't they? Particularly the home-grown ones.

Just before the Second War, I listened several times to Air Force generals discuss with a humor that soon turned into obsession the ease with which the White House could be seized, the Congress sent home, and the nation kept out of the war that the Jew Franklin D. Rosenfeld was trying to start against Hitler. Although Hitler was a miserable joker (and probably a crypto-Jew), he was doing our work for us by killing commies. I do not think this sort of thinking is by any means dead today. I once asked Fletcher Knebel what gave him his idea for *Seven Days in May,* a lively and popular thriller about the possibility of a military coup in Washington. "Talking to Admiral Radford," he told me. "He scared me to death. I could just see the Joint Chiefs kicking Kennedy out."

The United States has now been a garrison state for thirty-two years. To justify all those billions of dollars spent, the military likes to have a small war going on somewhere in the world. Or as General Van Fleet (W.P. 1915) said with some satisfaction, "Korea has been a blessing. There has to be a Korea either here or some place in the world." And so these blessings continued to shower upon us until August 15. Has peace at last come to our restless empire? Well, several weeks ago the new secretary of defense warned Congress that the Soviet's iron fist is still powerful within that velvet glove. If this striking image does not get the money out of Congress, a military crisis in the Middle East, or a small war in Chile, say, ought to keep the money flowing in the right direction.

Galloway and Johnson are, I think, too hard on the individual shortcomings of the West Pointers. After all, if we didn't want them to be the way they are (militantly anti-communist, anti-politician, anti-dissenter) they would be different. A class of this sort is made not born. I have known a good many West Pointers of the imperial generation and found them to be men of considerable virtue though none had, I should say, much sense of the civilian world. But then how could they? Their education was fifth-rate; their lives remote from everyday cares; their duty and honor directed not toward the republic but toward one another.

For a half century now West Pointers have been taught that communism is America's number one enemy without ever being told what communism is. Paradoxically, fascist-minded Americans tend to admire the communist societies once they actually visit them. The Nixons and the Agnews particularly delight in the absence of dissent; not to mention the finality of all social arrangements. Certainly the world of Mao (less some of his subtler thoughts) is nothing but the civilian world as West Point would like it to be. And if Mao is not an admirer of elites—well, neither (officially) were the founders of the American republic and just look what we have created! Anomalies are the stuff of political systems.

Certainly the West Pointers would approve the puritanism of the communist societies. Galloway and Johnson give a grim picture of the sexual deprivation of the cadets which, they maintain, makes for a lifetime of uneasy relations with women—not to mention "the entire company [that] once masturbated together in the showers." Life on the Hudson was even more austere in my father's day. But there were occasional mavericks. Although G.V. never much liked Eisenhower ("a sour cuss, always on the make"), he did give Ike credit for having managed, under the most perilous conditions, to lay the wife of the post dentist. Obviously *supreme* commanders are made early.

The military-industrial-West Point complex is more than a century old. One of the first functions of the Academy was to supply engineers to the nation. West Pointers built the first railroads as well as many roads and dams. Working as engineers for the early tycoons, West Pointers were brought into close contact with the business elite of the country and the result has been a long and happy marriage.

The military was also used to protect American business interests overseas. On at least one occasion the business interests tried to get the military to overthrow a president. In 1933 the Liberty League secretly approached Major General Smedley Butler and asked him to help them remove President Roosevelt. Butler turned them down flat. He also launched the most devastating attack ever made on American capitalism. Of his thirty-three years in the Marine Corps, he declared,

> I spent most of my time being a high-class muscle-man for Big Business, for Wall Street, and for the Bankers. In short, I was a racketeer, a gangster for capitalism . . . Like all members of the military profession, I never had an original thought until I left the service. . . . I helped make Mexico—and especially Tampico—safe for American oil interests in 1914. I decided to make Haiti and Cuba a decent place for the National City Bank boys to collect revenues in. . . .

He also lists among his field of operations Nicaragua, the Dominican Republic, China (where the Marines protected Standard Oil's interests in 1927). Butler summed up, "Looking back on it, I feel that I might have given Al Capone a few hints. The best he could do was operate his racket in three districts. I operated on three continents."

Our military today operates on all five continents with results that no longer please anyone except those businesses that make weapons and pay for presidential elections. The final irony is that despite all the money we pour into our military establishment it probably could not win a war against anyone—except perhaps the American people. The disaster in Vietnam showed that the services could not fight a war in a primitive country against a "highly motivated" enemy. Naturally, the West Pointers blame this defeat on the commie-weirdo-fags (and/or politicians) who forced them in the President's elegant phrase, "to fight with one arm tied behind them." Whatever that meant: after all, the military were given a half-million American troops and more than 100 billion dollars to play with. Admittedly there were a few targets they were told not to bomb, like hospitals in Hanoi—or Peking or Moscow—but secretly president and generals bombed pretty much whatever they wanted to. Perhaps the generals felt betrayed because they could not use hydrogen bombs on the jungles and dikes of North Vietnam, or attack China. Yet even the bloodthirstiest of the Pentagon hawks did not want another go 'round with Chinese ground troops after the rout we suffered in Korea.

It should be noted that the American fighting man has been pretty lousy from the beginning of the republic, and more power to him. He has no desire to kill strangers or get hurt himself. He does not like to be told what to do. For him, there is neither duty nor honor; his country is his skin. This does not make for a world conqueror. In fact, according to a 1968 study of American performance in World War II and Korea, "the US side never won unless it had a 2-to-1 superiority of forces over the other side."* Shades of George Washington, who disliked taking on the British unless he was certain to outnumber them, preferably five to one. Even then, Washington's troops were usually beaten. Like the Italians, we Americans are killers for personal profit or revenge; the large-scale stuff doesn't really grip us.

Stuart H. Loory's *Defeated: Inside America's Military Machine* is an analysis of the state of the armed forces today. If his report is true, let us hope that the Soviet military machine is in just as big a mess as ours. Loory begins with the usual but always staggering statistics. Between 1946 and 1972 five million citizens of a free republic were drafted into the "peacetime" [*sic*] armed forces.

---

*From "Ideology and Primary Group," a paper delivered by John Helmer to the annual meeting of the American Sociological Association on August 27, 1973. The material in this paper will be included in the *Deadly Simple Mechanics of Society*, to be published by the Seabury Press early next year.

Year in, year out, 37 percent of the national budget goes to the military. Of all military expenditures by every nation in the world, the United States accounts for 27.6 percent. The army's PX system is America's third largest retailer. The Defense Department owns land equivalent in area to the state of Ohio. And so on.

But what are we getting in exchange for all this money spent? A fifth-rate "ticket punching" officer corps, according to Loory. Apparently no officer is allowed to stay in any job long enough to learn to do anything well. In order to be promoted, he must get his ticket punched: a brief time in the field, then to command school, to the Pentagon, etc. This moving about ("personnel turbulence" is the army's nice phrase) has resulted in what appears to be a near-total demoralization of the basic units of the army. Officers are shipped out just as they get to know the names of the men in their outfits while the problems of drugs and race occupy most of the time of the commanders, particularly in Europe. Even the nuclear forces of SAC, forever guarding the free world, are in disarray. Obviously the second law of thermodynamics is in operation, and irreversible.

Mr. Loory contrasts American troops in Germany unfavorably to the soldiers of the Bundwehr. Apparently American troops are assigned to broken-down barracks and constantly oppressed with that mindless chicken shit which so appeals to the traditional "West Point mind": if you have nothing to do, police the area. The Germans, on the other hand, have modern barracks, interesting training, a good deal of freedom, and of course a stronger currency. In a nice reversal of history, the Americans are now the Prussians—in a sloppy sort of way—while the Prussians behave as if the private soldier is actually an intelligent member of the same race as his officers.

In the wake of the defeat of the American military machine in Asia and the resulting shocks to our institutions at home, a good many questions are bound to be asked about what sort of a country we want. Fatigue and lack of resources have stopped the long march from the Atlantic to the borders of China. The West Point elite have not served us well even though they have never disguised the fact that we are number three on their list of priorities. Yet even when they try to work peacefully for the country, they are often a menace. The Army Corps of Engineers has made such an ecological mess of our rivers and lakes that Justice

Douglas has termed them "public enemy number one."

Not unnaturally, the West Pointers are most successful at creating miniature West Points, particularly in Latin America (though Ethiopia and several other exotic countries have been seeded with Duty, Honor, Country academies). All around the world West Pointers are turning out military elites trained to fight not wars but those who would extend democracy at home. Galloway and Johnson have a particularly fascinating chapter on the links between West Pointers and their opposite numbers in Latin America, particularly with the dictator of Nicaragua, Tachito Somoza (W.P. 1946).

Galloway and Johnson favor placing the Academy's four regiments in four different cities, making them closer to the grass roots of, say, Harlem or of San Francisco. They feel that this would in some way acquaint the cadet corps with their third loyalty. I doubt it. I agree with Davy Crockett and Senator Wade: an aristocratic military elite is deeply contrary to the idea of this republic and its constitution. Since the next great war will be fought by computers and by highly trained technicians, we have no need of a peacetime army of two million or even of two hundred thousand. Certainly a large army controlled by the West Point elite will continue, as it has done for nearly a quarter century, to squander money and create wars.

Forgetting the morality of a republic trying to be an empire, we now lack the material resources to carry on in the old way (LBJ ran out of bombs one afternoon downstairs in his war room; later, Nixon was to run out of kerosene for his bombers). What money we have would be better used for internal improvements, in Henry Clay's phrase. After all, the two most successful nations in the world today are Japan and Germany—and neither has much of a military establishment. This simple lesson ought to be plain to America's capitalists; yet many of our magnates are as bemused by military grandeur as any plebe, misty-eyed at the thought of the Long Gray Line and by the resonant self-aggrandizing horseshit the late Douglas MacArthur used so successfully to peddle.

Self-delusion is a constant in human affairs. Certainly without self-delusion on the grandest scale we could never have got into our present situation; and West Point has certainly made its contribution. But reality has never been West Point's bag. According to George A. Custer (W.P. 1861), "The Army is the Indian's best friend." While according to West Point's current version of what happened in Vietnam, "The War . . . ended in August of 1968 when sorely battered Communist troops were unable to engage the allied war machine." With historians like that who needs generals?

There is also mounting evidence that today's soldier will not endure much longer West Point's traditional oppression. John Helmer's thesis in "Ideology and Primary Group" makes this pretty plain. According to Helmer, the division between the West Point officer class and today's working-class soldier is now almost unbridgeable. Since middle-class men were able to stay out of the worst of the Vietnam war, the working class provided the combat troops. They quickly got the point that "in the search and destroy tactics most commonly used [the infantryman] was, strictly speaking, the bait to catch the enemy. According to the plan he was intended to be a target, a sitting duck for the other side to attack at its ultimate cost."

The same cynical use of men is at work in Europe, where working-class American troops are, if not exactly bait, political hostages to ensure a "proper" American response in case of a Soviet strike. These men don't have to be good soldiers; they don't have to be anything but on the spot. It does not take great prescience, however, to know that should a Soviet army ever occupy Paris, the United States would abandon its own troops as swiftly as it would its allies. The American empire is not about to lose a single of its cities to save all Europe—much less three hundred thousand fuck-ups (in the eyes of the West Point elite) with their drugs, their brawling, their fragging of officers whom they regard as an alien and hostile class.

Today the first order of business in the United States is the dismantling of the military machine. Obviously, we must continue to make it disagreeable for anyone who might decide to attack us (this could be done of course by not provoking other nations but that is too much to ask). Nevertheless the military budget must be cut by two thirds; and the service academies phased out.

What to do with the officer corps? That is a delicate point. West Pointers are now more and more into politics and, as always, they are on the side of reaction. Their web of connections with the military academies they have created in Latin America, Asia, and Africa makes them truly international. Also their creations may give them dangerous ideas. It is not inconceivable that a coup of the sort that General Butler refused to lead might one day prove attractive to a group of the Honor, Duty, Country boys. Let us hope that Richard Nixon never asks General Haig (W.P. 1947) to send home Congress and Supreme Court so that the sovereign might get on with the country's true business, which is the making of armaments and small wars. Finding suitable employment for our officer caste will be, as they say, a challenge.

I look guiltily at the silver cup, and think of the generals who gave it to me. On a bright day in May four years ago I stood beside my uncle, General F.L. Vidal (W.P. 1933), at the edge of an Air Force runway near Washington, D.C. Awkwardly, my uncle held what looked to be a shoebox. "It's *heavy*, " he muttered in my ear. I shuddered. Like the contents of the box (my father's ashes), I am a lifelong thanatophobe. Behind us stood a dozen of G.V.'s classmates. Among them the solemn, pompous, haggard Leslie Groves —himself to die a few months later; and that handsome figure of the right wing, General Wedemeyer.

After the helicopter departed on its mission, the old generals of the empire commiserated with one another. The icon of their generation, the lovely athlete of a half century before, was now entirely gone, ashes settling upon the Virginia countryside. The generals looked dazed; not so much with grief as with a sense of hurt at what time does to men, and to their particular innocence. Although I have always found poignant (yes, even honorable) the loyalty of West Pointers to one another, I could not help thinking as I walked away from them for the last time that the harm they have done to this republic and to the world elsewhere far outweighs their personal excellence, their duty, their honor. But then the country that they never understood was always last in their affections and so the first of their loyalties to be betrayed.

The New York Review of Books
October 18, 1973

The Art and Arts
of E. Howard Hunt

From December 7, 1941, to August 15, 1973, the United States has been continuously at war except for a brief, too little celebrated interregnum. Between 1945 and 1950 the empire turned its attention to peaceful pursuits and enjoyed something of a golden or at least for us not too brazen an age. The arts in particular flourished. Each week new genius was revealed by the press; and old genius decently buried. Among the new novelists of that far-off time were Truman Capote (today a much loved television performer) and myself. Although we were coevals (a word that the late William Faulkner though meant evil at the same time as), we were unlike: Capote looked upon the gorgeous Speed Lamkin as a true tiger in the Capotean garden where I saw mere lambkin astray in my devouring jungle.

The one thing that Capote and I did have in common was a need for money. And so each of us applied to the Guggenheim Foundation for a grant; and each was turned down. Shocked, we compared notes. Studied the list of those who had received grants. "Will you just look," moaned Truman, "at those *ahh*-full

pee-pull they keep giving *muh*-nee to!" Except for the admirable
Carson McCullers who got so many grants in her day that she was
known as the conductress on the gravy train, the list of honored
writers was not to our minds distinguished. Typical of the sort
of novelist the Guggenheims preferred to Capote and me in 1946
was twenty-eight-year-old (practically middle-aged) Howard
Hunt, author of *East of Farewell* (Random House, 1943); a novel
described by the publishers as "probably the first novel about this
war by an American who actually helped fight it." The blurb is
unusually excited. Apparently, H.H. "grew up like any other
American boy" (no tap-dancing on a river boat for him) "going
to public schools and to college (Brown University, where he
studied under I.J. Kapstein)."

A clue. I slip into reverie. Kapstein will prove to be my Rosebud. The key to the Hunt mystery. But does Kapstein still live?
Will he talk? *Or is he afraid?* I daydream. "Hunt . . . E. Howard
Hunt . . . ah, yes. Sit down, Mr. . . . uh, Bozell? Forgive me
. . . this last stroke seems to have . . . Where were we? Howie.
Yes. I must tell you something of the Kapstein creative writing
method. I require the tyro pen-man to copy out in longhand some
acknowledged world masterpiece. Howie copied out—if memory
serves—*Of Human Bondage.*"

But until the Kapstein Connection is made, I must search
the public record for clues. The dust jacket of H.H.'s first novel
tells us that he became a naval ensign in May 1941. "There followed many months of active duty at sea on a destroyer, on the
North Atlantic patrol, protecting the life-line to embattled
England. . . ." That's more like it. My eyes shut: the sea. A cold
foggy day. Slender, virile H.H. arrives (by kayak?) at a secret
rendezvous with a British battleship. On the bridge is Admiral
Sir Leslie Charteris, K.C.B.: it's Walter Pidgeon, of course.
"Thank God, you got through. I never thought it possible.
There's someone particularly wants to thank you." Then out of
the fog steps a short burly figure; the face is truculent yet somehow indomitable (no, it's not Norman Mailer). In one powerful
hand he holds a thick cigar. When He speaks, the voice is the very
voice of human freedom and, yes, dignity. "Ensign Hunt, seldom
in the annals of our island story has this our embattled yet still
mightily sceptered realm owed to but one man . . ."

H.H. is a daydreamer and like all great dreamers (I think particularly of Edgar Rice Burroughs) he stirs one's own inner thea-

ter into productions of the most lurid sort, serials from which dull fact must be rigorously excluded—like the Random House blurb. "In February 1942, Howard Hunt was detached from his ship and sent to Boston." Now if the dates given on the jacket are accurate, he served as an ensign for no more than nine months. So how many of those nine months could he have spent protecting England's embattled life-line? H.H.'s naval career ends when he is "sent to Boston, to take treatment for an injury in a naval hospital." This is worthy of the Great Anti-Semanticist Nixon himself. Did H.H. slip a disk while taking a cholera shot down in the dispensary? *Who's Who* merely records: "Served with USNR, 1940–42."

I turn for information to Mr. Tad Szulc, H.H.'s principal biographer and an invaluable source of reference. According to Mr. Szulc, H.H. worked for the next two years "as a movie script writer and, briefly, as a war correspondent in the Pacific." *Who's Who* corroborates: "Movie script writer, editor March of Time (1942–43); war corr. Life mag. 1942." Yet one wonders what movies he wrote and what stories he filed, and from where.

Limit of Darkness (Random House, 1944) was written during this period. H.H.'s second novel is concerned with a naval air squadron on Guadalcanal in the Solomons. Was H.H. actually on Guadalcanal or did he use as source book Ira Wolfert's just published *Battle for the Solomons?* Possible clue: the character of war correspondent Francis H. O'Bannon . . . not at first glance a surrogate for H.H., who never casts himself in his books as anything but a Wasp. O'Bannon is everything H.H. detests—a low-class papist vulgarian who is also—what else?—"unhealthily fat and his jowls were pasty." The author contrasts him most unfavorably with the gallant Wasps to whom he dedicates the novel: "The Men Who Flew from Henderson."

They are incredibly fine, these young chaps. They ought to be, with names like McRae, Cordell, Forsyth, Lambert, Lewis, Griffin, Sampson, Vaughan, Scott—not a nigger, faggot, kike, or wop in the outfit. Just real guys who say real true simple things like "a guy who's fighting just to get back to the States is only half fighting. . . ." A love scene: " 'Oh, Ben, if it only would stop.' She put her face into the hollow of his shoulder. 'No,' he said. . . . 'We haven't killed enough of them yet or burned their cities or bombed them to hell the way we must. When I put away my wings I want it to be for good—not just for a few years.' " A key motif in the H.H. *oeuvre:* the enemy must be defeated once and for all so that man can live at peace with himself in a world where United Fruit and ITT know what's best not only for their stockholders but for their customers as well.

An academic critic would doubtless make something of the fact that since the only bad guy in the book is a fat, pasty Catholic newspaperman, H.H. might well be reproaching himself for not having flown with the golden gallant guys who gave so much of themselves for freedom, to get the job done. In their numinous company, H.H. may very well have *felt* like an overweight Catholic—and all because of that mysterious accident in the naval hospital; in its way so like Henry James's often alluded to but never precisely by the Master named disability which turned out to have been—after years of patient literary detective work—chronic constipation. Academic critics are not always wrong.

The actual writing of *Limit of Darkness* is not at all bad; it is not at all good either. H.H. demonstrates the way a whole generation of writers ordered words upon the page in imitation of what they took to be Hemingway's technique. At best Hemingway was an artful, careful writer who took a good deal of trouble to master scenes of action—the hardest kind of writing to do—while his dialogue looks most attractive on the page. Yet unwary imitators are apt to find themselves (as in *Limit of Darkness*) slipping into aimless redundancies. Wanting to Hemingwayize the actual cadences of Wasp speech as spoken by young fliers, H.H. so stylizes their voices that one character blends with another. Although Hemingway worked with pasteboard cutouts, too, he was cunning enough to set his dolls against most stylishly rendered landscapes; he also gave them vivid things to do: the duck that got shot was always a real duck that really got shot. Finally, the Hemingway trick of repeating key nouns and proper names is simply not possible for other writers—as ten thousand novels (including some of Hemingway's own) testify.

In H.H.'s early books, which won for him a coveted (by Capote and me) Guggenheim grant, there is a certain amount of solemnity if not seriousness. The early H.H. liked to quote from high-toned writers like Pliny and Louis MacNeice as well as from that *echt* American Wasp William Cullen Bryant—whose radical politics would have shocked H.H. had he but known. But then I suspect the quotations are not from H.H.'s wide reading of world literature but from brief random inspections of *Bartlett's Familiar Quotations.*

H.H.'s fliers are conservative lads who don't think much of Roosevelt's Four Freedoms. They fight to get the job done. That's all. Old Glory. H.H. is plainly dotty about the Wasp aristocracy. One of the characters in *Limit of Darkness* is almost unhinged when he learns that a girl he has met went to Ethel Walker. Had H.H. not chosen a life of adventure I think he might have made a good second string to John O'Hara's second string to Hemingway. H.H. has the O'Hara sense of irredeemable social inferiority which takes the place for so many Irish-American writers of original sin; he also shares O'Hara's pleasure in listing the better brand-names of this world. Even on Guadalcanal we are told of a pipe tobacco from "a rather good New Zealand leaf."

By 1943 H.H. was a promising author. According to *The New York Times*, "*East of Farewell* was a fine realistic novel, without any doubt the best sea story of the war." Without any doubt it was probably the *only* sea story of the war at that point but the *Times* has its own dread style to maintain. Now a momentous change in the daydreamer's life. With *Limit of Darkness* in the works at Random House, H.H. (according to *Who's Who*) joined the USAF (1943–46); and rose to the rank of first lieutenant. It would seem that despite "the injury in a naval hospital" our hero was again able to fight for human dignity, this time in the skies.

But according to Mr. Szulc what H.H. really joined was not the Air Force but the Office of Strategic Services, a cloak-and-dagger outfit whose clandestine activities probably did not appreciably lengthen the war. "As a cover, he was given the rank of Air Corps Lieutenant." Mr. Szulc tells us that H.H. was sent to China to train guerrillas behind the Japanese lines. Curiously enough, I have not come across a Chinese setting in any of H.H.'s novels. Was he ever in China? One daydreams. " 'Lieutenant Hunt reporting for duty, General.' The haggard face with the luminous strange eyes stared at him through the tangled vines. 'Lieutenant Hunt?' Wingate's voice was shrill with awe. 'Until today, no man has ever hacked his way through that living wall of slant-eyed Japanese flesh . . . !' "

In 1946, H.H. returned to civilian life and wrote what is probably his most self-revealing novel, *Stranger in Town* (Random House, 1947). This must have been very nearly the first of the returned-war-veteran novels, a genre best exemplified by Merle Miller's *That Winter;* reading it, I confess to a certain nostalgia.

Handsome, virile young Major Fleming returns to New York City, a glittering Babylon in those days before the writing ap-

peared on Mayor Lindsay's wall. Fleming has a sense of aliena-
tion (new word in 1947). He cannot bear the callous civilian world
which he contrasts unfavorably with how it was for us back there
in the Pacific in our cruddy foxholes with the frigging sound of
mortars overhead and our buddies dying—for what? How could
any black-marketing civilian spiv know what war was really like?

Actually, none of *us* knew what it was like either since, as far
as my investigations have taken me, no novelist of the Second
World War or returned-veteran-from-the-war novelist ever took
part in any action. Most were clerks in headquarter companies or
with *Yank* or *Stars and Stripes;* the manlier was a cook. H.H. may
have *observed* some of the war as a correspondent and, perhaps,
from behind the lines in China, but no foxhole ever held him, no
wolf ever fed him, no vastation overwhelmed him in the Galleria
at Naples. But the daydreamer of course is always there. And
how!

The book is dedicated to two dead officers (Wasp), as well as to
"The other gallant young men who did not return." Only a book
reviewer whose dues were faithfully paid up to the Communist
party could keep a tear from his eye as he read that line. Then
the story. It is early 1946. Major Fleming checks into the elegant
Manhattan flat of his noncombatant brother who is out of town
but has given him the flat and the services of a worthy black
retainer who could have played De Lawd in *Green Pastures.* A
quick resumé of Fleming's career follows.

Incidentally, each of H.H.'s narratives is periodically brought
to a halt while he provides the reader with highly detailed capsule
biographies written in *Who's Who* style. H.H. plainly enjoys composing plausible (and implausible) biographies for his characters
—not to mention for himself. In *Contemporary Authors,* H.H. composed a bio, for one of his pseudonyms Robert Dietrich, taking
ten years off his age, putting himself in the infantry during
Korea, awarding himself a Bronze Star and a degree from
Georgetown. A quarter century later when the grandmother-
trampler and special counselor to the President Charles W. Colson wanted documents invented and history revised in the interest of Nixon's re-election, he turned with confidence to H.H. He
knew his man—and fellow Brown alumnus.

As Fleming orders himself champagne and a luxurious meal
ending with baked Alaska (for one!), we get the bio. He has been
everywhere in the war from "Jugland" (Yugoslavia?) to the Far

East. He remembers good meals in Shanghai and Johnny Walker Black Label. Steak. Yet his memories are bitter. He is bitter. He is also edgy. "I can't go around for the rest of my life like somebody out of the Ministry of Fear."

Fleming is an artist. A sculptor. H.H. conforms to that immutable rule of bad fiction which requires the sensitive hero to practice the one art his creator knows nothing about. We learn that Fleming's old girl friend has married someone else. This is a recurrent theme in the early novels. Was H.H. jilted? Recipient of a Dear John letter? Get cracking, thesis-writers.

The civilian world of New York, 1946, annoys Fleming ("maybe the Far East has spoiled me for America"). He is particularly enraged by demobilization. "Overseas, the nineteen-year-old milksops were bleeding for their mothers, and their mothers were bleeding for them, and the army was being demobilized, stripped of its powers. . . . He had had faith in the war until they partitioned Poland again. . . . Wherever Russia moved in, that part of the world was sealed off." Fleming has a suspicion that he is not going to like what he calls "the Atomic Age." But then, "They trained me to be a killer. . . . Now they'll have to undo it."

At a chic night club, Fleming meets the greasy Argentine husband of his old flame; he beats him up. It seems that Fleming has never been very keen about Latins. When he was a schoolboy at Choate (yes, Choate), he met an Italian girl in New York. She took him home and got his cherry. But "she smelled of garlic, and the sheets weren't very clean, and after it was all over when I was down on the street again, walking home, I thought that I never wanted to see her again." Ernest would have added rain to that sentence, if not to the scene.

The themes that are to run through H.H.'s work and life are all to be found in *Stranger in Town*. The sense that blacks and Latins are not quite human (Fleming is moderately attracted to a "Negress" but fears syphilis). The interest in pre-war jazz: Beiderbecke and Goodman. A love of fancy food, drink, decor; yet whenever the author tries to strike the elegant worldly note, drapes not curtains tend to obscure the view from his not so magic casements, looking out on tacky lands forlorn. Throughout his life's work there is a constant wistful and, finally, rather touching identification with the old American patriciate.

There is a rather less touching enthusiasm for war. "An atom bomb is just a bigger and better bomb," while "the only justifica-

tion for killing in war is that evil must be destroyed." Although
evil is never exactly defined, the killers for goodness ought to be
left alone to kill in their own way because "if I hired a man to
do a dirty job for me, I wouldn't be presumptuous enough to
specify what weapons he was to use or at what hour. . . ." Toward
the end of the book, H.H. strikes a minatory anti-communist
note. Fleming denounces pacifists and a "a new organization
called the Veterans Action Council" whose "ideals had been a
paraphrase of the Communist manifesto." Apparently these veterans prefer to follow the party line which is to disarm the U.S.
while Russia arms. A few years later when Joe McCarthy got
going, this was a standard line. But it was hot stuff in 1945, and
had the book-chat writers of the day like Orville Prescott and
Charles Poore not hewed so closely to the commie line *Stranger
in Town* would have been much read. As it was, the book failed.
Too avant-garde. Too patriotic.

The gullible *Who's Who* now tells us that H.H. was a "screen
writer, 1947–48; attaché Am Embassy, Paris, France, 1948–49."
But Mr. Szulc knows better. Apparently H.H. joined the CIA
"early in 1949, and after a short period in Washington headquarters, he was sent to Paris for nearly two years. Now for a cover,
he called himself a State Department reserve officer." But the
chronology seems a bit off.

According to the blurb of a John Baxter novel, the author
[H.H.] "worked as a screen writer until Hollywood felt the impact of TV. 'When unemployed screen writer colleagues began
hanging themselves aboard their yachts,' Baxter joined the Foreign Service." I slip into reverie. I am with Leonard Spigelgass,
the doyen of movie writers at MGM. "Lenny, do you remember E. Howard Hunt alias John Baxter alias Robert Dietrich
alias . . ." Lenny nods; a small smile plays across his handsome
mouth. "Howie never got credit on a major picture. Used to try
to peddle these foreign intrigue scripts. He was hipped on assassination, I recall. Poor Howie. Not even Universal would touch
him." But I fear that like Pontius Pilate in the Anatole France
story, Lenny would merely say, "E. Howard Hunt? I do not
recall the name. But let me tell you about Harry Essex . . ." If
H.H. *was* in Hollywood then he is, as a writer, unique. Not one
of his books that I have read uses Hollywood for background.
This is superhuman continence considering how desperate for
settings a man who writes nearly fifty books must be.

Who's Who puts H.H. in Paris at the Embassy in 1948. Mr. Szulc puts him there (and in the CIA) early 1949. Actually H.H. was working for the Economic Cooperation Administration at Paris in 1948 where he may have been a "black operator" for the CIA. With H.H. the only facts we can rely on are those of publication. *Maelstrom* appeared in 1948 and *Bimini Run* in 1949. *The Herald Tribune* thought that *Maelstrom* was a standard thriller-romance while *Bimini Run* was dismissed as "cheap, tawdry" (it is actually pretty good). That was the end. H.H. had ceased to be a contender in the big literary sweepstake which currently features several young lions of that day grown mangy with time's passage but no less noisy.*

In 1949, at popular request, the novelist Howard Hunt hung up the jock until this year when he reappeared as E. Howard Hunt, author of *The Berlin Ending*. Simultaneous with the collapse of his career as a serious author, his attempts at movie writing came to nothing because of "the impact of TV." Too proud to become part of our Golden Age of television, H.H. joined the CIA in 1948 or 1949, a period in which his alias Robert Dietrich became an agent for the IRS in Washington.

In Paris, H.H. met Dorothy Wetzel, a pretty girl herself given to daydreaming: she claimed to be a full-blooded Cherokee Indian to the consternation of her family; she may or may not have been married to a Spanish count before H.H. One reasonably hard fact (ritually denied) is that she was working as a secretary for the CIA in Paris when she met H.H. They were married in 1949 and had four children; their marriage appears to have been idyllically happy despite the fact that they were rather alike in temperament. A relative recalls that as a girl Dorothy always had her nose in a book—a bad sign, as we know. She also believed in the war against evil, in the undubiousness of the battle which at the end of her life last December seemed to be going against the good.

From Paris the two CIA employees moved on to Vienna where they lived a romantic life doing whatever it is that CIA agents do as they defend the free world, presumably by confounding the commies. According to *Who's Who*, H.H. was transferred to the American Embassy in Mexico City in 1950. Latin America was a natural field for H.H. (with the Guggenheim money he had gone

---

*My friends Irwin Shaw and James Jones were told by a journalist that I was referring to them. Actually, I was thinking of Norman Mailer and myself.

for a year to Mexico to learn Spanish). Also, in Latin America the struggle between good and evil might yet be resolved in good's favor. Europe was old; perhaps lost. John Baxter's *A Foreign Affair* (1954) describes H.H.'s life in those days and his settling views. *A Foreign Affair* also marks the resumption of H.H.'s literary career and the beginning of what one must regard as the major phase of his art. Between 1953 and 1973, H.H. was to write under four pseudonyms over forty books.

Three years in Mexico City. Two years in Tokyo. Three years at Montevideo (as consul, according to *Who's Who;* actually he was CIA station chief). During this decade 1950–60, H.H. created Gordon Davis who wrote *I Came to Kill* (Fawcett, 1954). In 1957 H.H. gave birth to Robert Dietrich who specialized in thrillers, featuring Steve Bentley, formerly of the CIA and now a tax consultant. Steve Bentley first appears in *Be My Victim* (1957). It is interesting that the Bentley stories are set in Washington, DC, a city which as far as I can judge H.H. could not have known at all well at the time. According to Mr. Szulc, H.H. was briefly at CIA headquarters in 1949; otherwise he was abroad until the 1960s. Presumably the city whose symbol was one day to be Watergate always had a symbiotic attraction for him.

From the number of books that H.H. began to turn out, one might suspect that he was not giving his full attention to the work of the CIA. Nevertheless, in 1954, H.H. found time to assist in the overthrow of the liberal government of Jacobo Arbenz in Guatemala.

H.H. has now published *Give Us This Day,* his version of what *really* happened at the Bay of Pigs. He also tells us something about the Guatemala adventure where he had worked under a Mr. Tracy Barnes who was "suave and popular . . . a product of Groton, Yale, and Harvard Law. Through marriage he was connected to the Rockefeller clan. . . ." Incidentally, both the OSS and its successor the CIA of the early cold war were manned by fun-loving American nobles. Considering H.H.'s love of the patriciate, it is not impossible that his principal motive in getting into the cloak-and-dagger game was to keep the best company. The hick from western New York who had gone not to Harvard but to Brown, who had not fought in the Second War but worked behind the lines, who had failed as a serious novelist found for himself in the CIA a marvelous sort of club where he could rub shoulders with those nobles whose *savoir-faire* enthralled him.

After all, social climbing is one of the most exciting games our classless society has to offer.

But as Scott Fitzgerald suspected, the nobles are not like those who would serve them on the heights. They are tough eggs who like a good time whether it is playing polo or murdering enemies of the state. They take nothing seriously except their pleasures and themselves. Their admirers never understand this. Commie-hunting which is simply fun for the gamesters became for their plebian friend a holy mission. And so it is the true believer H.H. who is in the clink today while his masters are still at large, having good times. Of course they make awful messes, as Fitzgerald noted; luckily the Howies of this world are there to clean up after them.

In recruiting H.H. for the Bay of Pigs, Barnes expected to use him as "on that prior operation—Chief of Political Action . . . to assist Cuban exiles in overthrowing Castro." This means that H.H. had worked with Guatemalan right-wingers in order to remove Arbenz. "The nucleus of the project was already in being —a cadre of officers I had worked with against Arbenz. This time, however, all trace of US official involvement must be avoided, and so I was to be located not in the Miami area, but in Costa Rica." Later in the book we learn that "the scheduled arrival of Soviet arms in Guatemala had determined the date of our successful anti-Arbenz effort." Arms which the American government had refused to supply.

During a meeting with President Idigoras of Guatemala (who was giving aid, comfort, and a military base to the anti-Castro forces) H.H. "thought back to the period before the overthrow of Colonel Arbenz when CIA was treating with three exiled leaders: Colonel Castillo Armas, Dr. Juan Cordova Cerna, and Colonel Miguel Idigoras Fuentes. As a distinguished and respected jurist, Cordova Cerna had my personal vote as provisional president . . ." But H.H. was not to be a kingmaker this time. Castillo Armas was chosen by the golden gamesters, only to be "assassinated by a member of the presidential bodyguard in whose pocket was found a card from Radio Moscow. . . ." They always carry cards—thank God! Otherwise how can you tell the bad from the good guys?

One studies the book for clues to H.H.'s character and career; daydreams are always more revelatory than night dreams. As I have noted, H.H. chose Washington, DC, as setting for the Robert Dietrich thrillers starring Steve Bentley. Although he could not have known the city well in the fifties, he writes knowledgeably of the broken-down bars, the seedy downtown area, the life along the wharfs—but of course low-life scenes are the same everywhere and I can't say that I recognize my native city in his hard-boiled pages.

Here is Georgetown. "In early Colonial times it was a center of periwigged fashion and Federalist snobbery that lasted a hundred years. For another eighty the close-built dwellings settled and tottered apart until only Negroes would live there, eight to a room. Then for the last twenty-five years, the process reversed. The New Deal's flood of bureaucrats claimed Georgetown as its own. . . . On the fringes huddle morose colonies of dikes and nances, the shops and restaurants have names that are ever so quaint, and sometimes it seemed a shame that the slaves had ever left." The narrator, Steve Bentley, is a tough guy who takes pride in the fact that Washington has "per capita, more rape, more crimes of violence, more perversion, more politicians, more liquor, more good food, more bad food . . . than any other city in the world. A fine place if you have enterprise, durability, money, and powerful friends." It also helps to have a good lawyer.

The adventures of Steve Bentley are predictable: beautiful girl in trouble; a murder or two. There is a great deal of heavy drinking in H.H.'s novels; in fact, one can observe over the years a shift in the author's attitude from a devil-may-care-let's-get-drunk-and-have-a-good-time preppishness to an obsessive need for the juice to counteract the melancholy of middle age; the hangovers, as described, get a lot worse, too. Mr. Szulc tells us that in real life H.H. had been known to tipple and on at least one occasion showed a delighted Washington party his CIA credentials. H.H.'s taste in food moves from steak in the early books (a precious item in wartime so reminiscent of today's peacetime arrangements) to French wine and lobster. As a student of H.H. I was pleased to learn that H.H. and his fellow burglars dined on lobster the night of the Watergate break-in. I think I know who did the ordering.

It is a curious fact that despite American right-wingers' oft-declared passion for the American Constitution they seem always to dislike the people's elected representatives. One would think that an enthusiasm for the original republic would put them squarely on the side of a legislature which represents not the

dreaded people but those special and usually conservative interests who pay for elections. But there is something about a congressman—any congressman—that irritates the American right-
winger and H.H. is no exception.

Angel Eyes (Dell, 1961) is typical. Beautiful blonde calls on Steve
Bentley. Again we get his philosophy about Washington. "A
great city. . . . All you need is money, endurance, and powerful
friends." The blonde has a powerful friend. She is the doxie of
"Senator Tom Quinby. Sixty-four if he was a day, from a back-
woods, hillbilly state that featured razorback hogs, turkey-neck
sharecroppers, and contempt for Civil Rights. . . . A prohibition-
ist and a flag-waving moralizer." One suspects a bit of deceit in
the course of the Steve Bentley thrillers. They are not as heavily
right-wing and commie-baiting as the Howard Hunt or John
Baxter or Gordon Davis works, while some of the coloreds are
actually OK guys in Steve Bentley's book. All the more reason,
however, to find odd the contempt for a tribune of the people
whose political views (except on prohibition) must be close to
H.H.'s own.

I suspect that the root of the problem is, simply, a basic loathing of democracy, even of the superficial American sort. The
boobs will only send boobs to Congress unless a clever smooth
operator like Representative Lansdale in *End of a Stripper* manages to buy an election in order to drive the country, wittingly
or unwittingly, further along the road to collectivism. It would
be much simpler in the world of Steve Bentley not to have elections of any kind.

Steve doesn't much cotton to lady publishers either. "Mrs. Jay
Redpath, otherwise known as Alma Ward" (or Mrs. Philip Graham, otherwise known as Kay Meyer) makes an appearance in
Angel Eyes, and hard as nails she is. But Steve masters the pinko
spitfire. He masters everything, in fact, but Washington itself
with its "muggers and heroin pushers and the whiteslavers and
the faggotry. . . . This town needs a purifying rain!" Amen to that,
Howie.

In 1960 H.H. published three Dietrich thrillers. In 1961 H.H.
published two Dietrich thrillers. In 1962 there was no Dietrich
thriller. But as John Baxter H.H. published *Gift for Gomala* (Lippincott, 1962). The dates are significant. In 1961 H.H. was involved
in the Bay of Pigs and so, presumably, too busy to write books.
After the Bay of Pigs, he dropped Robert Dietrich and revived

John Baxter, a straight if rather light novelist who deals with the not-so-high comedy of Kennedy Washington.

H.H. begins his apologia for his part in the Bay of Pigs with the statement that "No event since the communization of China in 1949 has had such a profound effect on the United States and its allies as the defeat of the US-trained Cuban invasion brigade at the Bay of Pigs in April, 1961. Out of that humiliation grew the Berlin Wall, the missile crisis, guerrilla warfare throughout Latin America and Africa, and our Dominican Republic intervention. Castro's beachhead triumph opened a bottomless Pandora's box of difficulties . . ." This is the classic reactionary's view of the world, uncompromised by mere fact. How does one lose China if one did not possess China in the first place? And what on earth did Johnson's loony intervention in the Dominican Republic really have to do with our unsuccessful attempt to overthrow Castro?

H.H. deplores the shortness of the national memory for America's disgrace twelve years ago. He denounces the media's effort to make JFK seem a hero for having pulled back from the brink of World War III. Oddly, he remarks that "The death of Jack Ruby and worldwide controversy over William Manchester's book for a time focused public attention on events surrounding the assassination of John Fitzgerald Kennedy. Once again it became fashionable to hold the city of Dallas collectively responsible for his murder. Still, and let this not be forgotten, Lee Harvey Oswald was a partisan of Fidel Castro, and an admitted Marxist who made desperate efforts to join the Red Revolution in Havana. In the end he was an activist for the Fair Play for Cuba Committee." Well, this is what H.H. and a good many like-minded people want us to believe. But is it true? Or special pleading? Or a cover story? A pattern emerges.

H.H.'s memoir is chatty. He tells how in 1926 his father traced an absconding partner to Havana and with an army Colt .45 got back his money. "Father's intervention was direct, illegal, and effective." Years later his son's Cuban work proved to be indirect and ineffective; but at least it was every bit as illegal as Dad's. Again one comes up against the paradox of the right-wing American who swears by law and order yet never hesitates to break the law for his own benefit. Either law and order is simply a code phrase meaning get the commie-weirdo-fag-nigger-lovers or H.H.'s Nixonian concept of law and order is not due process but vigilante.

As H.H. tells us how he is brought into the Cuban adventure, the narrative reads just like one of his thrillers with the same capsule biographies, the same tight-lipped asides. "I'm a career officer. I take orders and carry them out." It appears that ex-President Figueres offered to provide the anti-Castro Cubans with a base in Costa Rica (the same Figueres sheltered Mr. Vesco). But the Costa Rican government decided not to be host to the patriots so H.H. set up his Cuban government-in-exile in Mexico City, resigning from the Foreign Service (his cover). He told everyone he had come into some money and planned to live in Mexico. Privately, he tells us, he was dedicated to getting rid of the "blood-soaked gang" in Havana by shedding more blood.

This was the spring and summer of 1960 and Kennedy and Nixon were running for president. Since Kennedy's denunciations of the commie regime ninety miles off the coast of Florida were more bellicose than Nixon's, the exiled Cubans tended to be pro-Kennedy in the election. But not H.H. He must have known even then that JFK was a communist at heart because his chief support came from the pinko elements in the land. H.H. also had a certain insight into the new President's character because "JFK and I were college contemporaries" (what he means is that when Jack was at Harvard Howie was at Brown) "and I had met him at a Boston debut" (of what?) "where he was pointed out to me. . . . I freely confess not having discerned in his relaxed lineaments the future naval hero, Pulitzer laureate, Senator, and President."

Meanwhile H.H. is stuck with his provisional government in Mexico and he was "disappointed. For Latin American males their caliber was about average; they displayed most Latin faults and few Latin virtues." In other words, shiftless but not musical. What can an associate member of the Wasp patriciate and would-be killer of commies do but grin and bear it and try to make a silk purse or two of his Latin pigs' ears?

In 1960 Allen Dulles received the top team for a briefing on the proposed liberation of Cuba. H.H. was there and tells us of the plan to drop paratroopers at "Santa Clara, located almost in Cuba's geographic center" while "reinforcing troops would land by plane at Santa Clara and Trinidad . . . on the southern coast." Assuming that Castro's troops would be in the Havana area, the Brigade would "march east and west, picking up strength as they went." There would also be, simultaneously, a fifth column to "blow up bridges and cut communications." But "let me underscore that neither during this nor other meetings was it asserted

that the underground or the populace was to play a decisive role
in the campaign." H.H. goes on to explain that the CIA operation
was to be essentially military and he admits, tacitly, that there
would probably be no great uprising against Castro. This is candid but then H.H. wants no part of *any* revolution. At one point
he explains to us correctly that the American revolution was not
a class revolution but a successful separation of a colony from an
empire. "Class warfare, therefore, is of foreign origin."

The Kennedy administration did not inspire H.H. with confidence. Richard Goodwin, Arthur Schlesinger, Jr., Chester
Bowles "all had a common background in Americans for Democratic Action—the ADA." In H.H.'s world to belong to ADA is
tantamount to membership in the Communist party. True to
form, the White House lefties started saying that the Castro revolution had been a good thing until betrayed by Castro. This
Trotskyite variation was also played by Manolo Ray, a liberal
Cuban leader H.H. found as eminently shallow and opportunistic as the White House found noble. H.H. had his hands full with
the Consejo or government-to-be of Cuba.

Meanwhile, troops were being trained in Guatemala. H.H.
made a visit to their secret camp and took a number of photographs of the Brigade. Proud of his snaps, he thought they should
be published in order to "stimulate recruiting"; also, to show the
world that members of the Consejo were getting on well with the
Brigade, which they were not.

At this point in time (as opposed to fictional points out of time),
aristocratic Tracy Barnes suggested that H.H. meet Arthur
Schlesinger, Jr., at the White House where Camelot's historian
was currently "pounding out" the White Paper on Cuba for
Arthur the King. Arthur the historian "was seated at his desk
typing furiously, a cigarette clinging to his half-open mouth,
looking as disorderly as when we had first met in Paris a decade
before." Although H.H.'s style is not elegant he seldom comes up
with an entirely wrong word; it is particularly nice that in the
monster-ridden cellar of his brain the word "disorderly" should
have surfaced instead of "disheveled" for are not all ADA'ers
enemies of law'n'order and so *dis*orderly?

During this meeting, H.H. learns that Dean Rusk has vetoed
the seizure from the air of Trinidad because the world would
then know that the US was deeply implicated in the invasion.
(The word "incursion" had not yet been minted by the empire's

hard-working euphemists.) Then the supreme master of disorder appeared in the historian's office. Said Adlai Stevenson to aristocratic Tracy Barnes, " 'Everything going well, Tracy?' and Barnes gave a positive response. This exchange is important for it was later alleged that Stevenson had been kept in the dark about invasion preparations."

Later, waiting in the press secretary's office, "I sat on Pamela Turnure's desk until the getaway signal came and we could leave the White House unobserved, much like President Harding's mistress." This is Saint-Simon, as told to Harold Robbins!

D-Day. "I was not on the beachhead, but I have talked with many Cubans who were." Shades of the war novelists of a quarter century before! "Rather than attempt to write what has been written before, it is enough to say that there were no cowards on the beach, aboard the assault ships or in the air." But the Bay of Pigs was a disaster for the free world and H.H. uses the word "betrayal." As the sun set on the beachhead which he never saw, "only vultures moved." Although safe in Washington, "I was sick of lying and deception, heartsick over political compromise and military defeat." Fortunately, H.H.'s sickness with lying and deception was only temporary. Ten years later Camelot would be replaced by Watergate and H.H. would at last be able to hit the beach in freedom's name.

At least two other Watergate burglars were involved with the Bay of Pigs caper. "Co-pilot [of a plane that dropped leaflets over Havana] was an ex-Marine named Frank Fiorini," who is identified in a footnote: "Later, as Frank Sturgis, a Watergate defendant." That is H.H.'s only reference to Sturgis/Fiorini.* On the other hand, he tells us a good deal about Bernard "Bernie" L. Barker, "Cuban-born US citizen. First man in Cuba to volunteer after Pearl Harbor. Served as USAF Captain/Bombardier. Shot down and spent eighteen months in a German prison camp." H.H. tells us how Bernie was used by the CIA to infiltrate the Havana police so "that the CIA could have an inside view of Cuban antisubversive operations." Whatever that means. Bernie was H.H.'s assistant in Miami during the pre-invasion period. He was "eager, efficient, and completely dedicated." It was Bernie who brought Dr. Jose Miró Cardona into H.H.'s life. Miró is a right-wing "former president of the Cuban bar" and later head

---

*The hero of *Bimini Run* is called Sturgis.

of the Cuban revolutionary council. He had also been, briefly, Castro's prime minister.

Bernie later became a real estate agent in Miami. Later still, he was to recruit two of his employees, Felipe de Diego and Eugenio P. Martinez, for duty as White House burglars. According to Barker, de Diego had conducted "a successful raid to capture Castro government documents," while Martinez made over "300 infiltrations into Castro Cuba." At the time of Watergate Martinez was still on the CIA payroll.

Give Us This Day is dedicated "To the Men of Brigade 2506." The hero of the book is a very handsome young Cuban leader named Artime. H.H. prints a photograph of this glamorous youth with one arm circling the haunted-eyed author-conspirator. It is a touching picture. No arm, however, figuratively speaking, ever encircles the equally handsome Augustus of the West. H.H. is particularly exercised by what he believes to have been Kennedy's tactic "to whitewash the New Frontier by heaping guilt on the CIA." H.H. is bitter at the way the media played along with this "unparalleled campaign of vilification and obloquy that must have made the Kremlin mad with joy." To H.H., the real enemy is anyone who affects "to see communism springing from poverty" rather than from the machinations of the men in the Kremlin.

"On December 29, 1962, President Kennedy reviewed the survivors of the Brigade in Miami's Orange Bowl. Watching the televised ceremony, I saw Pepe San Román give JFK the Brigade's flag" (Footnote: "Artime told me the flag was a replica, and that the Brigade feeling against Kennedy was so great that the presentation nearly did not take place") "for temporary safekeeping. In response the President said, 'I can assure you that this flag will be returned to this Brigade in a free Havana.'" H.H. adds sourly, "One wonders what time period he had in mind."

Who's Who tells us that H.H. was a consultant with the Defense Department 1960–65. Mr. Szulc finds this period of H.H.'s saga entirely murky. Apparently H.H. became personal assistant to Allen Dulles after the Bay of Pigs. Mr. Szulc also tells us that in 1963 the American ambassador to Spain refused to accept H.H. as deputy chief of the local CIA station because of H.H.'s peculiar activities as station chief for Uruguay in 1959. After persuading that country's president Nardone to ask Eisenhower to keep him *en poste* in Uruguay, H.H. then tried to overthrow the same

President Nardone without telling the American ambassador. It was this tactless treatment of the *ambassador* that cost H.H. the Spanish post.

One of H.H.'s friends told Mr. Szulc, "This is when Howard really began losing touch with reality."* In *Give Us This Day* H.H. tells us how he tried to sell Tracy Barnes on having Castro murdered. Although H.H. gives the impression that he failed to persuade the CIA to have a go at killing the Antichrist, columnist Jack Anderson has a different story to tell about the CIA. In a column for January 25, 1971, he tells us that an attempt was made to kill Castro in March 1961, a month before the invasion. Castro was to be poisoned with a capsule in his food. Capsule to be supplied by one John Roselli—a Las Vegas mobster who was eager to overthrow Castro and re-open the mob's casinos. Also involved in the project was a former FBI agent Robert Maheu, later to be Howard Hughes's viceroy at Las Vegas.

It is known that Castro did become ill in March. In February–March 1963, the CIA again tried to kill Castro. Anderson wonders, not illogically, if Castro might have been sufficiently piqued by these attempts on his life to want to knock off Kennedy. This was Lyndon Johnson's theory. He thought the Castroites had hired Oswald. The Scourge of Asia was also distressed to learn upon taking office that "We had been operating a damned Murder, Inc., in the Caribbean." Since it is now clear to everyone except perhaps Earl Warren that Oswald was part of a conspiracy, who were his fellow conspirators? Considering Oswald's strenuous attempts to identify himself with Castro, it is logical to assume that his associates had Cuban interests. But which Cubans? Pro-Castro or anti-Castro?

I think back on the evidence Sylvia Odio gave the FBI and the Warren Commission's investigators.† Mrs. Odio was an anti-Castro, pro-Manolo Ray Cuban exile who two months before the assassination of President Kennedy was visited in her Dallas apartment by three men. Two were Latins (Mexican, she thought, they weren't the right color for Cubans). The third, she maintained, was Oswald. They said they were members of her friend Manolo Ray's organization and one of them said that their

---

**The New York Times Magazine*, June 3, 1973, p. 11.

†Warren Commission *Hearings*, Vols. XI:369–381 and XXVI:834–838; see also National Archives: Commission Document No. 1553.

companion Oswald thought Kennedy should have been shot after the Bay of Pigs. If Mrs. Odio is telling the truth, then whoever was about to murder Kennedy may have wanted the left-wing anti-Castro group of Manolo Ray to get the credit.*

During this period Oswald's behavior was odd but not, necessarily, as official chroniclers maintain, mad. Oswald was doing his best to become identified publicly with the Fair Play for Cuba Committee as well as setting himself up privately as a sort of Soviet spy by writing a mysterious "fact"-filled letter to the Soviet Embassy. That the Russians were genuinely mystified by his letter was proved when they turned it over to the American government after the assassination. Also, most intriguingly, Oswald visited Mexico City in September 1963, where H.H. was acting chief of the CIA station. Finally, Oswald's widow tells us that he took a pot-shot at the reactionary General Walker, the sort of thing a deranged commie would do. Was he then simply a deranged commie? The right-wing Cubans and their American admirers certainly want us to think so.

After the murder of the President, one of those heard from was Frank Fiorini/Sturgis, who was quoted in the Pompano Beach, Florida, *Sun-Sentinel* to the effect that Oswald had been in touch with Cuban Intelligence the previous year, as well as with pro-Castroites in Miami, Mexico City, New Orleans. A Mrs. Marjorie Brazil reported that she had heard that Oswald had been in Miami demonstrating in front of the office of the Cuban Revolutionary Council headed by our old friend Dr. Miró Cardona. A sister of one Miguel Suarez told nurse Marjorie Heimbecker who told the FBI that JFK would be killed by Castroites. The FBI seems eventually to have decided that they were dealing with a lot of wishful thinkers.

*The Warren Commission and the FBI never satisfactorily identified Mrs. Odio's visitors. Just before the Report was finished, the FBI reported to the Warren Commission that one Loran Eugene Hall, "a participant in numerous anti-Castro activities," had recalled visiting her with two other men, one of them, William Seymour, resembling Oswald. But after the Report appeared the FBI sent the Commission a report that Hall had retracted his story and that Mrs. Odio could not identify Hall or Seymour as the men she had seen. (See Richard H. Popkin, *The Second Oswald* [Avon, 1967], pp. 75–80.) Hall had already been brought to the Commission's attention in June 1964, under the names of "Lorenzo Hall, *alias* Lorenzo Pascillio." The FBI heard in Los Angeles that Hall and a man called Jerry Patrick Hemming had pawned a 30.06 rifle, which Hall redeemed shortly before the assassination with a check drawn on the account of the "Committee to Free Cuba." Hemming was identified in 1962 as one of the leaders of Frank Sturgis's anti-Castro brigade. (See Warren Commission Document 1179:296–298 and Hans Tanner, *Counter Revolutionary Brigade* [London, 1962], p. 127.)

Finally, Fiorini/Sturgis denied the story in the *Sun-Sentinel;* he said that he had merely speculated with the writer on some of the gossip that was making the rounds in Miami's anti-Castro Cuban community. The gossip, however, tended to be the same: Oswald had killed Kennedy, on orders from Castro or from those of his admirers who thought that the murder of an American president might in some way save the life of a Cuban president.

Yet the only Cuban group that would be entirely satisfied by Kennedy's death would be the right-wing enemies of Castro who held Kennedy responsible for their humiliation at the Bay of Pigs. To kill him would avenge their honor. Best of all, setting up Oswald as a pro-Castro, pro-Moscow agent, they might be able to precipitate some desperate international crisis that would serve their cause. Certainly Castro at this date had no motive for killing Kennedy, who had ordered a crackdown on clandestine Cuban raids from the United States—of the sort that Eugenio Martinez is alleged so often to have made.

I suspect that whoever planned the murder must have been astonished at the reaction of the American establishment. The most vengeful of all the Kennedys made no move to discover who really killed his brother. In this, Bobby was a true American: close ranks, pretend there was no conspiracy, do not rock the boat—particularly when both Moscow and Havana seemed close to nervous breakdowns at the thought that they might be implicated in the death of the Great Prince. The Warren Report then assured the nation that the lone killer who haunts the American psyche had struck again. The fact that Bobby Kennedy accepted the Warren Report was proof to most people (myself among them) that Oswald acted alone. It was not until several years later that I learned from a member of the family that although Bobby was head of the Department of Justice at the time, he refused to look at any of the FBI reports or even speculate on what might have happened at Dallas. Too shaken up, I was told.

Fortunately, others have tried to unravel the tangle. Most intriguing is Richard H. Popkin's theory that there were two Oswalds.* One was a bad shot; did not drive a car; wanted the world to know that he was pro-Castro. This Oswald was caught by the Dallas police and murdered on television. The other Oswald was seen driving a car, firing at a rifle range, perhaps talking to Mrs.

*Popkin, *The Second Oswald* (Avon, 1967).

Odio; he was hired by . . . ? I suspect we may find out one of these days.

In 1962, H.H. published *A Gift for Gomala* as John Baxter. This was an attempt to satirize the age of Camelot. Lippincott suggests that it is *"must* reading for followers of Reston, Alsop and Lippmann who are looking for comic relief." One would think that anyone who tried to follow all three of those magi would be beyond comic relief. The tale is clumsy: a black opportunist dresses up as a representative from a new African nation and tries to get a loan from Congress; on the verge of success, Gomala ceases to exist. Like Evelyn Waugh, H.H. thinks African republics are pretty joky affairs but he gives us no jokes.

For about a year during this period (1965–66) H.H. was living in Spain. Whether or not he was working for the CIA is moot. We do know that he was creating a new literary persona: David St. John, whose specialty is thrusting a CIA man named Peter Ward into exotic backgrounds with a bit of diabolism thrown in.

As Gordon Davis, H.H. also wrote *Where Murder Waits,* a book similar in spirit to *Limit of Darkness.* In the early work H.H. daydreams about the brave lads who flew out of Henderson, often to death against the foe. In *Where Murder Waits* H.H.'s dream self hits the beach at the Bay of Pigs, that beach where, finally, only vultures stirred. Captured, the hero spends nine months in the prisons of the archfiend Castro. Once again: Expiation for H.H. —in dreams begins self-love.

It is curious that as H.H. moves out of the shadows and into the glare of Watergate his books are more and more open about his political obsessions. *The Coven,* by David St. John, is copyrighted 1972. In July of 1971, on the recommendation of Charles W. ("If you have them by the balls their hearts and minds will follow") Colson, H.H. was hired by the White House and became a part-time criminal at $100 a day. Zeal for his new masters informs every page of *The Coven.* The villain is the hustling handsome rich young Senator Vane with "a big appeal to the young and disadvantaged" (i.e., commies)—just like Jack-Bobby-Teddy. The description of Mrs. Vane makes one think irresistibly (and intentionally) of Madame Onassis—not to mention Harold Robbins, Jacqueline Susann, and the horde of other writers who take such people and put them in books thinly revealed rather than disguised.

"The Vanes are legally married to each other and that's about all. Their private lives are separate. He's a terror among the chicks, and she gets her jollies from the artists, writers and beach boy types Vane gets public grants for." She also seduces her narrator. "I had seen a hundred magazine and newspaper photographs of her cutting ribbons, first-nighting, fox-hunting at Warrenton, and empathizing with palsied kids. . . ." But, as H.H. reminds us, "only a fool thinks there's any resemblance between a public figure's public image and reality." Fortunately the narrator is able to drive the Vane family out of public life (they are prone to taking off their clothes at orgies where the devil is invoked). H.H. believes quite rightly that the presidency must never go to devil-worshipers who appeal to the young and disadvantaged.

The chronology of H.H.'s life is a tangle until 1968 when he buys Witches Island, a house at Potomac, Maryland (his wife went in for horses). On April 30, 1970, the new squire retired from the CIA under a cloud—he had failed too often. But H.H. had a pension; he also had a lively new pseudonym David St. John; his wife Dorothy had a job at the Spanish Embassy. But H.H. has always needed money so he went to work for Robert R. Mullen and Company, a PR firm with links to the Republican party and offices not only a block from the White House but across the street from the Committee to Re-elect the President.

Mullen represented Howard Hughes in Washington. H.H. knew his way around the Hughes operation—after all, Hughes's man in Las Vegas was Robert Maheu, whose contribution to Cuban affairs, according to Jack Anderson,* was to "set up the Castro assassination" plot in 1961, and whose contribution to Nixon was to funnel $100,000 to Bebe Rebozo in 1970. But Hughes sacked Maheu late in 1970. In 1971 H.H. found a second home at the White House, assigned with G. Gordon Liddy to "the Room 16 project" where the administration prepared its crimes.

Room 16 marks the high point of H.H.'s career; his art and arts were now perfected. Masterfully, he forged; he burglared; he conspired. The Shakespeare of the CIA had found, as it were, his Globe Theatre. Nothing was beyond him—including tragedy. According to *Newsweek*, John Dean told Senate investigators that H.H. "had a contract" from "low-level White House officials" to murder the president of Panama for not obeying with sufficient

---

*Japan *Times*, January 23, 1971.

zeal the American Bureau of Narcotics directives. "Hunt, according to Dean, had his team in Mexico before the mission was aborted."*

As the world now knows, on the evening of June 16, 1972, H.H. gave a splendid lobster dinner to the Watergate burglars and then sent Bernie Barker and his Cubans into battle to bug the offices of the Democratic party because H.H. had been told by G. Gordon Liddy "that Castro funds were going to the Democrats in hopes that a rapprochement with Cuba would be effected by a successful Democratic presidential candidate." H.H. has also said (*Time*, August 27, 1973) that his own break-in of the office of Daniel Ellsberg's psychiatrist was an attempt to find out whether Ellsberg "might be a controlled agent for the Sovs."

One daydreams: "Dr. Fielding, I have these terrible headaches. They started just after I met my control Ivan and he said, 'Well, boychick, it's been five years now since you signed on as a controlled agent. Now I guess you know that if there's one thing we Sovs hate it's a non-producer so . . .' Dr. Fielding, I hope you're writing all this down and not just staring out the window like last time."

Now for the shooting of George Wallace. It is not unnatural to suspect the White House burglars of having a hand in the shooting. But suspicion is not evidence and there is no evidence that H.H. was involved. Besides, a good CIA man would no doubt have preferred the poison capsule to a gunshot . . . slipping ole George the sort of slow but lethal dose that Castro's powerful gut rejected. In an AP story this summer, former CIA official Miles Copeland is reported to have said that "senior agency officials are convinced Senator Edward Muskie's damaging breakdown during the presidential campaign last year was caused by convicted Watergate conspirator E. Howard Hunt or his henchman spiking his drink with a sophisticated form of LSD."†

When Wallace ran for president in 1968, he got 13 percent of the vote; and Nixon nearly lost to Humphrey. In May 1972, 17 percent favored Wallace for president in the Harris poll. Wallace had walked off with the Michigan Democratic primary. Had he continued his campaign for president as an independent or as a Democrat in states where he was not filed under his own party,

*Newsweek, June 18, 1973, p. 22.
†AP dispatch, London, August 17, 1973.

he could have swung the election to the Democrats, or at least denied Nixon a majority and sent the election to the House.

"This entire strategy of ours," Robert Finch said in March 1972, "depends on whether George Wallace makes a run on his own." For four years Nixon had done everything possible to keep Wallace from running; and failed. "With Wallace apparently stronger in the primaries in 1972 than he had been before," Theodore White observed, "with the needle sticking at 43 percent of the vote for Nixon, the President was still vulnerable—until, of course, May 15 and the shooting. Then it was all over."*

Wallace was shot by the now familiar lone assassin—a demented (as usual) busboy named Arthur Bremer. Then on June 21, 1973, the headline in the *New York Post* was "Hunt Tells of Orders to Raid Bremer's Flat."

According to the story by Bob Woodward and Carl Bernstein, H.H. told the Senate investigators that an hour after Wallace was shot, Colson ordered him to fly to Milwaukee and burglarize the flat of Arthur H. Bremer, the would-be assassin—in order to connect Bremer somehow with the commies? Characteristically, the television senators let that one slip by them. As one might expect, Colson denied ordering H.H. to Milwaukee for any purpose. Colson did say that he had talked to H.H. about the shooting. Colson also said that he had been having dinner with the President that evening. Woodward and Bernstein's "White House source" said, "The President became deeply upset and voiced concern that the attempt on Wallace's life might have been made by someone with ties to the Republican Party or the Nixon campaign." This, Nixon intuited, might cost him the election.†

May 15, 1972, Arthur H. Bremer shot George Wallace, governor of Alabama, at Laurel, Maryland; easily identified as the gunman, he was taken into custody. Nearby in a rented car, the police found Bremer's diary (odd that in the post-Gutenberg age Oswald, Sirhan, and Bremer should have all committed to paper their *pensées*).

According to the diary, Bremer had tried to kill Nixon in Canada but failed to get close enough. He then decided to kill George Wallace. The absence of any logical motive is now familiar to most Americans, who are quite at home with the batty

---

The Making of the President, 1972 (Atheneum, 1973), p. 238.
†*New York Post,* June 21, 1973, reprinting a *Washington Post* story.

killer who acts alone in order to be on television, to be forever
entwined with the golden legend of the hero he has gunned
down. In a nation that worships psychopaths, the Oswald-Brem-
er-Sirhan-Ray figure is to the general illness what Robin Hood
was to a greener, saner world.

Bremer's diary is a fascinating work—of art? From what we
know of the twenty-two-year-old author he did not have a literary
turn of mind (among his effects were comic books, some porno).
He was a television baby, and a dull one. Politics had no interest
for him. Yet suddenly—for reasons he never gives us—he decides
to kill the President and starts to keep a diary on April 4, 1972.

According to Mr. Szulc, in March 1972, H.H. visited Dita ("call
me Mother") Beard in Denver. Wearing a red wig and a voice
modulator, H.H. persuaded Dita to denounce as a forgery the
memo she had written linking ITT's pay-off to the Republican
party with the government's subsequent dropping of the best
part of its antitrust suit against the conglomerate. In May, H.H.
was installing the first set of bugs at the Democratic headquarters. His movements between April 4 and May 15 might be use-
fully examined—not to mention those of G. Gordon Liddy, et al.

For someone who is supposed to be nearly illiterate there are
startling literary references and flourishes in the Bremer diary.
The second entry contains "You heard of *One Day in the Life of
Ivan Dynisovich*'? Yesterday was my day." The misspelling of
Denisovich is not bad at all. Considering the fact that the name
is a hard one for English-speaking people to get straight, it is
something of a miracle that Bremer could sound the four syllables
of the name correctly in his head. Perhaps he had the book in
front of him but if he had, he would not have got the one letter
wrong.

The same entry produces more mysteries. "Wallace got his big
votes from Republicans who didn't have any choice of candidates
on their own ballot. Had only about $1055 when I left." This is
the first and only mention of politics until page 45 when he
describes his square clothes and haircut as "just a disguise to get
close to Nixon."

One reference to Wallace at the beginning; then another one
to Nixon a dozen pages later. Also, where did the $1,055 come
from? Finally, a minor psychological point—Bremer refers to
some weeds as "taller than me 5'6". I doubt if a neurotic twenty-
two-year-old would want to remind himself on the page that he

is only 5'6" tall. When people talk to themselves they seldom say anything so obvious. On the other hand, authors like this sort of detail.

Popular paperback fiction requires a fuck scene no later than a dozen pages into the narrative. The author of the diary gives us a good one. Bremer goes to a massage parlor in New York (he has told the diary that he is a virgin—Would he? Perhaps) where he is given an unsatisfying hand-job. The scene is nicely done and the author writes correctly and lucidly until, suddenly, a block occurs and he can't spell anything right—as if the author suddenly remembers that he is meant to be illiterate.

One of these blocks occurs toward the end of the massage scene when the girl tells Bremer that she likes to go to "wo-gees." This is too cute to be believed. Every red-blooded American boy, virgin or not, knows the word "orgy." Furthermore, Bremer has been wandering around porno bookstores on 42nd Street and the word "orgy" occurs almost as often in his favored texts as "turgid." More to the point, when an illiterate is forced to guess at the spelling of a word he will render it phonetically. I cannot imagine that the girl said anything that sounded like "wo-gee." It is as if the author had suddenly recalled the eponymous hardhat hero of the film *Joe* (1970) where all the hippies got shot so satisfyingly and the "g" in orgy was pronounced hard. On this page, as though to emphasize Bremer's illiteracy, we get "spair" for "spare," "enphaais" for "emphasis," and "rememmber." Yet on the same page the diarist has no trouble spelling "anticipation," "response," "advances."

The author of the diary gives us a good many random little facts—seat numbers of airplanes, prices of meals. He does not like "hairy hippies." A dislike he shares with H.H. He also strikes oddly jarring literary notes. On his arrival in New York, he tells us that he forgot his guns which the captain then turned over to him, causing the diarist to remark "Irony abounds." A phrase one doubts that the actual Arthur Bremer would have used. As word and quality, irony is not part of America's demotic speech or style. Later, crossing the Great Lakes, he declares "Call me Ismal." Had he read *Moby Dick?* Unlikely. Had he seen the movie on the Late Show? Possibly. But I doubt that the phrase on the sound track would have stayed in his head.

The diary tells us how Bremer tried to kill Nixon. The spelling gets worse and worse as Bremer becomes "thruorly pissed off."

Yet suddenly he writes, "This will be one of the most closely read pages since the Scrolls in those caves." A late April entry records, "Had bad pain in my left temple † just in front † about it." He is now going mad as all the lone killers do, and refers to "writing a *War+Peace.*"

More sinister: "saw 'Clockwork Orange" and thought about getting Wallace all thru the picture—fantasing my self as the Alek on the screen. . . ." This is a low blow at highbrow sex 'n' violence books and flicks. It is also—again—avant-garde. Only recently has a debate begun in England whether or not the film *Clockwork Orange* may have caused unbalanced youths to commit crimes (clever youths now tell the Court with tears in their eyes that it was the movie that made them bash the nice old man and the Court is thrilled). The author anticipated that ploy all right —and no matter who wrote the diary we are dealing with a true author. One who writes, "Like a novelist who knows not how his book will end—I have written this journal—what a shocking surprise that my inner character shall steal the climax and destroy the author and save the anti-hero from assasination!" Only one misspelling in that purple patch. But "as I said befor, I Am A Hamlet." It is not irony that abounds so much in these pages as professional writing.

May 8, Bremer is reading *R.F.K. Must Die!* by Robert Blair Kaiser. Like his predecessor he wants to be noticed and then die because "suicide is a birth right." But Wallace did not die and Bremer did not die. He is now at a prison in Baltimore, awaiting a second trial. If he lives to be re-examined, one wonders if he will tell us what company he kept during the spring of 1972, and whether or not a nice man helped him to write his diary, as a document for the ages like the scrolls in those caves. (Although H.H. is a self-admitted forger of state papers I do not think that he actually had a hand in writing Bremer's diary on the ground that the journal is a brilliant if flawed job of work, and so beyond H.H.'s known literary competence.)

Lack of originality has marked the current administration's general style (as opposed to the vivid originality of its substance; witness, the first magistrate's relentless attempts to subvert the Constitution). Whatever PR has worked in the past is tried again. Goof? Then take the blame yourself—just like JFK after the Bay of Pigs. Caught with your hand in the till? Checkers' time on the tube and the pulling of heartstrings.

Want to assassinate a rival? Then how about the Dallas scenario? One slips into reverie. Why not set up Bremer as a crazy who wants to shoot Nixon (that will avert suspicion)? But have him fail to kill Nixon just as Oswald was said to have failed to kill *his* first target General Walker. In midstream have Bremer—like Oswald—shift to a different quarry. To the real quarry. Make Bremer, unlike Oswald, apolitical. Too heavy an identification with the Democrats might backfire. Then—oh, genius!—let's help him to write a diary to get the story across. (Incidentally, the creation of phony documents and memoirs is a major industry of our secret police forces. When the one-man terror of the Southeast Asian seas Lieutenant Commander Marcus Aurelius Arnheiter was relieved of his command, the Pentagon put him to work writing the "memoirs" of a fictitious Soviet submarine commander who had defected to the Free World.)*

The White House's reaction to the Watergate burglary was the first clue that something terrible has gone wrong with us. The elaborate and disastrous cover-up was out of all proportion to what was, in effect, a small crime the administration could have lived with. I suspect that our rulers' state of panic came from the fear that other horrors would come to light—as indeed they have. But have the horrors ceased? Is there something that our rulers know that we don't? Is it possible that during the dark night of our empire's defeat in Cuba and Asia the American story shifted from cheerful familiar farce to Jacobean tragedy—to murder, chaos?

*The Arnheiter Affair by Neil Sheehan (Random House, 1971).

The New York Review of Books
December 13, 1976

What Robert Moses Did to New York City

"When coming up from Richmond by the night train, Mr. Laurence Oliphant, myself, and many more, arrived at Acquia Creek about one o'clock; the passage thence to Washington takes four hours; and as we were much fatigued, and had only these four hours for rest, we begged that the key of our berths might be given to us at once. 'I'll attend to you when I'm through,' was the only answer we could get; and we waited—a train of ladies, young folks, gentlemen—until the man had arranged his affairs, and smoked his pipe, more than an hour. Yet not one word was said, except by Mr. Oliphant and myself. The man was in office; excuse enough in American eyes for doing as he pleased. This is the kind of circle in which they reason; take away his office, and the man is as good as we are; all men are free and equal; add office to equality, and he rises above our heads. More than once I have ventured to tell my friends that this habit of deferring to law and lawful authority, good in itself, has gone with them into extremes, and would lead them, should they let it grow, into the frame of mind for yielding to the usurpation of any bold despot who may assail their liberties, like Caesar, in the name of law and order!"

This little sermon occurs in a book called *New America* published in 1867 by an Englishman named William Hepworth Dixon. Since Mr. Dixon was a journalist of absolutely no distinction, one must take very seriously what he says because he only records the obvious. After a year among us it was plain to him that in the name of law and order Americans are quite capable of building themselves a prison and calling it Happy Acres or Freedom Park and to reach this paradise all you have to do is take your first left at the Major Deegan Expressway out of New York; then your second right just past Hawthorne Circle and so on up the Taconic State Parkway to where the Caesarian spirit of Robert Moses will lead you into the promised land.

For thirty or forty years I have seen the name Robert Moses on the front pages of newspapers or attached to articles in that graveyard of American prose the Sunday *New York Times Magazine* section. But I never had a clear idea just who he was because I never got past that forbiddingly dull title Parks Commissioner. I associated him with New York City and I lived upstate. I now realize what a lot I have missed, thanks to someone called Robert A. Caro whose life of Moses has not only taken me a month to read (there are 1,246 pages) but not once—uniquely—did I find myself glumly riffling the pages still to be read at the back.

To begin at the beginning: The United States has always been a corrupt society. Periodically, "good" citizens band together and elect to office political opportunists who are presented to the public as *non*-politicians. Briefly, things appear to be clean. But of course bribes are still given; taken. Nothing ever changes nor is there ever going to be any change until we summon up the courage to ask ourselves a simple if potentially dangerous question: Is the man who gives a bribe as guilty as the man who takes a bribe?

For decades Vice President-designate Nelson Rockefeller has used his family's money to buy and maintain the Republican party of the State of New York while his predecessor but one, Spiro Agnew, was busy taking money from various magnates who wanted favors done—men who differ from the Rockefellers only in degree. Yet the Agnews are thought to be deeply wicked (if found out) while no sign of Cain ever attaches itself to their corrupters. It is a curious double standard—rather like those laws that put the hooker in jail for selling her ass while letting the john go free with a wink. But then we are a godly people and, as Scripture hath it, it is better to give than to receive. Blessed then are the Kennedys and the Rockefellers who buy directly or indirectly the votes of the poor and the loyalty of their leaders in order that public office might be won, and personal vanity hugely served.

"The fact is New York politics were always dishonest—long before my time." So testified Boss Tweed a hundred years ago. "There never was a time when you couldn't buy the Board of Aldermen. A politician in coming forward takes things as they are. This population is too hopelessly split up into races and factions to govern it under universal suffrage, except by the bribery of patronage, or corruption." This is elegantly put. As far as we know, Robert Moses did not take money for himself like Tweed or Agnew. He was more ambitious than that. Wanting power, Moses used the people's money to buy, as it were, the Board of Aldermen over and over again for forty-four years during which time, if Mr. Caro is to be believed, he was, without peer, the fount of corruption in the state.

Mr. Caro starts his long story briskly. At Yale Moses was eager to raise money for the undergraduate Minor Sports Association. To get money, Moses planned to go to an alumnus interested only in the swimming team and con him into thinking that his contribution would go not to the association but to the swimmers. The captain of the team demurred. "I think that's a little bit tricky, Bob. I think that's a little bit smooth. I don't like that at all." Furious, Moses threatened to resign from the team. The resignation was promptly accepted. There, *in ovo*, was the future career: the high-minded ends (at least in Moses's own mind) as represented by the Minor Sports Association; the dishonest means to attain those ends; the fury at being crossed; the threat of resignation which, in this instance, to his amazement, was accepted. For decades that threat of resignation brought presidents, governors, and mayors to their knees until Nelson Rockefeller turned him out—by which time Moses was approaching eighty and no longer the killer he had been.

Robert Moses came from a well-to-do German Jewish family, very much at home in turn-of-the-century New York City. Apparently mother and grandmother were arrogant, intelligent, domineering women. I think Mr. Caro goes on a bit too much about how like grandmother and mother Moses is. Yet it is interesting to learn that his mother abandoned Judaism for Ethical Culture and that her son was never circumcised or bar-mitzvahed. Later he was to deny that he was a Jew at all.

From Yale Moses went to Oxford where he succumbed entirely to the ruling-class ethos of that glamorous place. For young Moses the ruling class of Edwardian England was the most enlightened the world had ever known, and its benign but firm ordering of the lower orders at home and the lesser breeds abroad ought, he believed, to be somehow transported to our own notoriously untidy, inefficient, and corrupt land. Moses's Ph.D. thesis *The Civil Service of Great Britain* reveals its author as non-liberal, to say the least. Fearful that ignorant workers might organize unions and behave irresponsibly, he sternly proposed "the remorseless exercise of the executive power of suppression and dismissal to solve this problem."

Moses returned to New York, wanting to do good. He saw himself as a proto-mandarin whose education, energy and intelligence made him peculiarly suited to regulate the lives of those less fortunate. But pre-1917 New York was still the New York of Boss Tweed. The unworldly Moses did not realize that if you want to build a new slum for the teeming masses or create a playground for the not-so-teeming but deserving middle classes you must first buy the Board of Aldermen. Now this is never a difficult thing to do. In fact, these amiable men will give you as much money as you want to do almost anything you want to do (assuming that the loot is on hand) *if* you in turn will give them a slice of that very same money.

In the old days this was done in a straightforward way: the tin box full of cash (although one fairly recent mayor eccentrically insisted on money being delivered to him at Gracie Mansion in pillowcases). But as the years passed and the IRS began to cast an ever-lengthening shadow across the land, politicians became wary. They set up law offices (sometimes in the back bedroom of a relative's house) where "legal fees" from the city or the builder could be collected. Or they became associated with public relations firms: "fees" from the city or the contractors would then be laundered for personal use in much the same way that a now famous contribution to Nixon's re-election campaign surfaced as a pair of diamond earrings dangling from the pretty ears of the First Criminal's moll.

Robert Moses's early years as a reformer in New York City were not happy. He joined something called the Bureau of Municipal Research, an instrument for reform—neither the first nor the last. He annoyed his fellow reformers with his imperious ways; his formidable intelligence; his impatience. Then at the end of 1918, the goddess from the machine descended to earth and put him on the path to power. The name of the goddess was Belle Moskowitz. Although a reformer, Belle was a superb politician who had early on seen the virtues of one Al Smith, a Tammany vulgarian whom everyone misunderstood and, more seriously, underestimated. Belle brought Moses and Smith together. They were made for each other. And rose together.

The writing of legislation is perhaps the highest art form the United States has yet achieved, even more original and compelling than the television commercial. In tortured language, legislators rob the people of their tax money in order to enrich themselves and their friends. As an assemblyman from the city, Al Smith had become a power at Albany by the unusual expedient of reading all the bills that were introduced. Lacking education but not shrewdness, Smith very soon figured out who was getting the cash and why. An honest man (relatively speaking), Smith used his knowledge of bill-drafting to gain power over the other legislators; also, from time to time, he was able to blackmail them into occasionally doing something for the ridiculous masses who had elected them.

As a result of these gratuitous acts of kindness, Smith became governor of New York. In the process, governor's aide Robert Moses became a positive Leonardo of bill-drafting. One of his earliest masterpieces (equal to the *Virgin with St. Anne and St. John* or the *Turtle Oil Cosmetic two-minute TV spot*) was the State Reconstruction Commission. Masterfully, Moses rearranged the structure of the state, giving his friend Smith more power than any governor had ever before exercised. Moses also saw to it that he himself got full credit for this masterwork even though there were many apprentices in his atelier and at least one other master—the future historian Charles A. Beard whom Moses later accused of plagiarism when, in fact, Beard was using his own unacknowledged material from the commission report. Artists!

If Robert Moses had not taken a house at Babylon, Long Island, the history of New York City might have been very different.

Going from the city to Babylon and back again, Moses began to think about public parks and beaches, about diversions for the worthy middle classes of the city. After all, the age of the automobile was in its bright morning; and no one then living could have foreseen its terrible evening. Like most right-minded men of the day, Moses thought that anyone who owned a car ought to have a nearby park or beach to go to; those without cars were obviously not worthwhile and ought to stay home. As the automobile was the labarum in whose sign Moses would conquer, so the idea of mass transit was to be the perennial dragon to be slain whenever it threatened to invade any of his demesnes. Meanwhile, Long Island was full of empty beaches, promising sand bars, unspoiled woods. How to appropriate all this natural beauty for the use of the car owners?

Until 1923, the parks of New York State were run by sleepy patroons who simply wanted to conserve wild life for future generations. The patroons did not mind responsible campers and hikers wandering about their woods and lakes but they certainly did not want great highways to crisscross the wilderness or tons of cement to be poured over meadows in order to make shuffleboards, restaurants, and comfort stations for millions of visitors; nor did they think that every natural stream or pond ought to be rearranged by someone with a degree in civil engineering.

Unhappily for the patroons, Moses now had a Dream. He went to work to realize it. Exercising his formidable art, he drafted *A State Park Plan for New York*. Parks would be used for recreation as well as conservation. Parks would be reorganized into one system. The presidency of the Long Island State Park Commission would go to Moses; term of office—six years, longer than the governor's term. There are those who think that this bill was Moses's greatest masterpiece, even more compelling than the bill that set up the Triborough Authority. Certainly Moses displayed in its drafting a new maturity, as well as a mastery of every type of ambiguity. But I leave to Mr. Caro the task of being Walter Pater to this Gioconda. Enough to say that the principal joker in the bill was the use of an unrepealed 1884 law that gave the state the right to "appropriate" land "by simply walking on it and telling the owner he no longer owned it." This was power.

Jones Beach and other parks were connected with highways to the city and transformed into playgrounds. In the process a lot of people were "remorselessly" kicked off their land. But there are people and people. At first Moses wanted to put a parkway through the North Shore Long Island estates of such nobles as Stimson, Winthrop, Mills, and Otto Kahn. The lords objected and so, partly because Mr. Kahn was on good terms with Moses and partly because the other nobles owned the Republican party which controlled the state legislature, the parkway was diverted to a stretch of land inhabited by farmers who had no clout. The farmers were driven from their land.

Although Moses was always a profound conservative who only seemed to be liberal because he had a Dream about parks and highways, he was not above using the press to blast the "rich golfers" who stood athwart the people's right of way. Early on, Moses demonstrated a genius for publicity. Knowing that the New York press thrives on personal attacks, he gave them plenty. He also enjoyed the full support of *The New York Times* because he had managed to persuade one Iphigene Sulzberger that he was as interested in conservation as she was. For decades, with the connivance of the press, Moses was able to slander as "Pinkos" and "Commies" his many enemies. Also, the corrupter of others was careful to keep dossiers on those he had corrupted. But then to realize his Dream of an America covered with highways and of wilderness tamed to resemble fun fairs, Moses was remorseless since you cannot, he would observe, make an omelette with unbroken eggs (a line much used in those days by supporters of Hitler and Mussolini). He also liked to crow: "Nothing I have ever done has been tinged with legality."

The perfect public servant made only one serious error during this period. In 1934 he was Republican candidate for governor of New York against the incumbent Herbert Lehman. During the campaign Moses's contempt for all of the people all of the time was so open, so pure, so unremitting that he made Coriolanus seem like Hubert Humphrey. Even the docile press which had worked so hard to create a liberal image for Moses was appalled by the virulence of his *ad hominem* attacks on Governor Lehman —a decent man with whom Moses had always had good relations.

Suddenly his friend the governor was "a miserable, snivelling type of man . . . contemptible." Moses also charged that Lehman "created most of the state deficit." Actually, Lehman had reduced the deficit to almost zero. But then Moses has always had a Hitlerian capacity for the lie so big that it knocks the truth out of the victim who knows that his denial will never be played as big in

the press as the lie itself. Then Moses called Lehman "a liar"—
a word, one politician remarked, never before used in a guber-
natorial campaign. Eventually, the Mutual Broadcasting System
refused to broadcast Moses's speeches unless the Republican
party insured the network against libel. Moses's defeat was so
thorough that he never again offered himself to the public except
in controlled interviews conducted by admiring journalists. Soon
he was a hero again with his parks, highways, beaches. Was he
not incorruptible?

From time to time Mr. Caro feels that he ought to explain *why*
Moses is what he is and his narrative is occasionally marred by
vulgar Freudianisms in the Leon Edel manner. This is a pity
because the chief interest of biography is not *why* men do what
they do, which can never be known unless one turns novelist the
way Freud did when he wrote *Leonardo,* but what they do. One
does not want a theory explaining Moses's celebrated vindictiveness when examples of that vindictiveness are a matter of interesting record. For instance, after a run-in with Mayor Jimmy
Walker, Moses tore down the Casino in Central Park because
Walker had patronized it; yet the building itself was a charming
relic of the previous century and the people's property. Prematurely, he razed a yacht club because the members "were rude to
me." Shades of Richard Nixon! Petty revenge was certainly behind his desire to remove the Battery's most famous landmark—
the Aquarium in the old fort known as Castle Garden. Fortunately Eleanor Roosevelt got her husband the president to save
the fort itself through a Byzantine process involving the War
Department.

This was FDR's only victory over Moses. The two men despised each other; they were also somewhat alike. As an admiring
biographer of the president wrote, sadly, FDR had "a capacity for
vindictiveness which could be described as petty." When an earlier move against Moses failed, Roosevelt was criticized for petti-
ness by a friend. The great man's response was plaintive: "Isn't
the president of the United States entitled to one personal
grudge?"

In 1939 the Triborough Bridge was opened and the Moses empire was at its zenith. The bridge was—and is—a huge money-
maker. Money from those toll booths goes to an Authority and
the Authority (as adapted by Robert Moses) is the supreme example of his dark art. The Authority is responsible to no one except

those who hold its bonds. As a result, with Triborough money, Moses was now in a position to reward directly those who helped him and damage those who hurt him.

Mr. Caro quotes one city official as saying of Moses, "He gave everybody involved in the political set-up in this city whatever it was that they wanted." Tammany, Republicans, reformers, Fusionists . . . it made no difference. Either they were paid off through their law and insurance offices, their public relations and building firms, or they were attacked through the press, and hounded from office like Stanley Isaacs, the honest borough president of Manhattan.

Moses's achievement, according to Mr. Caro, "was to replace graft with benefits that could be derived with legality from a public works project." After all, the Authority had every right to hire someone's uncle to be a PR consultant just as the Authority was able to spend $500,000 a year on insurance premiums, a windfall for the insurers because, according to Moses's aide George Spargo, the Authority never filed or collected a claim during its first eighteen years. All perfectly legal and all perfectly corrupt. But who was to know? The books of the Authority could only be audited after a complaint by those who held the bonds of the Authority, and the trustee for those bond-holders was the Chase Manhattan Bank, the Rockefeller family's cosa nostra. Since the Authority was a great success, the bank was not curious about its inner workings.

From Triborough headquarters on Randall's Island, Moses presided over city and state. By the time the Second World War ended, he was uniquely powerful because the city, as usual, was broke and the only money available for building was either from the federal government or from the Triborough Authority, whose millions Moses could spend as he pleased—and it pleased him to cover as much of Manhattan as possible with cement while providing himself with a lavish way of life that included private yachts and a court theater at Jones Beach where his very own minstrel Guy Lombardo made a lot of money grinding out the sweetest music this side of coins clinking in toll booths. Why steal money to have a sumptuous life when you can openly use the public money to live gorgeously? Yet during all these years the press, led by the ineffable *New York Times*, praised Moses for his incorruptibility.

At one time or another most of the mayors and governors

Moses dealt with wanted to get rid of him; none dared. Moses was a god to the press and a master to the legislature. Finally, he alone had the money with which to create those public works that mayors must be able to point to with pride just before election time. To keep the irascible Mayor La Guardia happy, Moses built dozens of playgrounds and swimming pools (there was a pool *near* Harlem) so that the mayor could dash about greeting the kiddies and bragging. It was heady stuff. In time, however, the over-reacher overreaches, and one now begins to read Mr. Caro's text like a Greek tragedy, aware rather earlier than was usual at the Dionysos Theater of the hero's Tragic Flaw. Never having known just how Moses fell from power, I was glad that I could read the last sections of the book like a mystery novel: who would get him? and what would be the murder weapon?

The building of the Cross-Bronx Expressway might be the point where Moses found himself at the three roads, to maintain the classical analogy. He was then all-conquering and all-spend-ing: after the Second World War he built more than $2 billion worth of roads within the city. To do this, he expropriated thou-sands of buildings, not all of them slums, and evicted tens of thousands of people who were left to fend for themselves. Moses's elevated highways shadowed and blighted whole neighborhoods. The inner city began to rot, die. But no one could stop Moses for he had yet another Dream: exodus from the city to the suburbs but only by car, for there were to be no busses or trains on his expressways—just more and more highways for more and more cars, creating more and more traffic jams, while the once thriving railroads that had served the city went bankrupt, lingering on as derelict ghosts of what had been, fifty years before, a splendid mass transit system.

In 1952 East Tremont was a lower-middle-class Jewish neigh-borhood in the Bronx, reasonably content and homogeneous. Moses wanted his Cross-Bronx Expressway to go straight through the most populous part of East Tremont, razing 159 buildings and evicting 1,530 families. Alarmed, the people of this non-slum organized to save their homes. They prepared maps that showed how easy it would be to build an alternative route which would involve tearing down no more than six buildings. Except for the *World-Telegram* and the *Post*, the press ignored the matter. At first the politicians were responsive; but then, one by one, they succumbed to pressure and the community was duly destroyed. But Moses was now hated by the powerless millions who neither read nor are written about by *The New York Times.*

By the late fifties, however, even the newspaper of record was concerned about the lack of mass transport. City planners wanted Moses to put at the center of his expressways what Mr. Caro unhappily refers to as "a subway running at ground level." This would have made the city more escapable for the poor as well as for the car owners. It was also proposed that a train on the Van Wyck Expressway would get travelers from Pennsylvania Station to the airport at Idlewild in sixteen minutes. But Moses refused to listen. Criticism became more intense as the traffic jams increased. The city became more desperate and congested. Moses's answer: build more roads. When told that "the automobiles required to transport the equivalent of one trainload of commuters use about four acres of parking space in Manhattan," Moses spoke of huge skyscrapers filled with cars; he even built one but it was not practical at the price.

For Moses Long Island was now the promised land for the deserving middle class. "Figure out what sort of people you want to attract into Nassau County," he admonished. "By that I mean people of what standards, what income levels and what capacity to contribute to the source of local government. . . . Nassau should always be largely residential and recreational." This is as unmistakable an appeal as any ever made by Nixon-Agnew to the not-so-silent bigots of the heartland.

But now the master of corruption was growing insolent and careless from too much victory. A non-slum neighborhood on the West Side was marked for destruction by the Mayor's Slum Clearance Committee, chaired by Moses. The condemned six square blocks comprised 338 buildings worth $15 million. For $1 million the city sold the entire neighborhood to a group headed by Samuel Caspert, "a Democratic clubhouse figure" who was required to raze the area by 1954 in order to create something called Manhattantown. But politician Caspert and his friends were in no hurry. By October 1954, 280 buildings were still standing, and the tenants were paying rents to the Caspert cabal. The Senate Banking and Currency Committee thought this odd and began hearings. But Moses's perennial mouthpiece, the famed judge and friend of presidents Sam Rosenman, skillfully protected the Caspert gang and the scandal blew over.

In 1956 came the battle of the Tavern-on-the-Green. Moses

wanted to expand the Tavern's parking lot, removing in the process a bosky dell beloved of the affluent mothers of Central Park West. As usual, Moses won: at least before the injunctions arrived, the trees were bulldozed. But the West-siders stopped the parking lot, giving Moses a good deal of bad personal publicity in the process. Since the New York press is geared almost entirely to personalities, the real issue was ignored except by the *World-Telegram*, whose reporters saw fit to investigate Moses's connection with the manager of the Tavern-on-the-Green. During a four-year period the Tavern's gross income was $1,786,000 of which, thanks to Moses, the city got only $9,000 for the rental of a building that was city property. In exchange for this gift to the manager, Moses was able to use the Tavern as a private dining room.

But now two paladins appear on the scene, the journalists Gene Gleason and Fred Cook. They began a series of exposés in *World-Telegram*. Who was giving whose money to whom and for what? Eventually even *The New York Times* got interested in the corruption of the city, the exploitation of the poor, the lunatic set of priorities that had for decades put cars before people.

Pressure was put on Wagner to fire Moses. But Wagner could do nothing for, as Mr. Caro puts it, "the whole Democratic machine, the leaders of all five county organizations, on which Wagner depended, were on Moses's payroll." Those coins from the toll booths of the Triborough had bought the city's government.

In the end Moses was brought down not by the press or the reformers but by the true owner of the American republic, the family Rockefeller as personified by Nelson, who had begun his quest for the presidency in 1958 by spending a lot of the family's money to become New York's governor. Moses now confronted an arrogance equal to his own; a remorselessness quite as complete; and resources that were infinite. The two were bound to be enemies. After all, Rockefeller supported mass transit; liked to build things to celebrate himself; fancied parks; wanted no trouble or competition from the likes of Moses.

After a spat, on November 28, 1962, Moses sent the governor one of his many letters of resignation . . . carefully hedged with "tentatives" and "perhapses." With indecent briskness, Rocky accepted "with regret" Moses's resignation from the Long Island Park Commission. The governor then turned over the job to one of his brothers. Moses had a final brief orgy in the press. On the front page of the ever-loyal *New York Times,* he attacked the governor for nepotism. But, uncharacteristically, Moses ignored Machiavelli's famed advice—he had struck at a prince and not killed him. This was unwise. But perhaps Moses had deluded himself that he was as great a lord. Was he not still head of the Triborough Bridge and Tunnel Authority as well as creator of the World's Fair? No matter. The roof had begun to fall in.

Moses was never as interested in the New York World's Fair of 1964–65 as he was in the park that would succeed the fair. In setting up the fair, he managed, as usual, to offend a great many people, among them the representatives of the various European governments who decided to have nothing to do with the rude Mr. Moses. The result was a World's Fair without the world's involvement, and a series of breath-taking financial scandals that Mr. Caro has recorded with more than usual detail. All told, Moses had about $1 billion to play with while putting together the fair, and $1 billion can buy all sorts of loyalties and power in the land. The fair itself lost money.

By 1965 the Moses empire had shrunk to the Triborough Authority. The new mayor, John Lindsay, decided to get rid of Moses five years before the end of Moses's term. In a final bravura performance at Albany, Moses handed the mayor his beautiful head. Moses remained. But the end was near.

The sovereign at Albany desperately needed money to build things. The treasury of the Authority contained $110 million in cash and securities to which was added each year another $30 million. Rockefeller proposed to merge the Triborough with his own creature, the MTA (Metropolitan Commuter Transportation Authority). It should be noted that for all of Rockefeller's antagonism to Moses the man he has never ceased to emulate is Moses the power broker. According to Mr. Caro, "Rockefeller had created several giant 'public authorities' that were bastards of the genre because their revenue bonds would be paid off not out of their own revenues but out of the general revenues of the state."

Recently (September 2) *Time* magazine wrote an affectionate story on Vice President-designate Rockefeller. With a wry editorial smile, *Time* concedes that "Rockefeller was an expensive governor . . . as the budget kept rising, from $2 billion when he took office to $8.6 when he left, he devised a novel way of paying for his programs. Rather than going to balky state legislatures or to the voters, who might turn him down, he set up a host of quasi-independent agencies—the Metropolitan Transportation Authority, the Urban Development Corporation, the Housing Finance Agency—that issued bonds on their own initiative and repaid them with fees collected from users of the facilities that were constructed. 'The greatest system ever invented!' he exclaimed." Next to the sales tax, it *is* the greatest—until the taxpayer gets the bill. But long before that day of reckoning the governor moved on—and is now moving up. Terrific! Dubonnet on the rocks. Venezuela. Museum of modern Art. Attica. Hiya, fella!

Preparing for the showdown with Rockefeller, Moses did what might have been the most useful work of his career. He sat down and figured out what Rockefeller's various Authorities would eventually cost the state. The figures were staggering. For instance, the MTA's bond issue for $2.5 billion would eventually cost the taxpayers $1 billion in interest. But Moses's addition and multiplication were never published. The Rockefeller machine had begun to move against him. In 1967, Rockefeller arranged for Chase Manhattan (headed by his brother David) to blow the whistle on the Triborough Authority. The bank wanted a look at the Authority's books, a dangerous business if things were not in order, but necessary if the bonds were to be retired preparatory to merger. Thomas E. Dewey was hired as the bank's counsel.

Mr. Caro seems to think that if Moses had put up a fight, he might have staved off—or delayed—the merger with MTA. Certainly had he the public interest at heart, Moses ought to have revealed his arithmetic to a grateful nation. But, somehow, Moses was conned. He made no demur to the merger, and Chase Manhattan dropped its suit against the Authority. The merger went through and Moses found himself on the new payroll as a non-consulted consultant, with a car and driver. And that was the end of the line.

Last August 27, Moses released a 3,500-word attack on Mr. Caro's book through a public relations outfit named Edward V. O'Brien. So suspicious has Mr. Caro made me of PR firms that I want to know *which* O'Brien is Edward V. (the one on page 1,089 of *The Power Broker?*) and has he ever done any work for the city or the Triborough? For old times' sake *The New York Times* gave fair space to Moses's attack. According to the King Lear of Jones

Beach, Mr. Caro's book contains "hundreds of careless errors. Many charges are downright lies." But Moses does not mention any errors or lies except to deny that he ever had an affair with ex-Representative Ruth Pratt. Here I think Moses is on strong ground. The biographer of a living person ought never to address himself to the private life of his subject—particularly if the subject is someone like Moses whose *public* life is not only fascinating in itself but continues to affect us all. I did not enjoy reading about Moses's alcoholic wife or about the feud with his only brother Paul (whom Moses refers to, curiously, as "a brother of mine, now dead," as if there were hundreds of brothers to choose from and Mr. Caro, maliciously, picked the wrong one to interview).

Moses does confess that he may have been a bit rough at times in his career, again quoting his favorite cliché about eggs and omelettes. He also says that he personally favors mass transit but argues, disingenuously, that he did nothing about it because he was never in charge of mass transit—as if that was the point to his lifelong obstruction. He is still a lover of the automobile: "We live in a motorized civilization." Energy crisis, unlivable cities, pollution—none of these things has altered his proud Dream. But rather than make the obvious point that a man of eighty-six is now out-of-date, one ought instead to regard with a degree of awe his stamina and his continuing remorseless brilliance.

Finally, in looking back over all that Robert Moses has done to the world we live in and, more important, the way that he did it by early mastering the twin arts of publicity and of corruption, one sees in the design of his career a perfect blueprint for that inevitable figure, perhaps even now standing in the wings of the Republic, rehearsing to himself such phrases as "law and order," "renewal and reform," "sacrifice and triumph," the first popularly elected dictator of the United States.

Hiya, fella . . .

The New York Review of Books
October 17, 1974

Conglomerates

I n 1966 Edmund Wilson wrote in his journal (published as *Up-state*):

> Fred Dupee, who now lives on the Hudson, had invited a new
> neighbor, and IBM tycoon. The subject of Vietnam arose and the
> tycoon asked Dorothea Straus for her opinion on the subject. Doro-
> thea made the tactful reply that she took the war question so seri-
> ously that she would rather not talk about it. The tycoon said
> something invidious about her being Jewish. Dwight Macdonald
> became inflamed, and the tycoon offered to sock him in the
> jaw . . .

As second-hand stories go this is about par. Actually the threat
to Macdonald was made before Mrs. Straus was dismissed by the
tycoon as a mere Jewess (and so a Commie) while the *New Yorker's*
own Diderot responded to the threat of a sock in the jaw with
a fit of uninflamed giggles. Final correction: the tycoon was
employed by ITT, and according to Anthony Sampson's new

book,* he is today one of the six top executives of a vast conglomerate that owns everything from tasteless Wonderbread to most of the lousy telephone systems in Europe. At the time, I wondered how the Jewess-baiter could hold a job of importance in any firm anywhere. As the party crumbled, I asked several guests: What is—or are—ITT? No one knew. That was an innocent age.

Mr. Sampson has now turned his attention to the multinational conglomerates in general and to International Telephone and Telegraph in particular and, predictably, he views with alarm the way these nomadic holding companies have transformed themselves into sovereign states able to treat with nation states from a position of strength—witness, the current dealings between ITT and the pack of woolly lambs that presently gambol in the shadows of the Kremlin's onion domes.

ITT was invented by one Sosthenes Behn in 1920. A Virgin Islander of Danish-French extraction, Colonel Behn was curiously well-situated to be an international businessman, turning a buck wherever possible. The fact that the Colonel got on better with dictators than he did with democrats was not necessarily a sign of bad character: serious businessmen have always preferred paying off one man or his son-in-law to buying half a thousand members of a Congress the way they must do in Washington, DC, say—not to mention subsidizing the key figures of a permanent and ever-expanding bureaucracy.

When Peron took over ITT's telephone system in Argentina, the caudillo of the pampas made a gentlemanly settlement of the sort Castro (not exactly your average fanatic democrat) refused to make, causing Colonel Behn's successor Harold Geneen to present the exiled dictator Batista with a golden telephone—presumably for old times' sake.

After Hitler came to power, Colonel Behn increased his holdings in Germany to include 28 percent of Focke-Wulf, which manufactured Luftwaffe bombers. When war came, Colonel Behn saw no conflict of interest: like the Pope he regarded himself as belonging to all sinners. In fact, the Colonel had a pleasant meeting with Hitler in 1938 (apparently, the Führer was nicely groomed with the manners, thank heaven, of a gentleman), and ITT was allowed to keep its German holdings. Two years later Goering arranged the acquisition of ITT's local holdings "in

---

* *The Sovereign State of ITT* (Stein and Day, 1973).

exchange [for] the mysterious and prosperous company General Anilin and Film Corporation (GAF), an offshoot of the I.G. Farben cartel . . . seized by the United States Treasury Department" in 1942. Mr. Sampson leaves the unsavory story at this point. His readers might be amused to know that two decades later Attorney General R.F. Kennedy settled the matter of GAF's ownership with a fifty-fifty split between the Swiss group which claimed the company and the Justice Department which maintained that the company belonged to the US on the ground that it had been simply a cover for the Nazi I.G. Farben. Kennedy was inclined to be generous because, as Victor Navasky *(Kennedy Justice)* put it, "the Kennedys had appointed a number of family friends to various positions in and around the company."

Mr. Sampson takes us on a swift and generally entertaining— that is to say, chilling—tour of ITT's present horizon which is the great globe itself: Avis Cars, Sheraton Hotels, Levitt towns, and now the third largest insurance company in the world; cash in-flow is very important for a business which is in the business not of making things but of making money. I suspect that much of the nervousness the conglomerates excite in the American puritan's bosom is not so much their brutal devotion to making money as their indifference to the things that they are required to make in order to make the money. Of peripheral interest are the potato chips, rental cars, dog food, insurance. What matters to Geneen (an accountant) are loans, interest rates, currency fluctuations, corporate mergers, and the avoidance of paying taxes on profits anywhere on earth. According to Senator E. Kennedy, ITT—the eighth largest American company—paid no federal American tax in 1971.

In some detail Mr. Sampson describes ITT's attempted takeover of ABC, the third American television network. To the government ITT spoke glowingly of all the money that they would put into the network; to others they spoke coolly of what they intended to take out of it. Their lobbying was, as always, thorough; so too was their intimidation of their critics. One *New York Times* reporter discovered that the company was collecting a dossier on her private life. The Justice Department finally stopped the merger on the ground that ABC did not need ITT's financing. It was also felt that the network's news programs would be affected because of ITT's "close and confidential relation with foreign governments." But it was a close call for network freedom of speech which is, of course, no more than the heady freedom to paraphrase the demure editorials of the *Washington Post* and the *New York Times*.

During the last few years Geneen has taken a tack quite different from that of Colonel Behn. Instead simply of trying to get on with whatever government happens to be in charge of a country where he wants to make money, Geneen is now attempting to create the sort of governments that would be obliged to get on with him. So began the sinister comedy in Chile that involved not only Geneen but John McCone, a former head of the CIA and now an ITT director. Fearing that Allende's election as president would mean nationalization of ITT's telephone holdings in Chile, Geneen offered at least a million dollars to the CIA to help defeat Allende. As far as we know, the CIA sat that one out and Allende was duly elected.*

ITT then set about acquiring the Hartford Insurance Company, the biggest caper in their history thus far and as all major heists nowadays seem to do, it involved the 37th president whose eccentric notions of law (ignore it) and order (impose it) have to date been contained not by the Constitution or by the Congress or by the press but by his own eerie and rather touching propensity to fuck up.

Nixon wanted the Republican convention to be held in San Diego, his "lucky city." San Diego was not thrilled. Money would be needed, the city fathers said. In another part of the swamp Geneen was having trouble with the antitrust-buster Richard McLaren at the Justice Department. McLaren also wanted to take the case to the Supreme Court in order to clarify once and for all the antitrust laws. Attorney General Mitchell (now under indictment) and Vice President Agnew (still at large)†were both well-disposed to Geneen. Words were spoken on ITT's behalf; letters written. But McLaren soldiered on. Then a light went on in Geneen's head: donate through ITT's Sheraton hotel chain $400,-000 to the Republicans for their San Diego convention and . . . The offer was made. The offer was accepted. The trust suit against ITT was swiftly settled out of court, and to everyone's

---

*May 12, 1976, Mr. Geneen said to the ITT shareholders that he had not known that a "possible" $350,000 of ITT money had gone to Chile to support the "democratic anti-Communist cause."

†This was written before Agnew's crimes came to light. How did I know? Ah . . .

surprise, ITT was allowed to keep their most precious acquisition, Hartford. McLaren left the Department of Justice to become a federal judge.

Unfortunately for the funsters, ITT's Washington lobbyist Dita Beard wrote a memo giving the game away. Promptly, she went into the hospital (with a weak heart). In disguise (red wig, a voice modulator), novelist–CIA agent–presidential burglar E. Howard Hunt arrived from the White House with orders to get Dita in line. No doubt intimidated by the red wig, the altered voice, she recanted: the memo was a forgery, she said, or sort of. A year later E. Howard Hunt was arrested at the Watergate break-in and. . . . No, no. Enough. Linkage is all, as Nixon's Metternich would say.

Mr. Sampson ends his book with the nice irony of Geneen publicly deploring the collapse of the "free" world as Latin America goes Marxist while, simultaneously, putting together what promises to be a super deal with Moscow. Mr. Sampson comes to no precise conclusion. There is evidence that companies which are taken over by conglomerates usually become inefficient (when they are not simply gutted of their assets and discarded). It is also true that Geneen's crusading fervor and vigor is something new under the corporate sun. Instead of being embarrassed by all the dirty tricks he had been caught at, he takes the high line that in order to maintain the Western world's prosperity his is the only way and if the United States and Western Europe are to compete with a corporate nation-state like Japan, say, then more not less ITT is necessary.

Mr. Sampson tells us that he wrote this book at "high speed." I wish he had not. There are sentences which the elegant author of *The New Europeans* ought not to have allowed to wriggle onto the page ("Her relations were especially strained with Bill Merriam, a sociable aristocrat of 60 who had once been a friend of the Jack Kennedys, but who was much less adept at politics than her"). Those bracketing "hers" are Mid-Atlantic at its most refined.

Mr. Sampson ought to redo his book post-Watergate, if there should ever be such an era. For instance, two months ago, the Justice Department reopened the business of the Hartford merger because, according to Attorney General Richardson "the ITT inquiry has begun to overlap with the Watergate investigation." Will Mr. Sampson be obliged by events to call his sequel

Sovereign Empire? I think not. I have a feeling that like the joyous Cornfeld's paper pyramid, ITT, too, will pass, taking the currency of the Western world with it in a replay of 1929. So, puritans, take heart. We may be at the end of that paper money which has been for our rulers a puzzling and currently alarming fiat for their much loved barbarous metal; and for the poor, as someone once said, their blood. Absolute purity will then require us to return to the delights and challenges of barter, and to real things.

New Statesman
July 20, 1973

Political Melodramas

Recently *The New York Times* noted that, once again, the television viewer would be able to watch "Gore Vidal's political melodrama *The Best Man*." Over the years I have become so familiar with this listing that I no longer wonder why I am irritated by it. No longer, that is, until Watergate. I realize now that my distress was always with the word "melodrama." *The Best Man* was first written as a realistic play about two men at a political convention, fighting one another for the presidential nomination of their party.

In 1959 when I wrote the play, the Democratic rivals for the nomination were Adlai Stevenson (who was being smeared as a homosexual—and an indecisive one to boot), John F. Kennedy (who was being smeared as an altogether too active heterosexual as well as the glad beneficiary of his wealthy father's ability to buy elections) and the majority leader of the Senate, Lyndon Johnson (who was known to take cash for any political services rendered). In the background was Harry S Truman, whose campaign for election in 1948 nearly ended before it began. Unable to pay for the train in which he was to whistle-stop the country, giving hell to the rich, Truman turned to his crony Louis Johnson and asked for money quick. Johnson got the money from the "China Lobby," and ever after the grateful President loyally served the cause of Chiang Kai-shek. All of this was common knowledge to most of us who were involved in the life and politics of Washington, DC.

When I based the character of the wicked candidate in the play on Richard Nixon, I thought it would be amusing if liberal partisans were to smear unjustly that uxorious man as a homosexual. I was promptly condemned by a conservative columnist who said that my plot was absurdly melodramatic since no man could rise to any height in American politics if he were thought to be a fag. Yet this same columnist used to delight in making coy allusions in print to Stevenson's lack of robustness.

The noble, if waffling, character in the play was based on Adlai Stevenson. I thought it might be interesting if he were to have undergone some mild psychiatric therapy which the bad guy could seize upon as a sign of mental instability, maintaining solemnly that no one who had ever been to a psychiatrist ought to have access to the arrows that our imperial eagle-ensign holds in its claw—much less the eagle's sprig of laurel. This time a liberal pundit said that it was simply not possible for anyone who had undergone "serious" psychotherapy to be considered for high office. So, no doubt, thought the hapless McGovern when he took as his running mate shock-treated Senator Thomas Eagleton.

When faced with a moral issue most American commentators simply ignore it—or as Elaine May said to Mike Nichols in one of their skits, "I like a moral issue so much more than a real issue." Journalists who know quite as much or more than I about American politics seem never able to deal in print with the actual issues raised as opposed to the occasional muck raked. They black out because, well, the institution of the presidency must be preserved while the sanctity of Congress and the Supreme Court. . . . In other words, don't give away the game because we're all in this together, making a pretty good living out of USA, Inc. To describe the way things really are is to be a shit and we know what happens to shits: they are flushed away. Unfortunately, to complete this out-of-control metaphor, the waters of the Republic are now befouled from too much flushing, and we are poisoned when we drink.

In 1967 I published a novel called *Washington, D.C.* The narrative began in the Roosevelt era and ended as dawn struck the towers of Camelot. I invented two senators: one old-style, one new-style. Hoping to be president in 1940, my old senator raised money by doing the wrong kind of favor for a lobbyist. Since the senator was essentially a moral man (brought up on McGuffey's Eclectic Reader), he was literally demoralized by his crime, and fell. The young senator was very much in the Kennedy tradition and so was able to take without a second thought anything that was not nailed down because that's the way you play the game around here: that's what the word "pragmatism" means. At the end of the book it was fairly plain that he was presidential material. Across the land there was a chorus of distress from writers of book-chat as well as from political camp-followers. The author was traducing famous and honorable men, not to mention the greatest society the world had ever seen. Why was the writer such a shit? Because, God help us, he was filled with envy! Apparently anyone who criticizes anything or anyone in the land of the free does so because he is envious—proving, I suppose that this peculiar emotion must indeed be a prevailing national trait.

J.K. Galbraith wrote one of the few favorable reviews of *Washington, D.C.*, but even that lovable old cynic saw fit to admonish me in person: "You know things are not that bad in politics." I looked at him with, as they say in popular fiction, wonder. Surely Ken must have heard the funny story told by a Kennedy relation who, on his way to West Virginia, stopped at a barber's to have his hair cut and then hurried off, leaving behind his bag filled with dollars to be paid to the honest yeomen of West Virginia in exchange for their support of the family's candidate. Also, when I ran for Congress as a Democrat in 1960, I caught some Republicans buying votes. I wanted to prosecute but was dissuaded by a leader of my party. "If you nail them here, they'll nail us somewhere else in the state."

Last spring I felt obliged to offer my countrymen yet another glimpse of their masters in a play called *An Evening With Richard Nixon.* All of Nixon's dialogue in this entertainment was taken from his actual speeches and press conferences. The effect was properly devastating but, alas, the envious author was found guilty of having, this time, drawn attention to those small lapses which we are taught from childhood to paper over. ("If you can't be good be careful" is an American maxim.) Even the British drama reviewer for the *New York Times* was shaken by the unfair way I had treated a man whom he referred to with true reverence as "our President."

Was it ever thus? Yes. I fear the United States has always been a nation of ongoing hustlers from the prisons and disaster-areas of old Europe. Our grand British heritage is now wearing thin but still can be observed in our racism as well as in the spontaneous hypocrisy with which our public men respond to inconvenient disclosures and the self-serving rhetoric that swirls about them in time of crisis like squid's ink. The brilliant Alexander Hamilton was almost certainly corrupt during his years at the Treasury—his right-hand man went to jail. Hamilton was also a British secret agent, as was Benjamin Franklin. Jefferson's commanding general of the American army, James Wilkinson, was a Spanish agent (for political reasons the President protected him and thus condoned treason). Andrew Jackson's appointment of his Tammany friend Sam Swartwout to the collectorship of the Port of New York helped undermine the Jacksonian "revolution" (such as it was) because the President's political heir, Van Buren, was brought down, in part, by Swartwout's theft of more than $1 million from the port.

Growing up in the Washington house of my grandfather, Senator T.P. Gore of Oklahoma, I was intimately aware of the Teapot Dome scandal. My grandfather had once written a brief for one of the oil barons in the case. Although I do not think that my grandfather was on the take (senator from an oil state, he died poor), he was certainly unwise and for at least one troublesome election he was known irreverently as "Teapot Gore." When the poor but eloquent tribune of the people Senator William Borah (the lion of Idaho) died, several hundred thousand dollars were found in his safety deposit box. "He was my friend," said Senator Gore gravely to the press, "I do not speculate." In private, my grandfather was fairly certain that the money was from Hitler. Borah was a devoted isolationist and not above taking money from those whose interests he would have furthered anyway.

Last year a remarkable book was published in the United States, *Washington Pay-Off* by Robert N. Winter-Berger. At first hand, the author, a former lobbyist, described how the Speaker of the House of Representatives, John McCormack, rented space in his Capitol office to a master criminal named Nathan Voloshen. From the Speaker's office a team of influence-peddlers sold favors to innumerable clients. Eventually they were busted by US Attorney Robert Morgenthau. Voloshen went to jail. The Speaker was persuaded to retire from Congress. This horror story was one of several carefully detailed by Mr. Winter-Berger; each involved some of our most celebrated public men.

Needless to say, the book did not please the owners of the United States, a loose consortium that includes the editors of the *New York Times* and the *Washington Post*, the television magnates, the Rockefellers, Kennedys, ITT, IBM, etc. Winter-Berger's exposés were largely ignored by the press and television. The book did become a best seller but never became what it should have been, a subject for national debate. Intrigued by the silence the book had aroused, I rang Robert Morgenthau and asked him if he thought Winter-Berger a reliable witness (in the high Whittaker Chambers sense of the word). Morgenthau said that, all in all, the text was accurate. If so, the following scene was drawn from life.

Early in Johnson's reign, the President appears in the Speaker's office. Unaware that Winter-Berger is also in the room, the President denounces his former aide, Bobby Baker, who is under indictment. "John, that son of a bitch is going to ruin me. If that cocksucker talks, I'm going to land in jail." Thus, characteristically, spoke the emperor of the West, the scourge of Asia and shield to ungrateful Europe, the sole wielder of the arrows and the laurel. The Speaker draws Johnson's attention to the cowering Winter-Berger. The President wants to know if the witness is "all right." Winter-Berger swears loyalty to his sovereign, and listens raptly as LBJ outlines a plan to stay out of the clink. A message must be got to Baker: "I will give him a million dollars if he takes the rap."

Recently Bobby Baker left prison and it is said that he, too, may write a book. If he does, I suspect that a quorum of that senate whose secretary he was may yet convene itself in Lewisburg Federal Penetentiary. For my British readers who are now reeling in disbelief from line to line of this cheery report: yes, we do have laws of libel in the United States but they are less strict than yours. Even so, the scene with Johnson in the Speaker's office was published while the former President was still alive and capable of bringing action against publisher and author. He did neither.

I have nothing to add to the unfolding scandals of Watergate except to note that what has so far been revealed is only the tip of not an iceberg but a glacier. As a professional political melodramatist, however, I am struck by the tameness of my work. Like Clive, when I consider my opportunities I am impressed by my restraint.

During the last few days the owners of the United States have been telling us that to preserve the Republic everyone must now support a chastened Nixon and make it possible for him to govern. Why? To continue the devastation of Cambodia and Laos? The erosion of civil liberties? The stockpiling of redundant arms? The control of wages but not of profits? The curtailing of all programs that might make the poor less desperate?

I cannot for the life of me see the value of continuing this administration another day in office. More to the point, I do not think that the American system in its present state of decadence is worth preserving. The initial success of the United States was largely accidental. A rich almost empty continent was occupied and exploited by rapacious Europeans who made slaves of Africans and corpses of Indians in the process. They created a Venetian-style republic based on limited suffrage and dedicated to the sacredness of property. Now the land is no longer rich enough to support the pretensions of the inhabitants. Institutions that once worked well enough for the major stockholders are no longer adequate to bear the burden of all our mistakes. Yet I am certain that a majority of my countrymen would like things to continue pretty much as they are. If they do, then their only hope is the prompt impeachment and dismissal of this president. A ritual scapegoat is needed to absolve our sins and Nixon has obligingly put his head on the block. Certainly to allow him to go free makes us all accomplices. It also brings to a swift end the brief, and by the world no doubt unlamented, American imperium.

New Statesman
May 4, 1973

The State of the Union

"**H**ow can you say such awful things about America when *you live in Italy?*" Whenever I go on television, I hear that plangent cry. From vivacious Barbara Walters of the *Today* show (where I was granted six minutes to comment on last November's elections) to all the other vivacious interviewers across this great land of ours, the question of my residency is an urgent matter that must be mentioned as soon as possible so that no one will take seriously a single word that that awful person has to say about what everybody knows is not only the greatest country in the history of the world but a country where vivacious Barbara Walters et al. can make a very pretty penny peddling things that people don't need. "So if you no liva here," as sly fun-loving Earl Butz might say, "you no maka da wisecracks."

Usually I ignore the vivacious challenge: the single statement on television simply does not register; only constant repetition penetrates . . . witness, the commercials. Yet on occasions, when tired, I will rise to the bait. Point out that I pay full American income tax—50 percent of my earned income contributes to the support of the Pentagon's General Brown, statesman/soldier and keen student of the Protocols of the Elders of Zion. Remind one and all that I do spend a good part of my time in the land of the free, ranging up and down the countryside for months at a time discussing the state of the union with conservative audiences (no use talking to the converted), and in the process I manage to see more of the country than your average television vivacity ever does. In fact, I know more about the relative merits of the far-flung Holiday Inns than anyone who is not a traveling salesman or a presidential candidate.

Last fall I set out across the country, delivering pretty much the same commentary on the state of the union that I have been giving for several years, with various topical additions, subtractions. In one four-week period I gave fifteen lectures, starting with the Political Union at Yale and then on to various colleges and town forums in New York, New Jersey, West Virginia, Nebraska, Missouri, Michigan, Washington, Oregon, California . . .

October 29. Bronxville, New York. A woman's group. Ten-thirty in the morning in a movie house where Warhol's *Frankenstein* was playing. Suitable, I decide. In the men's room is a life-size dummy of a corpse that usually decorates the lobby. Creative management.

Fairly large audience—five, six hundred. Very conservative—abortion equals euthanasia. Watergate? What about Chappaquiddick? Our dialectic would not cause Plato to green with Attic envy.

I stack the cards of my text on the lectern. Full light on me. Audience in darkness. Almost as restful as the creative stillness of a television studio. I feel an intimacy with the camera that I don't with live audiences. Had I played it differently I might have been the electronic Norman Thomas, or George Brent.

I warn the audience: "I shall have to refer to notes." Actually, I read. Could never memorize anything. No matter how many times I give the same speech, the words seem new to me . . . like Eisenhower in 1952: "If elected in November," the Great Golfer read dutifully from a text plainly new to him. "I will go to . . . *Korea?*" The voice and choler rose on the word "Korea." No one had told him about the pledge. But go to Korea he did, resentfully.

I reassure the audience that from time to time I will look up from my notes, "in order to give an air of spontaneity." Get them laughing early. And often. Later the mood will be quite grim out there as I say things not often said in this great land of ours where the price of freedom is eternal discretion.

For some minutes, I improvise. Throw out lines. Make them laugh. I've discovered that getting a laugh is more a trick of timing than of true wit (true wit seldom provokes laughter; rather the reverse). I tell them that although I mean to solve most of the problems facing the United States in twenty-seven minutes —the time it takes to read my prepared text (question time then lasts half an hour, longer if one is at a college and speaking in the evening), I will not touch on the number one problem facing the country—the failing economy (this is disingenuous: politics is the art of collecting and spending money and everything I say is political). "I leave to my friend Ken Galbraith the solving of the depression." If they appear to know who Galbraith is, I remark how curious it is that his fame is based on two books, *The Liberal Hour,* published just as the right-wing Nixon criminals hijacked the presidency, and *The Affluent Society,* published shortly before we went broke. Rueful laughter.

I begin the text. Generally the light is full in one's eyes while the lectern is so low that the faraway words blur on my cards. I crouch; squint. My heart sinks as flash bulbs go off and cameras click: my second chin is not particularly noticeable when viewed straight on but from below it has recently come to resemble Hubert Humphrey's bull-frog swag. Do I dare to wear a scarf? Or use metal clamps to tuck the loose skin up behind the ears like a certain actress who appeared in a television play of mine years ago? No. Let the flesh fall to earth in full public view. Soldier on. Start to read.

"According to the polls, our second principal concern today is the breakdown of law and order. Now, to the right wing, law and order is often just a code phrase meaning 'get the niggers.' To the left wing it often means political oppression. When we have one of our ridiculous elections—ridiculous because they are about nothing at all except personalities—politicians declare a war on crime which is immediately forgotten after the election."

I have never liked this beginning and so I usually paraphrase. Shift lines about. Remark that in the recent Presidential election (November 7, 1972) 45 percent of the people chose not to vote. "They aren't apathetic, just disgusted. There is no choice."

Sometimes, if I'm not careful, I drift prematurely into my analysis of the American political system: there is only one party in the United States, the Property party (thank you, Dr. Lundberg, for the phrase) and it has two wings: Republican and Democrat. Republicans are a bit stupider, more rigid, more doctrinaire in their laissez-faire capitalism than the Democrats, who are cuter, prettier, a bit more corrupt—until recently (nervous laugh on that)—and more willing than the Republicans to make small adjustments when the poor, the black, the anti-imperialists get out of hand. But, essentially, there is no difference between the two parties. Those who gave Nixon money in '68 also gave money to Humphrey.

Can one expect any change from either wing of the Property party? No. Look at McGovern. In the primaries he talked about tax reform and economic equality . . . or something close to it. For a while it looked as if he was nobly preparing to occupy a long box at Arlington. But then he was nominated for president and he stopped talking about anything important. Was he insincere in the primaries? I have no idea. I suspect he was just plain dumb, not realizing that if you speak of economic justice or substantial change you won't get the forty million dollars a Democratic candidate for president needs in order to pay for exposure on television where nothing of any real importance may be said. Remember Quemoy? and her lover Matsu?

Once I get into this aria, I throw out of kilter the next section. Usually I do the Property party later on. Or in the questions and answers. Or not at all. One forgets. Thinks one has told Kansas City earlier in the evening what, in fact, one said that morning in Omaha.

Back to law and order.

"An example: roughly eighty percent of police work in the United States has to do with the regulation of our private morals. By that I mean, controlling what we drink, eat, smoke, put into our veins—not to mention trying to regulate with whom and how we have sex, with whom and how we gamble. As a result, our police are among the most corrupt in the Western world."

Nervous intake of breath on this among women's groups. Some laughter at the colleges. Glacial silence at Atlantic City. Later I was told, "We've got a lot of a very funny sort of element around here . . . you know, from Philadelphia, originally. Uh . . . like Italian." I still don't know quite what was meant.

"Not only are police on the take from gamblers, drug pushers, pimps, but they find pretty thrilling their mandate to arrest prostitutes or anyone whose sexual activities have been proscribed by a series of state legal codes that are the scandal of what we like to call a free society. These codes are very old of course. The law against sodomy goes back fourteen hundred years to the Emperor Justinian, who felt that there should be such a law because, as everyone knew, sodomy was a principal cause of earthquake."

"Sodomy" gets them. For elderly, good-hearted audiences I paraphrase; the word is not used. College groups get a fuller discussion of Justinian and his peculiar law, complete with quotations from Procopius. California audiences living on or near the San Andreas fault laugh the loudest—and the most nervously. No wonder.

"Cynically one might allow the police their kinky pleasures in busting boys and girls who attract them, not to mention their large incomes from the Mafia and other criminal types, *if* the police showed the slightest interest in the protection of persons and property, which is why we have hired them. Unhappily for us, the American police have little interest in crime. If anything, they respect the criminal rather more than they do the hapless citizen who has just been mugged or ripped off.

"Therefore, let us remove from the statute books all laws that have to do with *private* morals—what are called victimless crimes. If a man or woman wants to be a prostitute that is his or her affair. It is no business of the state what we do with our bodies sexually. Obviously laws will remain on the books for the prevention of rape and the abuse of children, while the virtue of our animal friends will continue to be protected by the S.P.C.A."

Relieved laughter at this point. He can't be serious . . . or is he?

"Let us end the vice squad. What a phrase! It is vice to go to bed with someone you are not married to or someone of your own sex or to get money for having sex with someone who does not appeal to you—incidentally, the basis of half the marriages of my generation."

Astonished laughter at this point from middle-aged women . . . and by no means women liberationists. I speak only to, as far as I am able, conservative middle-class audiences off the beaten track—Parkersburg, West Virginia; Medford, Oregon; Longview, Washington. If the women respond well, I improvise; make a small play: "Marvin may not be handsome but he'll be a *good provider* . . . and so Marion walks down the aisle a martyr to money." Encouraging that "nice" women are able to acknowledge their predicament openly. I got no such response five years ago.

"Let us make gambling legal. Those who want to lose their money gambling should have every right to do so. The principal objectors to legalized gambling are the Mafia and the police. *They* will lose money. Admittedly a few fundamentalist Christians will be distressed by their neighbors' gambling, but that is a small price to pay for the increased revenue to the cities, states and federal government, not to mention a police force which would no longer be corrupted by organized crime.

"All drugs should be legalized and sold at cost to anyone with a doctor's prescription."

Intake of breath at this point. Is *he* a drug addict? Probably. Also, varying degrees of interest in the subject, depending on what part of the country you are in. Not much interest in Longview because there is no visible problem. But the college towns are alert to the matter as are those beleaguered subs close to the major urbs.

"For a quarter of a century we have been brainwashed by the Bureau of Narcotics, a cancer in the body politic that employs many thousands of agents and receives vast appropriations each year in order to play cops and robbers. And sometimes the cops we pay for turn out to be themselves robbers or worse. Yet for all the legal and illegal activities of the Bureau the use of drugs is still widespread. But then if drugs were entirely abolished thousands of agents would lose their jobs, and that would be unthinkable."

Around in here I take to discussing the findings of one doctor who had recently appeared on television warning of the perils of pot. Apparently too much pot smoking will enlarge the breasts of young males (Myra Breckinridge would have had a lot to say on this subject but I may not) while reducing their fertility. I say, "Isn't this *wonderful?*" using a Nixon intonation; and recommend that we get all the males in the country immediately on pot. The women laugh happily; a sort of pill for the male has always been their dream. Equality at last.

I play around with the idea of Southern senators doing television commercials, pushing the local product: "Get your high with Carolina Gold." I imitate Strom Thurmond, puffing happily.

"How would legalization work? Well, if heroin was sold at cost in a drugstore it would come to about fifty cents a fix—to anyone with a doctor's prescription. Is this a good thing? I hear the immediate response: Oh, God, every child in America will be hooked. But will they? Why do the ones who get hooked get hooked? They are encouraged to take drugs by the pushers who haunt the playgrounds of the cities. But if the drugs they now push can be bought openly for very little money then the pushers will cease to push.

"Legalization will also remove the Mafia and other big-time drug dispensers from the scene, just as the repeal of Prohibition eliminated the bootleggers of whisky forty years ago."

I feel I'm going on too long. My personal interest in drugs is slight. I've tried opium, hashish, cocaine, LSD, and pot, and liked none of them except cocaine, which leaves you (or at least me) with no craving for more. Like oysters. If in season, fine. Otherwise, forget them. Pot and opium were more difficult for me because I've never smoked cigarettes and so had to learn to inhale. Opium made me ill; pot made me drowsy.

"The period of Prohibition—called the noble experiment— brought on the greatest breakdown of law and order the United States has known until today. I think there is a lesson here. Do not regulate the private morals of people. Do not tell them what they can take or not take. Because if you do, they will become angry and antisocial and they will get what they want from criminals who are able to work in perfect freedom because they have paid off the police.

"Obviously drug addiction is a bad thing. But in the interest of good law and good order, the police must be removed from the temptation that the current system offers them and the Bureau of Narcotics should be abolished.

"What to do about drug addicts? I give you two statistics. England with a population of over fifty-five million has eighteen hundred heroin addicts. The United States with over two hundred million has nearly five hundred thousand addicts. What are the English doing right that we are doing wrong? *They* have turned the problem over to the doctors. An addict is required to register with a physician who gives him at controlled intervals a prescription so that he can buy his drug. The addict is content. Best of all, society is safe. The Mafia is out of the game. The police are unbribed, and the addict will not mug an old lady in order to get the money for his next fix."

Eleanor Roosevelt maintained that you should never introduce more than one "new" thought per speech. I'm obviously not following her excellent advice. She also said that if you explain things simply and in proper sequence people will not only understand what you are talking about but, very often, they will begin to realize the irrationality of some of their most cherished prejudices.

One of the reasons I took the trouble to spell out at such length the necessity of legalizing drugs was to appeal not to the passions of my audience, to that deeply American delight in the punishing of others so perfectly exploited by Nixon-Agnew-Reagan, but to appeal to their common sense and self-interest. If you *give* an addict his drugs, he won't rob you. The police won't be bribed. Children won't be hooked by pushers. Big crime will wither away. Some, I like to think, grasp the logic of all this.

"I worry a good deal about the police because traditionally they are the supporters of fascist movements and America is as prone to fascism as any other country. Individually, no one can blame the policeman. He is the way he is because Americans have never understood the Bill of Rights. Since sex, drugs, alcohol, gambling are all proscribed by various religions, the states have made laws against them. Yet, believe it or not, the United States was created entirely separate from any religion. The right to pursue happiness—as long as it does not impinge upon others—is the foundation of our state. As a modest proposal, this solution to the problem of law and order is unique: *it won't cost a penny*. Just cancel those barbarous statutes from our Puritan past and the police will be obliged to protect us—the job they no longer do.

"Meanwhile, we are afflicted with *secret* police of a sort which I do not think a democratic republic ought to support. In theory, the FBI is necessary. For the investigation of crime. But in all the years that the FBI has been in existence the major criminals—the Mafia, Cosa Nostra—have operated freely and happily. Except for the busting of an occasional bank robber or car thief, the FBI has not shown much interest in big crime. Its time has been devoted to spying on Americans whose political beliefs did not please the late J. Edgar Hoover, a man who hated Commies, blacks and women in more or less that order."

This generally shocked the audience and never got a laugh. Needless to say, my last lecture was given before the FBI's scrutiny of "dissidence" became public; not to mention the CIA's subsequent admission that at least ten thousand Americans are regularly spied upon by that mysterious agency whose charter is to subvert wicked foreigners not lively homebodies.

"The FBI has always been a collaborating tool of reactionary politicians. The Bureau has also had a nasty talent for amusing presidents with lurid dossiers on the sex lives of their enemies.

"I propose that the FBI confine its activities to *organized* crime and stop pretending that those who are against undeclared wars like Vietnam or General Motors or pollution want to overthrow the government and its Constitution with foreign aid. Actually, in my lifetime, the only group of any importance that has come near to overthrowing the Constitution was the Nixon administration."

A number of cheers on this. When I am really wound up I do a number of Nixon turns. I have the First Criminal's voice down . . . well, pat. I do a fair Eisenhower, and an excellent FDR. Am working on Nelson Rockefeller right now. No point to learning Ford.

"So much, as General Eisenhower used to say, for the domestic front. Now some modest proposals for the future of the American empire. At the moment things are not going very well militarily. Or economically. Or politically.

"At the turn of the century we made our bid for a world empire. We provoked a war with Spain. We won it and ended up owning the Spanish territories of Cuba and the Philippines. The people of the Philippines did not want us to govern them. So we killed three million Filipinos, the largest single act of genocide until Hitler."

Much interest in this statistic. Taken from Galloway and Johnson's book, *West Point: America's Power Fraternity.* Recently I got a letter from a Filipino scholar who has been working on the subject. She says that no one will ever know the exact number killed because no records were kept. But whole towns were wiped out, every man, woman and child slaughtered. The American army does admit that perhaps a quarter million were killed during the "mopping up." The spirit of My Lai is old with us.

"The first and second world wars destroyed the old European empires, and created ours. In 1945 we were the world's greatest power, not only economically but militarily—we alone had the atom bomb. For five years we were at peace. Unfortunately those industries that had become rich during the war *combined* with the

military—which had become powerful—and together they concluded that it was in the best interest of the United States to
maintain a vast military establishment.

"Officially this was to protect us from the evil Commies. Actually it was to continue pumping federal money into companies
like Boeing and Lockheed and keep the Pentagon full of generals
and admirals while filling the pork barrels of congressmen who
annually gave the Pentagon whatever it asked for, *with* the
proviso that key military installations and contracts be allocated
to the home districts of senior congressmen."* Tough sentence
to say. Never did get it right.

"Nobody in particular was to blame. It just happened. To
justify our having become a garrison state, gallant Harry Truman
set about deliberately alarming the American people. The Soviet
was dangerous. We must have new and expensive weapon systems. To defend the free world. And so the cold war began. The
irony is that the Soviet was not dangerous to us *at that time.*
Millions of their people had been killed in the war. Their industries had been shattered. Most important, they did not have
atomic weapons and we did.

"So, at the peak of our greatness, we began our decline."

Absolute silence at this point.

"Instead of using the wealth of the nation to improve the lot
of our citizens, we have been wasting over a third of the federal
budget on armaments and on the prosecution of open and secret
wars. We have drafted men into the Army in peacetime, something the founders of this country would have been appalled at.
We have been, in effect, for thirty-three years a garrison state
whose main purpose has been the making of armaments and the
prosecution of illegal wars—openly as in Vietnam and Cambodia,
secretly as in Greece and Chile. Wherever there is a choice between a military dictatorship—like Pakistan—and a free government—like India—we support the dictator. And then wonder
why we are everywhere denounced as hypocrites.

"This is not good for character. This is not good for business.
We are running out of raw materials. Our currency is worth less
and less. Our cities fall apart. Our armed forces have been, literally, demoralized by what we have done to them in using them
for unjust ends.

*I notice that I am cannibalizing earlier pieces.

"In a third of a century the only people who have benefited from the constant raid on our treasury and the sacrifice of our young men have been the companies that are engaged in making instruments of war—with the connivance of those congressmen who award the contracts and those generals who, upon early retirement, go to work for those same companies.

"What to do? A modest and obvious proposal: cut the defense budget. It is currently about a quarter of the national budget—eighty-five billion eight hundred million dollars. Unhappily both Ford and Rockefeller are loyal servants of the Pentagon. *They* will never cut back. They will only increase a military budget that is now projected for the end of the decade to cost us one hundred fourteen billion dollars a year. This is thievery. This is lunacy.

"Conservative estimates say that we can cut the budget by ten percent and still make the world free for ITT to operate in. I propose we aim to cut it by two thirds in stages over the next few years. I propose also a reduction of conventional forces. We need maintain no more than an army, navy, air force of perhaps two hundred thousand highly trained technicians whose task would be to see that anyone who tried to attack us would be destroyed.

"A larger army only means that we are bound to use it sooner or later. To attack others. We have learned that from experience. Generals like small wars because there is a lot of money being spent and, of course, they get promoted. I might be more tolerant of their not unnatural bias *if* they could actually *win* a war, but that seems beyond their capacity. They prefer a lot of activity; preferably in an undeveloped country blasting gooks from the air.

"I would also propose phasing out the service academies. And I was born in the cadet hospital at West Point where my father was an instructor."

To relieve the tension that has started to build, I wander off the track. Describe how I was delivered by one Major Snyder. Later Ike's doctor. "It's only gas, Mamie," he is supposed to have said to Mrs. Eisenhower when the President was having his first heart attack.

"The academies have created an un-American military elite that has the greatest contempt for the institutions of this country, for democratic institutions anywhere. Over the years West Point graduates have caused grave concern. On two occasions in the last century the academy was nearly abolished by Congress. I do not think, despite the virtues of an Omar Bradley, say, that the system which has helped lock us into a garrison state ought to continue."

Often, at this point, I recall an evening at my family's house shortly after the second war began. A group of West Point generals took some pleasure in denouncing that Jew Franklin D. Rosenfeld who had got us into the war on the wrong side. We ought to be fighting the Commies not Hitler. But then F.D.R. was not only a kike, he was sick in the head—and not from polio but from syphilis. Anyway, everything could be straightened out— with just one infantry brigade they would surround the White House, the Capitol, remove the Jew . . .

My lecture tour ended just as General Brown made his memorable comments on international Jewry and its fifth column inside the United States. I've since heard from several people who said they'd not believed my story until General Brown so exuberantly confirmed what I'd been saying.

"The motto of the academy is 'Duty, Honor, Country.' Which is the wrong order of loyalties. Worse, the West Point elite has created all around the world miniature West Points. Ethiopia, Thailand, Latin America are studded with academies whose function is to produce an elite not to fight wars—there are no wars in those parts of the world—but to *limit* democracy.

"West Point also trains many of these past and future oligarchs —like the present dictator of Nicaragua, Somoza. Retired West Pointers also do profitable business in those nations that are dominated by West Point–style elites.

"Finally, the best result of ceasing to be a garrison state would be economic. Until the energy crisis, the two great successes in the world today were Japan and Germany and they have small military establishments. The lesson is plain: no country needs more military power than it takes to deter another nation from attacking it.

"Now none of these proposals is of much use if we do not reduce our population. The US is now achieving a replacement rate of population. This is a startling and encouraging reduction of population but there are still too many of us and we ought to try by the next century to reduce our numbers by half. The problem is not lack of room. In area we have a big country, though we are gradually covering the best farmland with cement and poisoning the lakes and rivers.

"The problem is our way of living. With six percent of the

world's population we use forty percent of the world's raw resources. This unnatural consumption is now ending. We are faced with shortages of every kind and we will have to change the way we live whether we want to or not.

"Obviously fewer Americans means less consumption and more for everybody. How do we stop people from breeding? First, by not constantly brainwashing the average girl into thinking that motherhood must be her supreme experience. Very few women are capable of being good mothers; and very few men of being good fathers. Parenthood is a gift, as most parents find out too late and most children find out right away."

This never fails to please.

"More radically, I would say that no one ought to have a child *without* permission from the community. A sort of passport must be issued to the new citizen. How these passports will be allotted I leave to the wisdom of the democracy. Perhaps each girl at birth might be given the right to have one child with the understanding that if she decided to skip the hard work of motherhood she could pass that permission on to a woman who wanted two or three or four children.

"For those who gasp and say that this is interfering with man's most sacred right to add as many replicas of himself as he likes to the world, let me point out that society does not let you have more than one husband or wife at a time, a restriction which I have heard no conservative complain of, even though any Moslem would find it chilling, and Mrs. Richard Burton would find it square."

Mrs. Burton is thrown in, cheaply, to reduce the tension that is mounting. Most members of the audience believe that the right to have as many children as they want is absolute; and to limit population by law seems a terrible imposition. Yet most of them take for granted that the government has the right to control most aspects of our private lives (remember the legendary prisoner of Alcatraz who served time for going down on his wife?).

During the question-and-answer period someone always says that I have contradicted myself. On the one hand, I would allow free drugs, prostitution, gambling, and all sorts of wickedness while, on the other, I would restrict the right to have children— well, isn't that interfering with people's private lives?

The answer is obvious: adding a new citizen to a country is a public not a private act, and affects the whole community in a way that smoking pot or betting on horses does not. After all, the new citizen will be around a long time after his parents have departed. Doesn't it then make sense that if there is insufficient space, food, energy, the new citizen ought not to be born?

"In an age of chronic and worsening shortages, I would propose that all natural resources—oil, coal, minerals, water—be turned over to the people, to the government."

Two years ago when I made this proposal, the response was angry. The dread word "communism" was sounded. Now hardly anyone is much distressed. Even die-hard conservatives have fallen out of love with the oil industry.

"But since none of us trusts our government to do anything right—much less honest—national resources should be a separate branch of the government, coequal with the other three but interconnected so that Congress can keep a sharp eye on its funding and the courts on its fairness. The president, any president, on principle, should be kept out of anything that has to do with the economy.

"Much of today's mess is due to Johnson's attempt to conquer Asia without raising taxes, and to Nixon's opportunistic mucking about with the economy at election time. These presidential ninnies should stick to throwing out baseballs, and leave important matters to serious people."

At this point, without fail, a hot-eyed conservative will get to his feet and say that it is ridiculous to nationalize anything since it is not possible for a government agency to operate efficiently or honestly.

I then ask: isn't this a democratic society? and aren't those who do the government's work not an abstract enemy to be referred to as "them" but simply ourselves? Are you trying to say that we are, deep down, a nation of crooked fuck-ups? (Naturally, I euphemize.)

The point still does not penetrate. So I shift ground. Agree that the United States was founded by the brightest people in the country—and we haven't seen them since. Nice laugh. Tension relaxes a bit.

I agree that most people who go into government are second-raters. The bright ones go into the professions or into money-making. This flatters the audience. I suggest that we ought to "change our priorities." Businesslike phrase. Perhaps our schools should train a proper civil service. Train people who prefer payment in honor rather than in money. England, France, Scandinavia attract bright people into government despite low salaries.

This deeply disturbs the audience. First, you must never say that another country handles anything better than we do. Second, although the word "honor" makes no picture at all in the American head, "money" comes on as a flashing vivid green—for *go*.

Someone then says that socialist Sweden is a failure because everybody commits suicide, the logic being that a society without poverty will be so boring that death is the only way out. When I tell them that fewer Swedes commit suicide than Americans (we falsify statistics; they don't) they shake their heads. *They know.*

The next questioner says that England's National Health Service is a flop. This is not true but he would have no way of knowing since the newspapers he reads reflect the AMA's dark view of socialized medicine. Incidentally, England is always used as an example of what awful things will happen to you when you go socialist.

I point out that England's troubles are largely due to the energy crisis and an ancient unsolved class war. I mention England's successful nationalization of steel some years ago. I might as well be speaking Greek. The audience has no way of knowing any of these things. Year after year, the same simple false bits of information are fed them by their rulers and they absorb them, like television commercials.

I do find curious and disturbing the constant hatred of government which is of course a hatred of themselves. Do these "average" Americans know something that I don't? Is the world really Manichaean? Perhaps deep down inside they really believe we *are* all crooked fuck-ups, and murderous ones, too (thank you, Lieutenant Calley, President Johnson). After all, the current national sport is shoplifting. For once, I am probably too optimistic about my country.

"Now those who object to nationalizing our resources in the name of free enterprise must be reminded that the free enterprise system ended in the United States a good many years ago. Big oil, big steel, big agriculture avoid the open marketplace. Big corporations fix prices among themselves and thus drive out of business the small entrepreneur. Also, in their conglomerate form, the huge corporations have begun to challenge the very legitimacy of the state.

"For those of you who are in love with Standard Oil and

General Motors and think that these companies are really serving you, my sympathy. I would propose, however, that the basic raw resources, the true wealth of the country, be in our hands, not in theirs. We would certainly not manage our affairs any worse than they have.

"As for the quality of our life, well, it isn't much good for most people because most people haven't got much money. Four point four percent own most of the United States. To be part of the four point four you must have a net worth of at least sixty thousand dollars."

This projected figure is from the IRS and I find it hard to believe. Surely individual net worth must be higher. In any case, recent figures show that most of the country's ownership is actually in the hands of one percent with, presumably, a higher net capital.

"This gilded class owns twenty-seven percent of the country's real estate. Sixty percent of all corporate stock, and so on. They keep the ninety-five point six percent from rebelling by the American brand of bread and circuses: whose principal weapon is the television commercial. From babyhood to grave the tube tells you of all the fine things you ought to own because other people (who are nicer-looking and have better credit ratings than you) own them.

"The genius of our ruling class is that it has kept a majority of the people from ever questioning the inequity of a system where most people drudge along, paying heavy taxes for which they get *nothing* in return while ITT's taxes in 1970 diminished, despite increased earnings."

For any Huey Long in embryo, I have a good tip: suggest that we stop paying taxes until the government gives us something in return for the money we give it.

"We got freedom!" vivacious Barbara Walters positively yelled into my ear during our six minutes on the *Today* show. To which the answer is you don't have freedom in America if you don't have money and most people don't have very much, particularly when what they do make goes to a government that gives nothing back. I suppose vivacious Barbara meant that the people are free to watch television's God-awful programming which they pay for when they buy those overpriced shoddy goods the networks advertise.

"I would propose that no one be allowed to inherit more than, let us say, a half million dollars, while corporate taxes obviously must be higher.

"We should also get something back for the money we give the government. We should have a national health service, something every civilized country in the world has. Also, improved public transport. Also, schools which do more than teach conformity. Also, a cleaning of the air, of the water, of the earth before we all die of the poisons let loose by a society based on greed.

"Television advertising should be seriously restricted if not eliminated. Although the TV commercial is the only true art form our society has yet contrived, the purpose of all this beauty is sinister—to make us want to buy junk we don't need by telling us lies about what is being sold.

"Obviously, the bright kids know that what is being sold on the screen is a lot of junk but that is corruption, too, because then everyone who appears on the screen is also thought to be selling junk and this is not always true, even at election time.

"Fascism is probably just a word for most of you. But the reality is very much present in this country. And the fact of it dominates most of the world today. Each year there is less and less freedom for more and more people. Put simply, fascism is the control of the state by a single man or by an oligarchy, supported by the military and the police. This is why I keep emphasizing the dangers of corrupt police forces, of uncontrolled *secret* police, like the FBI and the CIA and the Bureau of Narcotics and the Secret Service and Army counterintelligence and the Treasury men—what a lot of sneaky types we have, spying on us all!

"From studying the polls, I would guess that about a third of the American people at any given moment would welcome a fascist state. This is because we have never been able to get across in our schools what the country was all about. I suspect that the reason for this failure is the discrepancy between what we were meant to be—a republic—and what we are—a predatory empire —is so plain to children that they regard a study of our Constitution as just another form of television commercial and just as phony. This is sad. Let us hope it is not tragic. The means exist to set things right."

Now for the hopeful note, struck tinnily, I fear. But the last "solution" I offer is a pretty good one.

"In the end we may owe Richard Nixon a debt of gratitude. Through his awesome ineptitude we have seen revealed the total corruption of our system. From the Rockefellers and the Kennedys who buy elections—and people—to the Agnews and Nixons who take the money from those who buy, we are perfectly corrupt. What to do?

"How do we keep both the corrupting Kennedys and Rockefellers as well as the corrupted Nixons and the Agnews *out* of politics?

"I propose that no candidate for any office be allowed to buy space on television or in any newspaper or other medium. This will stop cold the present system where presidents and congressmen are bought by corporations and gangsters. To become president you will not need thirty, forty, fifty million dollars to smear your opponents and present yourself falsely on TV commercials.

"Instead television (and the rest of the media) would be required by law to provide prime time (and space) for the various candidates.

"I would also propose a four-week election period as opposed to the current four-year one. Four weeks is more than enough time to present the issues. To show us the candidates in interviews, debates, *un*controlled encounters in which we can actually see who the candidate really is, answering tough questions, his record up there for all to examine. This ought to get a better class into politics."

There is about as much chance of getting such a change in our system approved by Congress as there is of replacing the faces on Mt. Rushmore with those of Nixon and company. After all, the members of the present Congress got there through the old corrupt route and, despite the occasional probity of an individual member, each congressman is very much part of a system which now makes it impossible for anyone to be elected president who is not beholden to those interests that are willing to give him the millions of dollars he needs to be a candidate.

Congress's latest turn to the screw is glorious: when paying income tax, each of us can now give a dollar to the Presidential Election Campaign Fund. This means that the two major parties can pick up thirty million dollars apiece from the taxpayers while continuing to receive, under the counter, another thirty or so million from the milk, oil, insurance, etc., interests.

"Since Watergate, no one can say that we don't know where we are or who we are or what sort of people we have chosen to govern us. Now it remains to be seen if we have the power, the

will to restore to the people a country which—to tell the truth
—has never belonged to the ninety-five point six percent but
certainly ought to, as we begin our third—and, let us not hope,
terminal—century."

I ended the series with a noon lecture at a college in Los
Angeles . . . not UCLA. They told me this so often that now I've
forgotten what the school was actually called. No matter. They
have doubtless forgotten what I've said. In a sense, I've forgotten
too. The act of speaking formally (or informally, for that matter)
is rather like the process of writing: at the moment it is all-
absorbing and one is absolutely concentrated. Then the great
eraser in one's brain mercifully sweeps away what was said,
written.

But impressions of audiences do remain with me. The young
appear to have difficulty expressing themselves with words.
Teachers tell me that today's students cannot read or write with
any ease (having read the prose of a good many American academics, I fear that the teachers themselves have no firm purchase
on our beautiful language).

Is television responsible? Perhaps. Certainly if a child does not
get interested in reading between six and thirteen he will never
be able to read or write (or speak) well and, alas, the pre-pubes-
cent years are the years of tube addiction for most American
children.

Naturally that small fraction of one percent which will maintain the written culture continues, as always, but they must now
proceed without the friendly presence of the common reader who
has become the common viewer, getting his pleasure and instruc-
tion from television and movies. A new kind of civilization is
developing. I have no way of understanding it.

As I re-do these notes, I am troubled by the way that I responded to the audiences' general hatred of any government. Yes,
we are the government—but only in name. I realize that I was
being sophistical when I countered their cliché that our government is dishonest and incompetent with that other cliché: *you* are
the government.

Unconsciously, I seem to have been avoiding the message that
I got from one end of the country to the other: we hate this system
that we are trapped in but we don't know who has trapped us or
how. We don't know what our cage really looks like because we
were born in it and have nothing to compare it to but if anyone

has the key to the lock then where the hell is he?

Most Americans lack the words, the concepts that might help them figure out what has happened; and it is hardly their fault. Simple falsities have been drummed into their heads from birth (socialism = Sweden = suicide) so that they will not rebel, not demand what is being withheld them . . . and that is not Nixon's elegant "a piece of the action" but justice. Social justice.

The myth of upward social mobility dies hard; but it dies. Working-class parents produce children who will be working-class while professional people produce more professionals. Merit has little to do with one's eventual place in the hierarchy. We are now locked into a class system nearly as rigid as the one that the Emperor Diocletian impressed upon the Roman empire.

Yes, I should have said, our rulers *are* perfectly corrupt but they are not incompetent: in fact, they are extremely good at exercising power over those citizens whom they have so nicely dubbed "consumers." But the consumers are not as dopey as they used to be and when they have to listen to exhortations from old-style Americans like myself, telling them *they* are the government and so can change it (underlying message: this bad society is what you dumb bastards deserve), they respond with the only epithets they can think of, provided them for generations by their masters: it's the Commies, pinkos, niggers, foreigners, it's *them* who have somehow screwed it all up.

But the consumers still have no idea who the enemy *they* are, no idea who really is tearing the place apart. No one has dared tell them that the mysterious *they* are the rich who keep the consumers in their places, consuming things that are not good for them, and doing jobs they detest. Witness, the boredom and fury of the younger workers on the Detroit assembly lines; no doubt made more furious—if not bored—by the recent mass firings, as the depression deepens.

Not since Huey Long has a major political leader come forward and said we are going to redistribute the wealth of the country. We are going to break up the great fortunes. We are going to have a just society whose goal will be economic equality. And we can do this without bloody revolution (although knowing the clever resourcefulness of our rulers, I suspect it will be a terrible time—Attica on a continental scale).

True revolution can only take place when things fall apart in the wake of some catastrophe—a lost war, a collapsed economy. We seem headed for the second. If so, then let us pray that that somber, all-confining Bastille known as the consumer society will fall, as the *first* American revolution begins. It is long overdue.

Esquire
May 1975

About the Author

GORE VIDAL was born at West Point in 1925. In 1943 he graduated
from the Phillips Exeter Academy and enlisted in the army.
While in the Pacific, at the age of nineteen, he wrote the much
praised novel *Williwaw*. Among his other novels are *The City and
the Pillar*, *Julian*, *Myra Breckinridge* and American Trilogy: *Burr*,
1876, *and Washington, D.C.*